LANGUAGE AND LITER/

Dorothy S. Strickland, Foundi
Donna E. Alvermann and María Paula

MW01034770

ADVISORY BOARD: Richard Allington, Kathryn Au, Bernice Cullinan, Colette Daiute,
Anne Haas Dyson, Carole Edelsky, Mary Juzwik, Susan Lytle, Django Paris, Timothy Shanahan

continued

For volumes in the NCRLL Collection (edited by JoBeth Allen and Donna E. Alvermann) and the Practitioners
Bookshelf Series (edited by Celia Genishi and Donna E. Alvermann), as well as other titles in this series,
please visit www.tcpress.com.

Language and Literacy Series, *continued*

Culturally Sustaining Literacy Pedagogies

Honoring Students' Heritages, Literacies, and Languages

Edited by

Susan Chambers Cantrell
Doris Walker-Dalhouse
Althier M. Lazar

TEACHERS COLLEGE PRESS

TEACHERS COLLEGE | COLUMBIA UNIVERSITY
NEW YORK AND LONDON

Published by Teachers College Press,® 1234 Amsterdam Avenue, New York, NY 10027

Front cover design by adam bohannon design. Photos (clockwise from top right): asierromero / Iiona Virgin / Anna Om / sitthiphong / Prostock-studio / Stuart Monk / Flamingo Images, all via Adobe Stock.

Library of Congress Cataloging-in-Publication Data

Names: Cantrell, Susan Chambers, editor. | Walker-Dalhouse,
    Doris, editor. | Lazar, Althier M., editor.
Title: Culturally sustaining literacy pedagogies : honoring students'
    heritages, literacies, and languages / edited by Susan Chambers
    Cantrell, Doris Walker-Dalhouse, and Althier M. Lazar.
Description: New York : Teachers College Press, 2022. | Series: Language
    and literacy series | Includes bibliographical references and index.
Identifiers: LCCN 2022004658 (print) | LCCN 2022004659 (ebook) |
    ISBN 9780807767023 (paperback) | ISBN 9780807767030 (hardcover) |
    ISBN 9780807781067 (epub)
Subjects: LCSH: Reading—Language experience approach. | Language
    arts—Correlation with content subjects. | Culturally-relevant pedagogy.
Classification: LCC LB1050.35 .C85 2022 (print) | LCC LB1050.35 (ebook) |
    DDC 370.117—dc23/eng/20220310
LC record available at https://lccn.loc.gov/2022004658
LC ebook record available at https://lccn.loc.gov/2022004659

ISBN 978-0-8077-6702-3 (paper)
ISBN 978-0-8077-6703-0 (hardcover)
ISBN 978-0-8077-8106-7 (ebook)

Printed on acid-free paper
Manufactured in the United States of America

Contents

Acknowledgments

We are grateful for all of the teachers and teacher educators who have contributed generously to this project. The book would not have been possible without the rich contributions of the chapter authors who not only agreed to write chapters for the book, but who also deepened our understanding of culturally sustaining literacy pedagogy (CSLP). We acknowledge the many Literacy Research Association (LRA) Study Group presenters and participants over the years who have engaged in lively and informative discussions about CSLP and stretched our thinking about this area of research and practice. We especially appreciate Rebecca Powell, who initially proposed the study group from which this book emanated and who has helped us think about policy implications of our work.

Finally, we thank the individuals who provided support throughout the development of this book, including Gail Clark, who prepared the manuscript for production, and Teachers College Press editor Emily Spangler, whose feedback and responses to our inquiries were invaluable in the development of this book.

Introduction

Culturally Sustaining Literacy Pedagogy: From Relevance to Permanence

Althier M. Lazar, Doris Walker-Dalhouse, and Susan Chambers Cantrell

In 2012 Django Paris unveiled the concept of culturally sustaining pedagogy (CSP) in *Educational Researcher* as a transformative vision for teaching and curriculum design that "seeks to perpetuate and foster— to sustain—linguistic, literate, and cultural pluralism as part of the democratic project of schooling" (p. 95). We take this vision into classrooms to show how literacy teaching can be centered around the lives and experiences of Black, Indigenous, and other people of color (BIPOC) as part of a larger campaign for racial justice (Willis et al, 2021). The murder of George Floyd by Minneapolis police, the brutality toward Asian Americans during the COVID-19 pandemic, and attempts by our own legislators to suppress BIPOC voters' rights are all manifestations of a society built on White supremacy. These recent events have amplified the need to decenter whiteness and empower BIPOC students' voices, experiences, and heritage in our literacy classrooms through CSLP– culturally sustaining *literacy* pedagogy. Realizing that we are far from full-scale adoption of CSLP, we offer this volume to bring us closer to this goal.

CSLP aligns with and is situated in several equity-driven educational paradigms including culturally relevant pedagogy (Ladson-Billings, 1995a), culturally responsive pedagogy (Gay, 2010), critical pedagogy (Freire, 1970), critical care (Rolón-Dow, 2005), humanistic pedagogy (Salazar, 2013), historically responsive pedagogy (Muhammad, 2020), critical literacy (Lewison et al., 2002), abolitionist teaching (Love, 2019), and antiracist Black language pedagogy (Baker-Bell, 2020a) with a primary goal of ensuring academic success for all students, with special attention to those in nondominant cultural communities. CSP has become a buzz-phrase in teaching circles, but it lacks sufficient grounding in practice. To honor the 10-year anniversary of Paris's vision of CSP, we bring you real classroom models that show how educators are using it to advance students' literacy learning.

We are three organizers of a Literacy Research Association Study Group who have met each December over the last 6 years to explore CSP and how it translates to K–12 literacy classrooms and teacher education programs. The study group has been a dedicated space for teachers, graduate students, researchers, and teacher educators to discuss what CSLP looks like and what it could look like, and to grapple with the challenges of translating it into practice. Participants have used the group to report on their successes and failures, to get feedback from other like-minded colleagues, and to hone their orientations and approaches. Mostly we have used each other for support because CSLP is complex. It is not simply a set of teaching lessons but rather an *orientation* toward children, literacy, language, teaching, learning, and the very purpose of education. Its complexity requires that educators collaborate in professional forums such as the LRA Study Group to make sense of CSLP and teach in ways that align with the concept.

We now wish to bring these conversations to you so that you can see possibilities of CSLP for your own classroom or school. Right now, CSLP is not widely understood or practiced. While the term *culture* is frequently tossed around in educational circles, literacy pedagogy in many schools is not centered on students' experiences, knowledge traditions, or heritage. It is much more centered around standardized testing, standardized programs, and deficit notions of what "at-risk" students might need. This is why robust discussions of CSLP are needed to give it permanence in our classrooms and schools. We provide these discussions in this book.

This chapter begins with a historical tour of how culturally sustaining pedagogy came to be and how it is currently conceived. Then we will look at some key factors that have undermined CSLP over the last few decades. At the end of this chapter we present an overview of the book and invite you to think about how you can add to the conversation based on your own experiences. It is our hope that you will use the author contact information we provide in the About the Editors and Contributors section at the end of the book so that you can be part of an ongoing conversation to make CSLP a reality in your school, classroom, and program.

CULTURALLY SUSTAINING LITERACY PEDAGOGY: A BRIEF HISTORY

The origins of culturally sustaining pedagogy are rooted in research done during the 1970s and through the 1990s to try to explain why disproportionate numbers of students in culturally marginalized communities were not succeeding in school. Across much of this research, findings pointed to the disjuncture between school-valued discourses, expectations, and routines that have been largely based on White, English-speaking, and middle-class norms and lifestyles, and the diverse ways of communicating, learning, being, and doing that many students in nondominant communities bring from their homes and communities (Au, 1980; Au & Jordan, 1981; Erickson, 1987; Irvine, 1991; King & Mitchell, 1995; Mohatt & Erickson, 1981; Philips, 1983). These studies revealed that school failure can be and often is a result of several levels of cultural disjuncture in school for those who are not weaned on school-valued ways of doing and communicating. Indeed, for many students whose languages and literacies are considered deficit and illegitimate, school has been and continues to be a hostile and alienating place (Heath, 1983; Purcell-Gates, 1997).

Many studies done in the 1990s uncovered resourced-based pedagogies (Au & Kawakami, 1994; Ball, 1995; E. Garcia, 1993; Lee, 1995; McCarty & Zepeda, 1995; Moll & Gonzales, 1994) that centered on the qualities of teachers and teaching that advanced students' learning and identification with academic achievement. According to Paris (2012), this research "repositioned the linguistic, cultural, and literate practices of poor communities—particularly poor communities of color—as resources to honor, explore, and extend in accessing Dominant American English (DAE) language and literacy skills and other White, middle-class dominant cultural norms of acting and being that are demanded in schools" (p. 94).

Especially groundbreaking was the concept of *funds of knowledge* based on research done in the homes and communities of Mexican American families in Tucson, Arizona (Moll et al., 1992). In tracking families' everyday practices and discourses, including those around learning and teaching, the team uncovered a range of "historically accumulated and culturally developed bodies of knowledge and skills essential for household or individual functioning and well-being" (p. 133). In working with teachers in after-school study groups, researchers shared their developing understandings about families' funds of knowledge and invited teachers to envision how these discoveries could be used to inform their instructional practice. Working with the research team, teacher Cathy Amanti learned that many of the children in her class sold candy. She then created a literacy-based "candy-making and selling" inquiry unit that addressed many areas of the curriculum, including math, science, health, consumer education, cross-cultural practices, advertising, and food production.

Resource-based pedagogical research revealed that students' cultural dislocation in school did not need to be a given, especially if they are in the presence of knowledgeable, committed, and culturally aware teachers. In her landmark study, Gloria Ladson-Billings examined the pedagogical practices of eight exemplary teachers of African American students which resulted in her book, *The Dreamkeepers: Successful Teachers of African American Children* (1994). These teachers demonstrated particular orientations toward themselves, students, teaching, and society which she translated as central tenets of culturally relevant pedagogy (CRP). These include:

1. Students whose educational, economic, social-political, and cultural futures are most tenuous are helped to become intellectual leaders in the classroom. (p. 117)
2. Students are apprenticed in a learning community rather than taught in an isolated and unrelated way. (p. 117)
3. Students' real-life experiences are legitimized as they become part of the "official" curriculum. (p. 117)
4. Teachers and students participate in a broad conception of literacy that incorporates both literature and oratory. (p. 117)
5. Teachers and students engage in a collective struggle against the status quo. (p. 118)
6. Teachers are cognizant of themselves as political beings. (p. 118)
7. When students are treated as competent, they are likely to demonstrate competence. (p. 123)
8. When teachers provide instructional "scaffolding," students can move from what they know to what they need to know. (p. 124)
9. The focus of the classroom must be instructional. (p. 124)
10. Real education is about extending students' thinking and abilities. (p. 125)
11. Effective teaching involves in-depth knowledge of both the students and the subject matter. (p. 125)

Ladson-Billings (1995b) proposed that culturally relevant pedagogy would "produce students who can achieve academically, produce students who demonstrate cultural competence, and develop students who can both understand and critique the existing social order" (p. 474). She urged educators to demand students' academic excellence by maintaining high expectations, recognizing their assets, and inspiring them to see academic achievement as part of their cultural legacy. Further, Ladson-Billings envisioned classrooms where students' cultural competence could be maintained through a variety of means, including using cultural referents to teach new concepts, welcoming parents or community members into classrooms to share their expertise, or by encouraging students to express themselves in their home languages. Further, she indicated that developing students' sociopolitical consciousness would help prepare them to question and work against structures and institutions that produce and maintain social inequities.

In his article, "Culturally Sustaining Teaching: A Needed Change in Stance, Terminology, and Practice" (2012), Paris credited Ladson-Billings and others for providing the field with a coherent theoretical position on culturally relevant and responsive pedagogy. He wrestled, however, with whether the terms "relevance" and "responsive" accurately captured the research findings and teaching practices that have informed a pedagogical orientation that is based on students' cultural assets and ideas of cultural pluralism. He also wondered whether these terms "go far enough in their orientation to the languages and literacies and other cultural practices of communities marginalized by systemic inequalities to ensure the valuing and maintenance of our multiethnic and multilingual society" (p. 93).

For instance, in the area of "cultural competence," Paris urged readers to ask "if the research and practice being produced under the umbrella of cultural relevance and responsiveness is, indeed, ensuring maintenance of the languages and cultures of African American, Latina/o, Indigenous American, Asian American, Pacific Islander American, and other long-standing and newcomer communities in our classrooms" (p. 94). He also questioned whether culturally relevant pedagogies are actually developing students' consciousness about social inequity in the ways envisioned by Ladson-Billings and others who have contributed to this work.

Paris references Alim's (2007) research on teaching and learning based on hip-hop traditions. Alim distinguished between centering a curriculum on students' cultural-linguistic assets and realities, versus one that is merely "*culturally appropriate, culturally responsive, culturally relevant*, or whatever other term we have produced to describe classroom practices that use the language and culture of the students to teach them part of the 'acceptable' curricular cannon" (Paris, 2012, p. 95). Paris's (2012) key point is that the terms *relevance* and *responsive* do not "guarantee in stance or meaning that one goal of an educational program is to maintain heritage ways and to value cultural and linguistic sharing across difference, to sustain and support bi- and multilingualism and bi- and multiculturalism" (p. 95). He argued "it is quite possible to be relevant to something or responsive to it without ensuring its continuing presence in a student's *repertoires of practice* (Gutiérrez & Rogoff, 2003), and so its presence in our classrooms and communities" (p. 95).

Culturally sustaining pedagogy more accurately represents the goal of *centering instruction on students' cultural and linguistic competence* while also offering students access to culturally dominant competencies. Further, Paris warns about simplified translations of CSP that consider heritage and traditional practices in teaching without paying attention to the continuously shifting practices of students and their communities. Paris (2012) writes "it is important that we do not essentialize and are not overly deterministic in our linkages of language and other cultural practices to certain racial and ethnic groups in approaching what it is we are seeking to sustain" (p. 95). He points to the ways African American youth, for instance, navigate identities through African American Language (AAL) and hip-hop cultures while those who identify as Latinx may appropriate these cultural modes in addition to those connected with Caribbean American cultures. Youth communities embrace traditional cultural practices while they continue to add to and change these practices. What is considered "cultural practice" is constantly in flux, requiring that educators become students of the youth cultures they serve.

A recent addition to the conversation about culturally sustaining instruction is Gholdy Muhammad's (2020) concept of *historically responsive literacy,* a framework that informs literacy teaching. Historically responsive literacy practice is rooted in the literary societies of the 1800s in which Black citizens met regularly to "construct knowledge and engage one another toward cultivating a literary culture" (p. 8). Literacy society members understood the transformative power of literacy to improve self and society, and used their literacy knowledge to confront and alter the extreme racism they faced during this time period. Muhammad's central goal is to help students of color connect with the power of literacy by identifying with the courageous literary engagements of those who operated in these societies. Based on this history, she argues for a reconceptualization of literacy education that includes four goals: (1) identity development, (2) skill development, (3) intellectual development, and (4) criticality. Connecting these goals to the history of engagement in literacy societies, Muhammad explains:

Each time early Black readers came together to read, write, think, and learn, they were making sense of who they were (identity), developing their proficiencies in the content they were learning within (skills), becoming smarter about something or gaining new knowledge and concepts in the world (intellect), and finally, developing the ability to read texts (including print text and social contexts) to understand power, authority and anti-oppression (criticality). (p. 12)

In her book, *Cultivating Genius: An Equity Framework for Culturally and Historically Responsive Literacy* (2020) Muhammad translates these ideas into historically responsive lessons that include explicit goals for cultivating students' identities, skills, intellectualism, and criticality. Criticality aligns with the concept of *critical literacy*, or using texts to examine issues of power within society. Operating from a criticality or critical literacy perspective means that students use texts to (1) disrupt the commonplace, (2) consider multiple viewpoints, (3) focus on the sociopolitical, and (4) take action to make the world more socially just (Lewison et al., 2002). These lessons provide a clear roadmap for teachers and school leaders for how they might build literacy programs around equity goals. Such clarity is needed in order to make culturally sustaining and historically centered literacy teaching practices a reality in classrooms.

HOW WIDESPREAD IS CRP/CSP?

In the years following Paris's call to embrace culturally sustaining pedagogy (CSP) as a necessary force against deficit and dehumanizing approaches to education, we turn to discuss its prevalence, or lack thereof, in today's classrooms. The good news is that over the last decade, research on culturally sustaining pedagogy has grown exponentially. In 2013, one year after Paris's *Educational Researcher* publication, the number of Google Scholar citations with the term *culturally sustaining pedagogy* was about 20 thousand. Today, this term is cited over 121,000 times on Google Scholar. This trend is reflected in literacy research circles as well. In 2002, there were only 6 mentions of *culturally responsive* or *culturally relevant* pedagogy in the National Reading Conference program. By 2020, the terms *culturally responsive, culturally relevant, culturally welcoming*, and *culturally sustaining* appeared 29 times in LRA's program guide, with related terms such as *humanizing* (3 mentions), *social justice* (22 mentions) and *equity* (22 mentions) also appearing in the conference program. Each of these latter two terms appeared only twice in the 2002 program.

While there is increased attention among educators toward culturally centered pedagogies, no comprehensive studies have been done to find out the existence of these practices in classrooms. Research on novice teachers offers a sobering picture of the difficulties they experience when trying to act in ways that align with CSP. Studies find that most novice teachers who construct understandings about culturally centered pedagogies within their teacher education programs might begin their professions being committed to the ideas of CSP and might exhibit some elements of CSP over time, but very few are able or are willing to advocate to sustain students' cultural ways of being in classrooms (Whipp, 2013; Whipp & Buck 2014).

Joan Whipp and Brandon Buck (2014) studied 17 graduates of a 4-year teacher education program that focused on preparing critically caring teachers based on the central concepts of CSP, including combining emotional warmth and high expectations, connecting with students' families, drawing from students' funds of knowledge (Gonzalez et al., 2005), building students' cultural competence, and developing the ability to be activists on behalf of their students. Data collected and analyzed during the first three years of their practice found that 13 graduates displayed some dispositions and actions that were consistent with CSP principles, but only three teachers described efforts to advocate for their students. Researchers found that schooling structures such as scripted teaching and standardized testing limited many of their study participants from being able to act on behalf of their students. This was the case for Angela, an African American woman who the researchers describe as engaging in several instructional practices consistent with CSP, including honoring the language traditions of her students. She discussed the importance of holding her students to high academic expectations and exhibited a "warm demanding" orientation in her classroom. Angela was asked to teach a new curriculum which she found to be too easy for her students, yet she "felt unable to change district mandates which required her to strip her curriculum down to scripted test prep lessons. Rather than fight these mandates, she decided to 'roll with it'" (Whipp & Buck, p. 15). Angela's case shows how novice teachers who are initially committed to CSP principles may have difficulty enacting them when they are pressured to teach a standardized curriculum. Federal initiatives such as No Child Left Behind (NCLB), Race to the Top, and the adoption of Common Core State Standards have contributed to the curriculum standardization movement. We will touch briefly on these initiatives and how the educational landscape has evolved in relation to CSP.

UNEVEN LANDSCAPES FOR CULTIVATING CSP

The enactment of NCLB in 2001 fundamentally changed the national educational landscape in ways that confined CRP to the margins of instructional practice. NCLB authorized states to close student achievement gaps by testing students in reading and math in grades 3 through 8 and holding school districts accountable for students' academic progress. School administrators and teachers were required to demonstrate that all of their students were making adequate yearly progress (AYP) based on standardized test performance. If schools failed to do so for multiple consecutive years, they could be reconstituted or turned over to state or private agencies to run. For many educators, this threat drove decisions about what and how to teach. The pressure on educators in underfunded schools to meet AYP was especially great, resulting in the widespread practice of prioritizing test preparation and test-taking skills over culturally centered practices. Many teachers were expected to implement test-driven practices like these under a looming threat of unemployment if they did not comply. Among the graduates of our own teacher education programs, many reported having to pledge fidelity to scripted curricula and testing practices as a condition of employment. Novice and experienced teachers alike felt pressed to challenge the NCLB-influenced policies imposed on them from above, hampering possibilities for widespread adoption of culturally centered pedagogies.

The adoption of Common Core State Standards (CCSS) in 2009 was another large-scale movement that has shaped the nature of teaching and learning across U.S. schools, with ramifications for CSP. CCSS were intended to provide a clear blueprint for what K-12 students should know and be able to do in math and English language arts. The standards emphasize critical thinking and problem solving—skills that prepare students for the complex thinking that is demanded in college and the real world. CCSS supporters argued that wide-scale adoption of the standards would better ensure students' access to classrooms where complex thinking is prioritized no matter where they live. Moreover, the website specifies that the CCSS do not dictate to teachers how they should teach.

In reality, however, teacher practice in many states has been narrowed by CCSS because these standards were linked to a massive standardized testing program, launched in 2009 under President Obama's Race to the Top initiative. States could qualify for grant funding if they adopted college and career-ready standards. States spent billions of dollars to phase in the standards, prepare students to take tests linked to the standards, and buy technology to administer online standardized testing. As a result, students were spending many hours either taking or preparing for tests. Further, scripted curricula aligned with CCSS goals were used in an effort to boost student performance on standardized tests. The combination of standardized testing and scripted teaching undermined the equity goals that CCSS were designed to meet (Ravitch, 2016), leaving teachers with less authority to make decisions about what and how to teach, including culturally sustaining approaches to literacy instruction. In theory, teachers are able to sustain students' cultural and linguistic knowledge while also meeting the higher-level thinking demands that are outlined in the CCSS, but the ongoing pressures of testing and adhering to prescribed curriculum guides reduce the probability that teachers can direct their energies to finding spaces within their programs to nurture students' home and community knowledge and language.

The nature of literacy instruction is further complicated by each state's interpretation of CCSS, with some states making explicit provisions for validating students' cultural lives and experiences. For instance, Wisconsin's CCSS for English language learners (ELL) state:

> Every student learns. Although no two students come to school with the same culture, learning strengths, background knowledge, or experiences, and no two students learn in exactly the same way, every student's unique personal history enriches classrooms, schools, and the community. This diversity is our greatest education asset. (Wisconsin Department of Public Instruction, 2011, p. 13)

These guidelines further describe the assets that emergent bilingual students bring to classrooms:

> ELLs bring with them many resources that enhance their education and can serve as resources for schools and society. Many ELLs have first language and literacy knowledge and skills that boost their acquisition of language and literacy in a second language; additionally, they bring an array of talents and cultural practices and perspectives that enrich our schools and society. (p. 14)

In our experience as we work with teachers, we wonder whether these calls to recognize students' cultural talents and practices have much traction in school districts that support standardized literacy instruction and testing. Our experiences in schools indicate that the residual effects of No Child Left Behind, Race to the Top, and the widespread adoption of Common Core State Standards has undermined opportunities for culturally sustaining literacy pedagogy, particularly for children in culturally and linguistically diverse communities. While some states have relaxed their testing programs somewhat, we still tend to see test-driven and prescriptive teaching practices in many classrooms that serve large populations of minoritized students, including those who speak languages other than English.

All of us have spent time in classrooms and work directly with teachers, literacy coaches, and school leaders. We have all observed teachers who are disillusioned with having to spend inordinate amounts of time on test preparation routines that are disconnected to authentic, critical, and culturally informed literacy practices. We have seen how entire writing programs in schools have been centered on test preparation. In one school, teachers were expected to have their students write short essays in response to test questions that were anticipated on the state exam. Students practiced writing formulaic passages with regurgitated topic sentences taken from test questions to be followed by a prescribed sequence of supporting details and a concluding sentence. No one other than teachers read these essays. Stripped of all communicative intent, writing instruction like this is completely inconsistent with tenets of CSP because students' cultural and linguistic assets are not recognized or built on, nor are their life experiences welcomed and validated. Students learn little about the purposes and functions of writing through practices like these. Yet these sorts of practices exist.

Simultaneously, we see the absence of these restrictive practices in Whiter, more affluent communities. Teachers in these communities are not as tied to such prescriptive and inauthentic, teaching-to-the-test practices in their literacy classrooms. Thus the federal policies designed to give minoritized students a leg up have actually reduced their access to meaningful, purposeful literacy learning opportunities. We believe that such an inequitable distribution of culturally centered, high-quality literacy teaching is a form of systemic racism. Susan shares an example of a school in which she and Rebecca Powell implemented a grant for culturally responsive practices while the district was mandating a scripted reading program for "failing" schools (Powell et al., 2017). Teachers' forced enactment of the scripted program led to negative outcomes for students and had a negative impact on teachers' psychological well-being. While some teachers demonstrated agency by quietly implementing more authentic instruction, several teachers fled to more affluent (whiter) schools, leaving many minoritized students to be taught by the most inexperienced teachers.

Added to these elements is a push from the political right to abolish ethnic studies programs and those that promote multilingualism (Garcia & Kleifgen, 2018; Paris, 2012). These factors contribute to a cultural void where whiteness, monoculturalism, monolingualism, and pedagogies centered on middle-class norms and lifestyles have continued to dominate in literacy classrooms. Holding all students to Eurocentric (white) literacy and language standards becomes a form of symbolic violence that is routinely perpetrated against students of color (Baker-Bell, 2020). Further exacerbating this problem is the existence of a primarily White and middle-class teaching force. Attempts to reconceptualize literacy teaching around CSP principles must include investments in hiring teachers, school leaders, and teacher educators of color (Bristol & Mentor, 2018; Haddix, 2017; Kohli & Pizzaro, 2016).

These are some of the factors that explain why CSLP has not gained more ground across U.S. schools, although we do see educators who have embraced this orientation toward students and literacy teaching. Their efforts have not been widely discussed or researched, but the work they have done offers an exciting glimpse of what we could see happening in many more schools as we become more knowledgeable about what CSLP looks like in practice. Paris (2012) argues that sustaining, perpetuating, and fostering students' knowledge and competencies in school must be viewed as a necessary and enduring campaign given the racist and persistent push by the political right for educational policies and programs based on White, Western, English-only/monolingual experiences and heritage.

WHERE WE ARE AND WHAT WE AIM TO DO IN THIS BOOK

We see the enormous potential of CSLP to gain a foothold in literacy classrooms. Efforts to reconceptualize literacy teaching around CSLP goals is one part of a larger campaign to democratize and humanize our schools. Achieving this goal will require a massive commitment to more equitable school funding, a serious shift toward supporting teacher authority and decision-making, and hefty investments in hiring educators of color. In addition, CSLP is predicated on educators understanding how issues of race and racism live within themselves and society. Educators need to be racially literate if they are to truly advocate for BIPOC learners through CSLP and other antiracist efforts (Sealey-Ruiz, 2021). In recognizing the limits of our roles as LRA Study Group organizers, we feel compelled to share what teachers and teacher educators are currently doing in the name of promoting CSLP in literacy classrooms.

First, we recognize that literacy educators need many more examples of how teachers and teacher educators have succeeded in creating humanizing learning spaces built around CSLP goals and how students are thriving because of these efforts. We've been able to enter (vicari-ously) classrooms centered on the language and practices of youth—where literacy events such as spoken word poetry, praise songwriting, and community-based movie and podcast production capitalize on the already-present literacies of youth. We have addressed practices ground-ed by raciolinguistic and translinguistic perspectives and how teachers can leverage students' linguistic assets in the literacy classrooms. We feel compelled at this stage to bring these practices to a wider audience through this book.

We also want to share examples of how educators have addressed the barriers that continue to undermine CSLP. Admittedly, this has been most difficult part of our LRA Study Group discussions. Many of our conversations about culturally sustaining literacy teaching have led to intellectual hair-pulling sessions that have left us drained and without clear resolutions. In the 2020 session, for instance, participants talked about the inability of teachers to deviate from strict curricular expecta-tions which they viewed at odds with their understandings about CSLP. We talked about the lack of availability of substitute teachers that would allow teachers to observe CSLP in action. We even discussed the inad-equacies of teacher coaching to cultivate culturally centered teaching approaches. All of these problems have no easy answers, but the study group has become a forum for talking about and trouble-shooting ways to mitigate and navigate around the barriers that tend to marginalize CSLP in schools. We want to make all of these efforts visible for new and practicing teachers and teacher educators. We also want to play a role in establishing a research agenda that fills the voids in the literature about designing, evaluating, and implementing CSLP.

This book brings together profiles of culturally sustaining practice in literacy classrooms across the United States. All of the authors work from Paris's conception of CSP as *an asset-based and critical orienta-tion toward teaching that is focused on maintaining students' cultural and linguistic competence, supporting students in questioning societal inequalities, and offering students access to culturally dominant compe-tencies.* Each chapter shows what culturally sustaining literacy pedagogy in K–12 classrooms looks like.

From the models presented in these chapters, readers will note themes critical to successful enactment of CSP in literacy contexts. First, chapter authors show how the internal work of self-examination and personal reflection about how one's own identities, biases, and assump-tions impact literacy teaching and learning in classrooms. Next, chapters address the tensions in curriculum and instruction that occur as teachers enact CSP while working to ensure students attain mandated outcomes.

Another theme that appears across chapters is the need to interrogate and push back against hegemonic processes and practices that are rooted in White ways of knowing and being, including the standards and school mores that create barriers for CSP.

Part 1 illustrates models of CSLP in elementary classrooms. In Chapter 1 Olivia Murphy, Jennifer D. Turner, Chrystine Cooper Mitchell highlight multimodal composing practices such as multiliterate repertoires (e.g., reading, writing, viewing, speaking, listening) that students leverage to design digital and nondigital texts that express meanings through images, words, gestures, movement, and other communicative modes (New London Group, 1996). Multimodal composing practices enable students of color to play with diverse representation(s) as well as to resist and critique dangerous dominant narratives (Vasudevan et al., 2010). In contrast to traditional practices which center whiteness, Chapter 1 shows how multimodal composition creates space for students to demonstrate their rich knowledge, cultural practices, and ways of being through drawings, photography, family storytelling, and producing picture books. Similarly, in Chapter 2 Kelly K. Wissman shows how traditionally deficit-oriented intervention practices were resisted as 1st- and 2nd-grade emergent bilinguals within an intervention setting engaged with diverse picture books that inspired dialogic conversations and authentic writing about immigration, language, and faith traditions. The chapter provides a case study of how a young Muslim girl, Alina, took up and created opportunities to read, respond to, and create texts that drew on her full linguistic and cultural resources.

Part 2 focuses on implementing CSLP with adolescents and youth. In Chapter 3 Britnie Delinger Kane and Rachelle S. Savitz examine curricular and instructional tensions that occur in bringing together disciplinary literacy and CSP. The authors suggest specific instructional practices that middle and high school ELA teachers might draw upon as they show how critical inquiry can integrally comprise the tenets of culturally sustaining pedagogies, support students' conceptually rich development in literacy and content-specific learning, and promote students' abilities to become more resilient participants in the political and social worlds in which they live (Spires et al., 2020). In Chapter 4 Sarah N. Newcomer and Kathleen M. Cowin provide an example of a culturally sustaining middle school literacy lesson as taught by a teacher candidate enrolled in their university's teacher education program. The lesson takes a strong asset-based approach to literacy instruction and focuses on maintaining students' linguistic and cultural competencies while developing proficiency in English. The authors address tensions teachers face between standards-based lessons and enacting CSP. In Chapter 5

Aimee Hendrix-Soto, Erica Holyoke, Heather Dunham, and Melissa Mosley Wetzel provide insight into how 5th- and 12th-grade teachers facilitated this using critical literacy pedagogies to raise students' critical consciousness in intermediate and secondary classrooms in underserved schools in one district. The authors showed how teachers prioritized youths' literacies and lives even under the pressures of standardized testing and accountability by analyzing three key teacher moves: (1) critical pedagogical approaches creating space for youth to drive the official curriculum, (2) centering local and larger issues in literacy pedagogies, and (3) employing a broad conceptualization of literacy, specifically multi-modal and digital literacies.

Part III addresses considerations and practices for implementing CSLP in K–12 classrooms. In Chapter 6 Kelli A. Rushek and Ethan Seylar exemplify self-examination as they highlight the critical reflective practices Seylar, a preservice English language arts (ELA) teacher, and Rushek, an English education instructor, undertook to critically examine how CSLP can be bridged from theory to practice in the development of one text set curation project in Ethan's teacher education program. The authors offer metacognitive reflections that highlight how they, as two critically informed White teachers, examined this secondary ELA unit through a CSLP lens in order to revise this unit in more culturally sustaining ways. In Chapter 7 Susan V. Bennett, AnnMarie Alberton Gunn, Alexandra Panos, Steven M. Hart, & Jenifer Jasinski Schneider illuminate specific culturally sustaining literacy elements for teachers to utilize in their K–12 classrooms. Based on an observational and interview study of 20 of the teachers to see how they enacted CSP with their students, the authors connect the theoretical basis of CSP into actual practice while addressing the political obstacles that impede changing deeply rooted hegemonic practices. Finally, Chapter 8 brings together the individual essays in the book into a cohesive set of takeaways for the audience around the book's central themes. The editors make explicit the ways in which the chapters collectively contribute new insights into CSLP.

Part I

MODELS OF CSLP IN ELEMENTARY CLASSROOMS

CHAPTER 1

Writing Their Stories

Using Culturally Sustaining Multimodal Composing Practices to Transform Writer's Workshop

Olivia Murphy, Jennifer D. Turner, and Chrystine Cooper Mitchell

The process of composing has changed over the last few decades in ways that allow authors to convey messages more meaningfully. More than ever before, student authors in K–5 classrooms have the opportunity to connect with their audiences using diverse mediums, including words, images, and multimedia, and think more critically about their purposes for composing. These multifaceted messages create space for multimodal communication, thus establishing a dynamic where the messages students construct are artistic, expressive, and purposeful (S. Miller & McVee, 2013). In particular, multimodal composing practices that are culturally sustaining open up a world of possibilities for students to convey their community knowledge and histories, affirm their racial and linguistic identities and experiences, and critique their sociopolitical realities.

Within multimodal texts, authors use multiple and interconnecting modes including text, images, gestures, sound, movement, and visual design elements (e.g., font size, color) to communicate meaning (Kress & Jewitt, 2003). Students of color compose multimodal meanings that are situated within broader socioracial contexts, leverage their cultural and linguistic repertoires, and represent their family and community literacies (Cappello et al., 2019; Turner, 2020). Accordingly, multimodal composition can achieve the goals of culturally sustaining pedagogy (Paris & Alim, 2014) by encouraging students of color to be culturally and linguistically dexterous in their writing; inviting them to explore and develop their racial, gendered, and linguistic knowledge through the writing process; and visibly celebrating myriad social, cultural, and academic identities in the classroom through the process of composing and sharing texts.

This chapter explores how such culturally sustaining multimodal composing practices can transform writer's workshops in K–5 classrooms. Calkins (2020) describes *writer's workshop* as a student-centered framework where teachers can provide student authors with opportunities to learn about being a writer. The workshop model enables teachers to engage students in predictable routines, explicitly teaching the parts of the writing process and involving students in authentic writing. Writer's workshop involves four distinct components:

1. The minilesson (5 to 20 minutes). The minilesson is a brief, focused lesson surrounding a key writing skill, concept, or strategy at the beginning of writer's workshop. The minilesson begins by connecting to previous learning, moves to teacher modeling, offers an opportunity for student engagement, and finishes with a link out to independent writing time where students practice what they learned in the minilesson.
2. Independent writing time (20 to 45 minutes). The majority of writer's workshop time is devoted to extensive time for students to write independently. Student authors create their multimodal texts during independent writing time, practicing the skill from the minilesson as they work. Independent writing time occurs simultaneously as conferencing is happening between peers and with the teacher.
3. Conferencing (during independent writing time). As students work on their writing, the teacher and/or peer pairs or small groups meet to check in and support the writing process. These conferences are brief, and include questions such as, "What are you working on currently?" or "What did you mean when you said ___; how might you make that more clear?" Conferences can also be used to reinforce specific skills, or to plan next steps for the student author's piece.
4. Author share (5 to 15 minutes). Author share is a space at the end of writer's workshop for student authors to share their work. Author shares can be full class or in pairs or small groups, and during author share time the teacher highlights exemplary student work related to the minilesson skill that the class can use as examples to strengthen their own writing.

Throughout the four components of the writer's workshop framework, teachers intentionally choose high-quality mentor texts that demonstrate how authors use various craft features in their writing. Teachers also use anchor charts that contain useful reminders about writing process procedures and strategies. Anchor charts are often constructed by both students and the teacher and are displayed in the classroom so that students can refer to them while writing.

Drawing on the writer's workshop model, we focus on four specific culturally sustaining composing practices that can be used during writer's workshop: (1) composing with drawings, (2) composing with photographs, (3) personal and family storytelling and (4) producing picture books. Specifically, we highlight how these multimodal composing practices expand the traditional literacy skills of children of color while simultaneously nurturing and sustaining their social and cultural identities (e.g., race, gender, language). By infusing multimodality with principles of culturally sustaining pedagogy—particularly the goals of perpetuating cultural and linguistic pluralism through meaningfully including and fostering students' cultures, home and community knowledges, and languages into the classroom (Paris & Alim, 2014)—we recognize that student authors, specifically students of color in K–5 classrooms, can use multiple modes to affirm their cultural and linguistic identities, communicate content learning, and advocate for social justice with classrooms and society (Cappello et al., 2019).

CONTEXT AND POSITIONALITIES

The composing practices described in this chapter were drawn from our work as teachers, teacher educators, and literacy scholars. Olivia is a White woman whose K–12 teaching experience, student teacher mentoring, and research endeavors have all been in urban schools in Brooklyn, New York, and the Maryland counties surrounding Washington, DC. Her entire career has been spent with students and colleagues with diverse racial, cultural, and linguistic repertoires. Being surrounded by students, educators, families, and community members with identities different from her own has given her the opportunity to learn culturally sustaining practices in an authentic way from and within multilingual, multicultural, and multiracial communities that these practices are primarily designed to serve. Jennifer is a Black female literacy scholar and teacher educator who has supported the cultural responsivity of preservice and inservice teachers for nearly twenty years. The practical examples highlighted in this chapter emanate from Jennifer's experiences as the mother of two African American sons and from her research on multimodal pedagogies with Black and Latinx youth aged 6 to 12 attending a summer reading program in Maryland. Chrystine is a White female teacher educator and former elementary teacher who has spent the greater part of her career considering how to infuse culturally responsive practices into her own elementary classroom as well as with her work with undergraduate and graduate students. Her experience working with the urban children in Trenton, New Jersey, and Reading, Pennsylvania, have informed her work and served as motivation to reach each and every child, focusing on what they bring to the classroom and what they need to be successful.

MULTIMODAL COMPOSING PRACTICES FOR WRITER'S WORKSHOP

Composing With Drawings

Composing with drawings is a time-honored practice in the primary grades (K–2), as young children of color often use sketches and other visualizations in their writing that help them imagine and reimagine their worlds and their learning (Cappello et al., 2019; Dyson, 2003). However, my (Jennifer's) work also demonstrates the benefits that drawings have for students in the intermediate grades (3 through 5) (Albro & Turner, 2019; Griffin & Turner, 2021). During our 4-week study, a veteran teacher and I invited intermediate-grade students to compose visual texts (i.e., drawings, collage) as a springboard for a career dream unit that culminated with a nonfiction writing project (Albro & Turner, 2019). Guided by a culturally sustaining approach to writing instruction that centered students' personal identities, interests, and goals, our career exploration unit provided opportunities for African American and Latinx students to author their own futures through composing multimodal texts. Career futures is a culturally sustaining topic because African American and Latinx children rarely have the opportunity to use their multiliteracies to freely dream about and (re)claim their own futures in traditional literacy classrooms (Albro & Turner, 2019; Turner, 2020). Through this career-focused unit, the African American and Latinx children leveraged their multimodal composing skills to determine their own life goals and values, articulate their career aspirations, and challenge and disrupt dominant societal narratives that (mis)characterize their future trajectories as illiterate, violent, and tragic (Albro & Turner, 2019; Griffin & Turner, 2021; Turner, 2020).

We launched the unit with three minilessons that facilitated students' composition of multiple visual texts related to their career aspirations and dreams. During these minilessons, we invited students to discuss the kinds of careers that they wanted to have as adults, and to create drawings of their aspirations. Students completed a graphic organizer with space for creating a quick sketch of their career dream and writing a sentence explaining why they aspired to those particular occupations. In the next minilesson, students used these graphic organizers as the basis for an expanded drawing of a scene from their work. We used the following series of prompts to foster reflective drawing:

- Imagine yourself at your workplace.
- What job are you doing?
- What do you see around you? What does your workplace look like?
- What tools are you using to do your job?
- Who is there at your workplace? What are those people doing?

After sharing their drawings, students created career collages on poster-sized boards with magazine images. To complement students' visual compositions, we implemented interactive read alouds of occupational-oriented books, which helped students think more specifically about their careers and the kinds of work they wanted to do. We also played several career-oriented games (e.g., Guess the Career) to build students' career vocabulary and their knowledge of specialized career fields. Career-specific knowledge was helpful for students like Joselina, a 9-year-old Latinx girl, who initially wanted to be a doctor. During the unit, Joselina came to realize that she was interested in neurology, and in turn focused her career collage and written report on that more specific career goal (see Figure 1.1).

Figure 1.1. Page from Joselina's Career Report

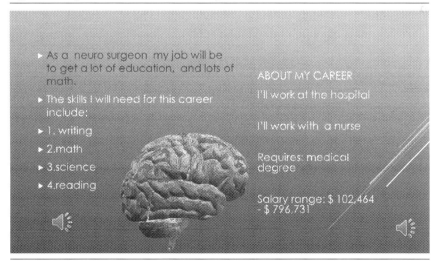

Finally, we invited community leaders from various fields (e.g., engineering, education, nursing) based on our students' career aspirations to speak with the class. Our guest speakers shared an overview of their daily job activities, the educational pathways they took to achieve their careers, and the skills required for them to fulfill their professional responsibilities. Students reported that they enjoyed these sessions immensely, because these authentic career experiences enabled them to make real-world connections to their own goals and aspirations.

In addition to composing visual texts, students completed multiple career-related writing activities, including completing a career interest questionnaire, developing a résumé, and writing a letter to a person who might help them achieve their career goals. These activities, in conjunction with the visual texts, led to a culminating writing project: a digital career report. The digital career reports used a PowerPoint template and included information on topics such as About My Career, Who Will Help Me Achieve This Career Goal? and My Path to Career Success. Students conducted research on their careers using print and online resources and used their research notes to prepare the presentation slides. We also encouraged students to incorporate their visual compositions (e.g., drawings, career collages) and other online images related to their careers, into their presentations. Students were often animated as they narrated these images; for example, as he described an image of a blue futuristic car, Nathan exclaimed , "I can't wait to become an engineer so I can build this cool car!" Students revised their slides based on teacher and peer feedback, then composed a script to narrate their presentations. During author share time, students presented their digital career reports to their families and friends. Through this unit, we learned that visual texts, including drawings, collage, and online images, are not just for students in the primary grades. Rather, visual texts, especially those composed by intermediate students, can be empowering because they surface their career interests and illuminate future literacies and possibilities.

Composing With Photographs

Teachers may incorporate photography into writer's workshop in a number of ways, two of which are outlined here. First, schools across the United States have employed the Literacy Through Photography (LTP) curriculum, a visual teaching approach developed by artist/educator Wendy Ewald in partnership with the Center for Documentary Studies at Duke University and Durham Public Schools (n.d.). When employed as a central component of writing instruction, LTP fosters students' creativity, voice, and criticality as they learn to read pictures and compose textual artifacts with photographic images and words. In addition, teachers who are not using LTP curricula may also incorporate culturally relevant photographs that teachers and/or students generate into the writing curriculum to highlight cultural traditions and celebrations, community events (e.g., ethnic festivals), and memorable experiences with family or friends (Cappello & Hollingsworth, 2008; Laman & Henderson, 2018). Such multimodal composing and storytelling with photos sustains students' identities and cultures in the classroom, while also helping teachers connect more with students and their families to better support learning (Strickland et al., 2010).

To help diverse writers compose with photographs, teachers may implement several minilessons about photography as part of writer's workshop. Students who compose using photographs greatly "benefit from learning about perspective, angle, and light to tell their stories. This process provides students with a new perspective and also builds on the traditional skills of comprehension and literary analysis" (Wiseman et al., 2016, p. 538). Prompts that help students to think about and analyze photographs include:

- Who is in this photo?
- What is happening in this photo?
- What do you notice about this photo?
- How does this photo make you feel?
- What do you think the photographer was trying to accomplish?
- What mood does the photograph create?

After these minilessons, students can work independently on their own multimodal photography projects that incorporate photographic images, words, and other communicative modes (e.g., music) that are accessible to students. Examples of vibrant photography projects include: (1) ABC books, where photographic images capture aspects of the local community that are meaningful to students; (2) "Best Part of Me" self-portraits, where students photograph their "best" physical abilities and traits; and (3) African proverbs, where students create photographs to represent their understanding of the morals in African proverbs (Laman & Henderson, 2018; Wiseman et al., 2016).

For these projects, students can either take their own photographs outside school and bring them to school to share, find or take photos while at school, or a combination of the two. For example, in the aforementioned Best of Me Project, the teacher requested that students bring in props in order to photograph their "best parts" at school. For instance, if a student liked the way they played soccer, they might bring in a ball for the photograph. Students also could have taken these pictures at home or at soccer practice or at a community soccer game and brought them in for the project. Both options are culturally sustaining in that they allow students to explore and share meaningful aspects of their knowledge, interests, families, and communities. Once the source of photos has been decided, the teacher might focus a minilesson on a read aloud of a book that connects with the theme of the project. For example, in the Best of Me portrait project, the teacher read the book *The Best Part of Me* (Ewald, 2002) which served as a mentor text for student writers. Next, students sketched and talked about their best physical traits (e.g., eyes, smile) or body parts (e.g., arms, feet) with peers. Finally, students create their photographic images and compose textual interpretations to accompany the photographs.

Peer and teacher conferencing is especially beneficial for students composing with photography. Peers and teachers can raise questions about the photographs that may help student writers to deepen or expand their interpretive writing. Teachers can also invite students to discuss the aspects of photography that have supported their writing process. Ella, an African American 3rd-grader in Wiseman et al.'s (2016) study, believed that the photographs in the Best Part of Me project helped her visualize ideas for stories, add more specific details in her compositions, and clarify her writing. Other students have found that photographs energize their writing by giving them a concrete visual text to consider (Cappello & Hollingsworth, 2008). Understanding the way students use photographs when composing is useful for teachers as they plan photography-oriented minilessons, read alouds, and projects in support of their diverse student writers.

Personal and Family Storytelling

Personal and family storytelling is an important culturally sustaining literacy practice in three specific ways. First, personal and family storytelling allows students of color to share significant aspects of their selves and cultures while also learning about and making connections with others. Second, storytelling in the classroom is a way to honor the oral traditions that make up an important part of many students' cultures, providing them with a familiar and exciting mode of literary expression. When students of color are storytellers in the classroom, their stories help counter traditional dominant cultural ideals that are replicated in many other curricular texts and activities with representations of the "rich practices of children, families, and communities . . . [to] be identified, honored, cultivated, and sustained" (Souto-Manning

& Rabadi-Raol, 2018, p. 214). Third, at its core, storytelling is an inherently multimodal activity that supports a variety of learning styles and needs while allowing students to share parts of themselves and their families, cultures, and communities.

Multimodal storytelling can be incorporated during each step of the writer's workshop model in culturally sustaining ways. During the minilesson portion of writer's workshop, teachers can focus on different elements of narratives to build students' storytelling skills. Some storytelling minilessons could center on narrative arcs (the structure and shape of a story), writing territories (the aspect[s] of one's life that students want to write about), character development, writing style, performance style, audience, and point of view. Teachers can introduce anchor text(s) in print, audio, and visual format, and guide students through an evaluation of one specific aspect of storytelling. To introduce and refine literary skills using a culturally sustaining approach, teachers can choose mentor texts that feature storytelling from Indigenous, African, Latinx, and other cultures with rich oral storytelling traditions. For example, PBS's Learning from the People' collection features a storytelling-focused writer's workshop series that teaches students about the key aspects of narratives while also allowing them to experience storytelling from a variety of cultures to inspire students' own cultural exploration through storytelling (PBS Learning Media, n.d.).

The very personal nature of storytelling also presents opportunities for culturally sustaining work during the conferencing portion of writer's workshop. In peer and small-group conferencing options, students' cultures and experiences are both affirmed and sustained through sharing with others while they simultaneously build their narrative writing skills with the help of their peers. In their description of a digital storytelling writer's workshop series, Bogard and McMackin (2012) explain that though it was not originally planned, regular writing partner conferences quickly became a norm during the series because of how well the students helped each other with narrative elements such as adding figurative and descriptive language, refining and clarifying their story arcs, and thinking about phrasing. For example, when listening to a partner's story, one student paused and asked to hear part of the story again and asked a clarifying follow-up question, which turned into a greater conversation between the two writing partners about adding more emotions to an entire section of the story (Bogard & McMackin, 2012). Throughout all of these conversations, and in the storytelling performances where students share their final pieces during author share, students are constantly sharing their stories and cultures and learning about their peers' lives, families, and cultures.

Incorporating multiple modalities of expression into the four stages of storytelling, writer's workshop not only enhances student expression, but also helps create a variety of entry points into the stories that students are composing and consuming. Previously in this chapter, we discussed composing with photographs, which can easily combine with personal and family storytelling. Students might choose to compose the story of a photograph or a series of photographs about themselves, their families, or their communities. They may also use photos to tell a story or as visual supports while storytelling to an audience of peers during author shares. Other student-generated artwork or artifacts can function similarly and also serve as conversational topics or starting points for peer and teacher conferencing. When conferencing, the teacher or peer may ask questions about the photo or picture to help students draw out, organize, or add more detail to their stories such as:

- What is the story of this photo/picture?
- Why is this photo important to you/why did you choose to draw this picture?
- What happened before/during/after this photo?
- Can you describe what is happening in this photo/picture?
- Why did you choose to include ____ in this picture? Where can you add these details into your story?
- How does this photo/picture make you feel? How do you want your story to make your listeners feel and what words can you choose to make them feel that way?

Finally, digital storytelling, specifically, has emerged over the past two decades as a powerful multimodal teaching tool that is engaging, familiar to the digital natives that all students now are, and allows students to combine a variety of multimedia elements like pictures, audio, and video to tell their stories (Robin, 2008). For teachers who have access to the technology to allow students to compose their stories digitally, a host of resources and opportunities are available. For example, websites like Voki.com and the free application Tellagami allow students to construct avatars—which create an opportunity for students to showcase elements of their personal, home, and community cultures and identities—and then have their avatar read their stories (with multiple language and accent options). On other sites like LittleBirdTales.com (specifically designed for elementary schoolers), and StoryboardThat.com, students can combine photos, artwork, other visual elements, music, and recorded audio together to tell their stories. When selecting elements for their stories, students can choose to incorporate photos, art, and voices from themselves, their families and communities, or from the Internet. During the author share portion of writer's workshop, students can play their stories in pairs, small groups, or even for the whole class. In addition to being great opportunities for students to learn, honor, and share their cultures and languages in the classroom, multimodal and digital storytelling are also particularly beneficial for students with diverse learning needs and multiple linguistic repertoires because they generate a variety of entry points for composition and sharing.

Producing Picture Books

For student authors, creating a picture book provides a space where they can convey meaning from written language, visual elements, design features, and the layout of the linguistic and visual elements throughout the book and on each page. Creating picture books can give students the opportunity to tell stories about their hobbies, families, neighborhoods, and interests using their own local languages, making it a culturally and linguistically sustaining writer's workshop choice. The writer's workshop model provides an invaluable vehicle for teachers to teach the necessary characteristics of picture book production through minilessons, and then have students apply those practices during independent writing time with the support of conferencing. This multimodal writing process of using visual narratives in writer's workshop can be illustrated in comic strip production (Reid & Moses, 2020) and the creation of digital picture books (Bogard & McMackin, 2012). Picture books have been shown to amplify a wide range of voices, including children of color and those with diverse linguistic and cultural backgrounds (McClung, 2018).

The prewriting stage is essential in the workshop process, recognizing that the first part of the creation of a story is the planning phase. Initial minilessons use modeling to focus on conventions of a good story and design features of picture books. The teacher models how to browse through books and takes note of the features of comic strips and graphic novels, having students look through them to notice their characteristics, specifically taking note of how culture and language are illustrated through author voice and drawings. Then the teacher leads students through an analytical reading of diverse and culturally relevant mentor texts, a similar process, while giving them time to discuss their wonderings with their partners (Reid & Moses, 2019). In their envisioning of this prewriting planning phase, Bogard and McMackin (2012) use graphic organizers to map out the macrostructure of a story, in particular, the beginning, middle, and end. Teachers often use *mentor texts*, high-quality examples where students can learn from authors, to illustrate what good picture books look like. Examples might include *Brown Sugar Babe* (Sherman, 2020), a story about beautiful shades of brown skin, or *The Arabic Quilt: An Immigrant Story* (Khalil, 2020), a picture book about a girl who wants to fit in with her peers at school. Throughout the picture book production process, minilessons continue to build on previous learning to highlight the characteristics and language of picture books and to depict how they can incorporate their own identity within their works.

During the next phase of writer's workshop, students can enact the learning that was modeled and practiced during the minilessons as they will have time and space to independently write their picture books. They can use the anchor charts that were co-created between teachers and students grounding the learning from those lessons. An example might include a T-chart that highlights how different authors incorporated language, culture, and voice into their books.

Figure 1.2 shows an example of a T-chart that illustrates how culture can be represented in picture books, specifically comparing a few of the culturally relevant picture books shared with students.

Figure 1.2. Anchor Chart Text Example

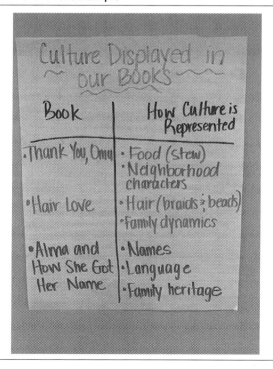

Students could use the anchor chart to apply their own understandings of language, culture, and voice into their picture books during independent writing, while the teacher is simultaneously conferencing with students to help them enhance their writing. The teacher walks students through the parts of a conference where together they research, decide, teach, and link (Calkins, 2020). During the research stage the teacher makes observations about the student author and asks meaningful questions that will help determine what small teaching moment the teacher can use to help strengthen the student's picture book. Example prompts might include:

- What parts of this story resemble your home or culture?
- What is the problem/solution in your story? How do the pictures support the problem/solution?
- What describing words would you use to portray your characters? How can you illustrate that through your pictures and wording?
- How is this story supposed to make the reader feel?

Since the goal of the conference is for students to become less dependent on the teacher and more reflective of their own writing, the "link" of the conference is a helpful mechanism to transfer the learning to a student's independent work.

Once the students complete their finished picture books, author shares are one way for students to celebrate their artifact and practice reading it aloud. Often, teachers will host classroom reading events where the students' work can be shared with loved ones (Reid & Moses, 2019), while other products are simply shared in the class together and then sent home for parents to celebrate (Bogard & McMackin, 2012). Student authors could also share parts of their picture books while they are being produced. For instance, students might choose to share the ways where they brought the language of their home culture into their picture book, or to celebrate how well a character is portrayed to exemplify the traits the student author was trying to convey. Students could similarly be asked to just share their story as they complete it, recognizing that not all students finish at the same time. Culturally sustaining practices can be woven throughout the workshop model from the resources that are selected, to the foci of the minilessons, to the conversations that occur between teachers, students, and peers. The lessons and conversations can become increasingly more sophisticated, weaving together how students see identity in picture books and emulating that through their own books.

DISCUSSION AND IMPLICATIONS

As classrooms in the United States become increasingly diverse, corner-stone frameworks and approaches to literacy instruction like writer's workshop must continue to evolve to meet the needs of all students, particularly students of color who bring an incredible wealth of cultural knowledge, languages, and literacies that have been historically repressed in schools. Culturally sustaining literacy practices support this evolution by encouraging students not only to bring their home and community cultural practices and knowledges into the classroom, but to nurture and expand them.

As demonstrated in this chapter, each component of writer's workshop can be infused with multimodal composing practices that help students sustain their cultures and languages. During minilessons, teachers should choose multimodal mentor texts ranging from photographs to audio stories to picture books that represent a range of cultures and identities that reflect the students in the classroom. During independent writing time, students should be encouraged to authentically compose stories of their lives, families, communities, and interests using a variety of both traditional and nontraditional composing tools including writing, drawing, speaking, photographs, digital voice recordings, and online platforms. When conferencing, teachers and peers should encourage and support student writers in using their knowledges, languages, and experiences to compose audio, visual, and written texts. Finally, during author shares, students should be encouraged to freely and proudly share their work—and therefore their cultures, selves, and communities—with their teachers and peers.

Infusing writer's workshop with multimodal composing practices such as composing with drawings and photographs, personal and family storytelling, and producing picture books has the power to teach students complex and important literacy skills while also affirming their multifaceted identities. Each of the approaches outlined above is easily implementable by any teacher who currently uses or plans to use writer's workshop in their classroom and can be aligned with any set of literacy goals and standards. We encourage elementary educators to begin incorporating these multimodal composing practices in their writer's workshops to create an atmosphere where social justice goals, self-empowerment, and literacy learning are all achieved through the nurturing and sustaining of students' complete selves.

CHAPTER 2

Learning From Alina

Culturally Sustaining Pedagogy Within an Elementary Reading Intervention Context

Kelly K. Wissman

I first met Alina (all names are pseudonyms) when she was 6 years old. I immediately noticed her bright brown eyes, at times watchful, at other times sparkling, especially when she perceived opportunities for connection or for a bit of fun. Nestled between her mother and father, she sat at a small table in the school library. Her smile grew as she looked from one parent to the other and then to her toddler brother who was charming the other families gathered at the surrounding tables. Her gaze then settled lovingly on her infant brother held in her mother's lap. The way Alina clasped her hands in front of her, her arms outstretched on the table, she looked proud—proud to be a big sister, proud to be surrounded by her parents, proud of the shimmery bracelet she showed me as I sat down at her table. Across the 2 years we would work together, this sharing of our jewelry—a ring, necklace, a bracelet—would become a signature greeting between us.

On this morning before the school day started, Alina's classroom classroom teacher, Lauren, and I, a university-based researcher, had gathered the five students in one of Lauren's reading groups and their families to introduce them to a project we were starting called Names, Dreams, and Journeys. Translators and English as a new language (ENL) teachers joined the multilingual children and families at the tables at this family breakfast. We started the project in response to Lauren's wish to bring more diverse picture books into her practice as a literacy specialist and to welcome her students' multilingual and immigrant families more intentionally into her teaching. As I explore below, this family breakfast in the school library was the first of many efforts within the project to bring a culturally sustaining lens (Paris & Alim, 2017) to the reading intervention setting.

In this chapter, I provide a portrait of how Alina took up opportunities to read, respond to, and create culturally sustaining texts within and outside a reading intervention context. My purpose is to render the possibilities of bringing a culturally sustaining lens to reading intervention in ways that position children and families, their multilingualism, and their heritage practices, as resources for literacy learning. In response to assertions that we need more descriptive accounts of how teachers translate culturally sustaining pedagogy (CSP) theory into classroom practice, I show how Lauren's choice of texts and teaching moves created an instructional context for Alina's multilayered literacies and identities to emerge. As I write about Alina's responses to Lauren's introduction of culturally sustaining picture books and family engagement efforts, I consider how Alina's literate identities were revealed in agentive, assertive, and creative ways. In contrast to dominant representations of learners in intervention contexts often characterized by what they do not know and cannot do, I illustrate how bringing a CSP lens to the setting allows us to view Alina as a knowledgeable, agentive, multilingual reader and writer of her world. In addition to describing how Lauren co-created a context for these identities to become more visible, I also discuss the challenges she navigated and provide recommendations to teachers facing similar constraints.

CULTURALLY SUSTAINING PEDAGOGY AND INTERVENTION

Decades of research have shown us that building on students' linguistic and cultural resources can lead to enhanced literacy learning (e.g., Keehne et al., 2018); however, within intervention contexts aimed at identifying and filling gaps in foundational literacy skills, these resources are often overlooked (Ascenzi-Moreno & Quiñones, 2020; Orosco & Klingner, 2010). Although grounded in aims to provide equitable learning opportunities for all students, many Response to Intervention (RTI) and Multi-Tiered System of Supports (MTSS) models promote the use of universal screenings, standard treatment protocols, and highly structured curricula that are not attuned to the assets of diverse multilingual learners (Klingner & Edwards, 2006; Moore & Klingner, 2014). Indeed, within an exhaustive analysis of legislation, policy, and reading research framed by critical race theory, Willis (2019a) concluded that racial disparities and disproportionalities have increased within RTI.

Students performing below grade-level expectations in reading frequently receive instruction that targets isolated skill deficits (Allington, 2013) and that minimizes exposure to authentic children's literature. Texts featured within core reading programs are often of questionable literary and social value (Maniates & Mahiri, 2011), and books featuring diverse characters, languages, and settings are limited in number and often problematic (Aukerman et al., 2019; Wu & Coady, 2010). In their critical content analysis of 20 books within the Fountas and Pinnell Leveled Literacy intervention system, D. Thomas and Dyches (2019) found that characters of color are routinely "demeaned and relegated to the margins" (p. 12).

Scholars have argued for the great potential of infusing children's literature into the curriculum to reflect multilingual students' lived experiences (Arizpe et al., 2014; Stewart, 2017), to showcase characters navigating transnational spaces (Brochin & Medina, 2017), and to illuminate how individuals utilize multiple languages in agentive, fluid, and socially transformative ways (Zapata, 2020). Yuyi Morales's (2018) picture book, *Dreamers*, has been widely praised for its multilayered rendition of an immigration experience as well as its translingual approach to moving fluidly between both English and Spanish in the narration and illustrations (Machado & Flores, 2021). Day and Ward (2019) have called the book a "resplendent, culturally rich addition to the children's literature canon" (p. 87). Given the ubiquity of core reading programs that rarely include such representations of multilinguals in these ways and given the restrictions some reading intervention teachers face in incorporating authentic children's literature into their instruction, however, it can be difficult for books like *Dreamers* to find a home in the reading intervention context.

Against this backdrop, Lauren and I endeavored to bring a culturally sustaining lens to reading intervention in both text selection as well as in the literacy opportunities offered to both families and children, many of whom were multilingual and recent immigrants. As chapters in this edited volume demonstrate, CSP highlights the need not only to foster, but also to sustain "linguistic, literate, and cultural pluralism as part of schooling for positive social transformation" (Paris & Alim, 2017, p. 1). Calling for a fundamental reenvisioning of pedagogical and assessment practices that uphold White middle-class monolingual norms to the exclusion of others, CSP asks educators to resist policies and practices meant to keep those norms in place. Bringing a culturally sustaining lens to the reading intervention setting inspired our practices and framed our inquiries in the following ways: (1) incorporating texts across the curriculum reflective of linguistic and cultural diversity; (2) engaging in inquiries arising from students' cultural worlds and critical questions; (3) offering ongoing invitations for multilingual, intergenerational story-telling; and (4) creating embedded opportunities for multiple languages, literacies, and heritage practices to travel fluidly across home and school contexts.

CONTEXT AND POSITIONALITY

This exploratory case study took place in a public urban elementary school in a midsize city in the Northeast with five emergent bilinguals (García, 2009b) and their teacher, Lauren, in a reading intervention set-ting. Within the school, 26% of the students were classified as "English as New Language Learners" (ENLs) and 78% qualified for free lunch. The five students who came to Lauren 3 to 4 times a week for 30 minutes of reading instruction spoke home languages of Arabic, Karen, Spanish, and Black Language (defined by Baker-Bell, 2020b). Four of the five families included members who were recent immigrants to the United States. When the study began, all five students were in the 1st grade and had scored below grade-level expectations in reading as determined by formal and informal assessment measures. Lauren, a teacher with whom I had an existing research relationship dating back 5 years pri-or to the start of this study, has been teaching for over 2 decades and holds advanced degrees in literacy. Both Lauren and I are White, cisgen-der women, middle class, and monolingual. These identities presented limitations to our pedagogical and research practice as we experienced difficulties in communicating with the multilingual participants as well as challenges in locating and teaching with linguistically diverse texts. Furthermore, we lacked the embodied understanding of participants' cultural and linguistic experiences.

Prior to the start of data collection, Lauren and I read and discussed a range of articles on CSP (e.g., Paris & Alim, 2014), diverse books (e.g., E. Thomas, 2016), and engagement with multilingual families (e.g., Rowe & Fain, 2013), as well as a selection of picture books featuring repre-sentations of multiple languages and diverse families. Lauren's reading intervention class was embedded in a broader school and district context that included fixed expectations related to curriculum, assessments, and student achievement, but also afforded flexibility in instructional choic-es. As a result, we concentrated on cultivating two central practices that she felt she could bring into her classroom: (1) interactive read alouds of diverse picture books accompanied by narrative writing invitations and (2) family engagement efforts that included family gatherings in the school library and sending home tote bags with books and a journal. These practices were not designed to replace direct, explicit, and systematic instruction in foundational skills, which Lauren continued to pursue in other aspects of her teaching, nor did we design the read alouds and family engagement efforts to serve as conduits for teaching those skills directly. Instead, the engagements with picture books and with families were designed to bring another dimension to Lauren's understanding of and support for her students across a range of their literate, cultural, and linguistic identities and to draw from families' linguistic and cultural knowledge as instructional resources.

We framed our work with the children and families through inquiries into names, dreams, and journeys. We chose these themes for their potential resonance with the lived experiences of families, many of whom were first generation immigrants, with multicultural backgrounds and multilingual language practices. We chose "names" because many researchers have found that students of color can find schools to be inhospitable in terms of learning and valuing their unique names (Kohli & Solórzano, 2012; Nash, et al., 2018). A focus on "dreams" highlighted participants' hopes and dreams, the possibilities of overcoming adversity, and the role of literacy in helping make dreams a reality. Finally, "journeys" invited inquiry and exploration of families' unique journeys in life and in the educational system (Souto-Manning & Martell, 2016).

These themes shaped the choice of interactive read alouds and the additional books sent home in tote bags (see Table 2.1). The tote bags also included a camera, markers, crayons, and a journal for the families to write, draw, or paste pictures in response to open-ended prompts (e.g., What's important to your family?) and more specific inquiries (e.g., the child's name story). Where possible, we drew on the assistance from English as a new language teachers and translators provided by the school to translate materials sent home in the tote bags into each family's home language. Given concerns about the accuracy of Google Translate and other online translation services, we used these tools sparingly. An overarching purpose of sending home the tote bags was to connect and enrich the in-school work by inviting families to read culturally sustaining texts together and to create texts reflective of their experiences and languages. The project culminated in a "book release party" where the children, families, teachers, and administrators gathered in the school library to celebrate the children's creation of their own picture books.

To varying degrees, Lauren and I both took on roles as researchers and as teachers throughout the study. By "studying side by side" (Erickson, 2006), we constructed knowledge within the immediate context

Table 2.1. Picture Books and Family Engagements

Focus	Picture Books	Family Engagements

Names	Interactive Read Alouds:
	
	• *Jonathan and His Mommy* by Irene Smalls
	• *Thunder Boy Jr.* by Sherman Alexie
	• *Golden Domes and Silver Lanterns: A Muslim Book of Colors* by Hena Khan
	• *Mommy's Khimar* by Jamilah Thompkins-Bigelow
	• *Dear Primo: A Letter to My Cousin* by Duncan Tonatiuh
	
	Books Within Tote Bags Sent Home:
	
	• Interactive Read Aloud Books
	• *Alma and How She Got Her Name* by Juana Martinez-Neal
	• *Marisol McDonald Doesn't Match/Marisol McDonald No Combina* by Monica Brown
	• *The Name Jar* by Yangsook Choi
	• *Rene Has Two Last Names/Rene Tiene Dos Apellidos* by Rene Colato Laínez
		• Family breakfast
		• Tote bags
		• Family journals:
		  » Family description and activities
		  » Child's name story
		  » Family photographs

Dreams	Interactive Read Alouds • *Dreamers* by Yuyi Morales • *Viva Frida* by Yuyi Morales Books Within Tote Bags Sent Home: • Interactive Read Aloud books • *My Pen* by Christopher Myers • *Drum Dream Girl* by Margarita Engle	• Classroom visits from families • Tote bags • Family journals: » Dreams for the family and child
Journeys	Interactive Read Alouds • *A Different Pond* by Bao Phi • *Lost and Found Cat: The True Story of Kunkush's Incredible Journey* by Amy Shrodes and Doug Kuntz • *Last Stop on Market Street* by Matt de la Peña Books Within Tote Bags Sent Home Interactive Read Aloud books	• Tote Bags • Family journals: » Family photographs • Book release party

of moment-by-moment instructional decisions as well as during reflections directly afterwards on what we were noticing and what pedagogical shifts might be considered next. Across the 2 years of the study, I was a participant observer in 44 reading group sessions, each averaging 30 minutes. I attended classes at Lauren's invitation that she identified would be most reflective of the study's goals (i.e., sessions that featured interactive read alouds of diverse books, discussions of the family journals, and the creation of the students' own picture books). For each session, I wrote observational fieldnotes and audio-recorded and transcribed classroom talk. When Lauren's schedule allowed, we spoke after class, resulting in 32 conversations, ranging from 3–30 minutes. Additional data sources included copies of student writing and family journals, fieldnotes from family engagement events, and fieldnotes from planning sessions.

CULTURALLY SUSTAINING LITERACY VIGNETTES

Bringing a culturally sustaining lens to the reading intervention setting was illuminating, enriching, and demanding. It required that Lauren and I had to be constantly looking for resources to ensure students and families had access to materials inclusive of their languages and access to pedagogical opportunities sustaining of the "lifeways of communities" (Paris & Alim, 2017, p. 1). Culturally sustaining pedagogy proceeds from an expansive and additive vision of schooling for students from culturally and linguistically diverse backgrounds. This vision centers the knowledge and resources of students, families, and communities. Rather than locating perceived deficits within individual students or pathologizing communities, CSP calls for a fundamental re-envisioning of past pedagogical and assessment practices centered in the White gaze, instead asking this question:

> What if . . . the goal of teaching and learning with youth of color was not ultimately to see how closely students could perform White middle-class norms but to explore, honor, extend, and, at times, problematize their heritage and community practices? (Paris & Alim, 2014, p. 86)

Bringing a CSP lens to intervention thus provided generative opportunities to see the children and their literacy and language practices in richer and more complex ways and to inspire the creation of pedagogical opportunities that reflected an expansive definition of culture. For example, CSP replaces static understandings of culture as an unchanging set of characteristics or a possession of a group of people, with a more dynamic understanding that emphasizes how individuals produce shifting, hybrid, and dynamic expressions of culture as lived across geographies, time, and language (Love, 2015). A CSP lens helped Lauren and me to seek out and be attuned to expressions of culture in terms of

language, religion, customs, and traditions, even as we also looked for
ways in which the children and their families were actively (re)making
culture in conversation with popular culture, diasporic practices, and
transnational literacies.

In the vignettes that follow, I present rich description of Lauren's
practice and how Alina took up and created her own learning opportunities in often agentive, assertive, and creative ways. Her actions reveal the interplay between her literate, religious, cultural, and linguistic
identities.

"We Are a Loving Muslim Family": A Family Journal Showcases Multiple Identities and Literacies

Shortly after the family breakfast in the school library that launched the
project, Lauren began to assemble materials to include in the tote bag to
be sent home with each child for 1 week at a time: picture books about
names, a family journal, markers and crayons, and a letter translated
into the family's home language. Sending home materials in this way to
the five students in this reading intervention setting was new to Lauren.
This practice added an often festive and lively energy to the setting. Each
time a family sent back the tote bag after keeping it for a week, Lauren
would suspend whatever lesson plans she had made for the session that
day to focus on the family's contribution to the journal and to engage
in storytelling.

On one of these celebratory days, the children gathered around the
kidney-shaped table as Lauren carefully opened each page from Alina's
family journal and paused, asking Alina to tell us about it. On one page,
Alina's mother drew pictures of each family member. Alina then pronounced each family member's name and pointed to them on the page.
Underneath the portraits of the family members Alina's mother wrote in
English, "We are a loving Muslim family. The best thing ever is to be
together in a family." Alina beamed as she read these words aloud to
us. The next page was fully devoted to one of Alina's younger brothers,
the boy Alina lovingly referred to as her "baby." Next to a hand-drawn
portrait, Alina's mother wrote in Alina's voice, "I love him very much
and I like to spend most of his time with him." On another page, Alina's
mother traced an image of Cinderella from one of Alina's coloring
books, which Alina then colored in with light blues for her dress and yel-
lows for her hair. Alina smiled as she glanced at the page. Next to it, her
mother wrote in Alina's voice, "I love watching Barbie and other clips
on YouTube. I love dancing." Across the pages, which also included
responses written in Arabic to questions about Alina's name story and a

description of the family's time in Yemen prior to coming to the United States, a devotion to family is displayed prominently within the words and images.

At the same time that family and religion are centered in the contributions to the family journal, allusions to popular culture figures and to multimedia are also present, suggesting the layers of Alina's identities finding expression across multiple modalities. Given that both popular culture figures referenced, Cinderella and Barbie, embody idealized notions of White femininity, it is possible to see here the ubiquity of these figures and how they circulate not only within popular media texts, but also within family rooms and all the way back into classrooms. Within the journal, Alina and her mother purposefully made visible their multiple languages, providing tangible representations of their cultural backgrounds that included their uptake of popular culture, and using multiple modalities to construct knowledge fluidly across contexts. Alina's family journal was thus reflective of a culturally sustaining approach in that it helped create entry points for Alina and her mother to draw on their languages, faith traditions, and cultural resources to support literacies and heritage practices across home and school settings.

"Oh! Muslim?": Embodied Responses to an Interactive Read Aloud

A few weeks later, Lauren conducted an interactive read aloud of *Golden Domes, Silver Lanterns: A Muslim Book of Colors* (H. Khan, 2015), with the five multilingual students in Alina's reading intervention class. As class began, Alina was sitting with her fellow classmates, Yasir, Lah Eh San, Salvador, and Tahir-Ra. When Lauren started the read aloud, Alina was still shifting in her seat and arranging the pencils in front of her, an uncustomary sour expression on her face. On this day, Alina hadn't had the best morning, but she brightened a bit when she glanced at the cover of the book. Upon hearing Lauren say the word *Muslim*, Alina's mood shifted further:

> *Lauren:* The story we're going to read is *Golden Domes and Silver Lanterns*. It's a Muslim book of colors.
> *Alina:* Oh! Muslim?!

It is difficult to render the eclectic mix of joy, surprise, and recognition in Alina's voice as she asked this question and as she realized the potential focus of the book. This one word, Muslim, reverberated in the room as both Alina and Yasir sat up straighter and the other students careened their necks to get a better look at the book's cover and to study the faces

of Alina and Yasir. Lauren affirmed that she had indeed said the word
Muslim and continued to introduce the book and engage the children in
a discussion of what they were noticing:

> *Lauren:* Yeah, Muslim.
> *Yasir:* Like me!
> *Lauren:* And you. [looking at Alina]
>
> *[Alina laughs]*
>
> *Yasir:* And you!
> *Lauren:* [laughs] I'm not Muslim, but you and Alina are Muslim.
>   Maybe Alina and Yasir, you'll recognize some of the things in
>   the story. If you do, let us know. OK? Tell us if you know what
>   these things are. It's called *Golden Domes and Silver Lanterns*.
>   Before we even read it, I would really like you to just look
>   at the pictures on the front cover and tell me what you think
>   about the pictures. What do you notice?
> *Lah Eh San:* It's like a castle.
> *Lauren:* Show me what you think is a castle.
> *La Eh San:* This!
> *Lauren:* This right here looks like a castle?
> *Alina:* That's the mosque.
> *Lauren:* You see that? Is that the mosque?
> *Yasir:* Yeah, that is the mosque . . . In Syria I go in the mosque to
>   pray.

Lah Eh San, who is not Muslim, initially identified the mosque as a
castle. In response, Alina definitively asserts that the building is not a
castle, but a mosque, while Yasir speaks about attending a mosque in
Syria before his family's move to the United States. Lauren's decision to
choose this particular text and to invite responses to it through the interactive read aloud created a context where both Alina and Yasir could
build on their background knowledge and their cultural and linguistic
resources to construct knowledge with their classmates.

As the read aloud continued, Alina began sharing some of her responses to the book in Arabic, something she had not done previously
in this setting. Lauren turned to her, and asked enthusiastically, "Is
that Arabic? Say it again! I want to hear it! I want to hear it." For the
remainder of the read aloud, Alina and Yasir made additional contributions in Arabic, mostly to each other, and sometimes to Lauren to tell
her the Arabic word for what she was reading or to correct her pro-
nunciation. Within only a few pages, the book helped create a context

for Alina and Yasir to show their expertise in multiple languages and knowledge of religious traditions as well as to invoke Yasir's own transnational crossing.

Later, when the little girl in the picture book describes the rug she prays on, Alina, without speaking, spontaneously jumped up from the table, glided to the class rug, and demonstrated how she prayed. In these moments, Alina's embodied responses reflected her bilingualism, her faith, and her cultural knowledge. She spoke Arabic to her classmates in a setting where she had not done so previously and brought together her faith tradition and her school learning in a spontaneous and physical demonstration of prayer. From a culturally sustaining lens, I would argue that Alina recreated the classroom space as one not just passively welcoming of her cultural and linguistic background, but one where she agentively cocreated it and invited others into it.

During this interactive read aloud, language, religion, and culture were "creatively foregrounded" (Paris & Alim, 2014, p. 87) in the choice of book, the children's meaning-making, and Lauren's creation of a context that encouraged spontaneous responses. Certainly, the choice of *Golden Domes, Silver Lanterns* (H. Khan, 2015) was important in what occurred here. Yet, I would also argue that the setting that Lauren cocreated with the children and families also played central roles. By gathering the families for the family breakfast and by inviting them to share stories in the family journal, Lauren had demonstrated a vital interest in and welcoming of multiple languages and families' lived experiences into school spaces. This constellation of invitations and opportunities helped contribute to a context in which Alina read, received, and acted upon Kahn's text in culturally sustaining ways.

"I Am Praying": Agentive Writing Across Modalities and Spaces

Over the months that followed, Lauren and the students continued their inquiries into names, dreams, and journeys through interactive read alouds, the family journals, and narrative writing invitations. As the school year began to draw to a close and as students began to compose their own picture books for eventual sharing at an end-of-school-year celebration, Alina asked Lauren to view *Golden Domes, Silver Lanterns* (H. Khan, 2015) again. The following week, Alina asked her mother to photograph her as she prayed. Lauren had the photographs developed and shared them with Alina. Without any prompting from Lauren, Alina then worked diligently to write step-by-step directions on how to pray and carefully placed photographs of herself by each step, incorporating a lyrical repetition of the line, "I am praying" next to each photo. Alina's picture book, which she shared at the children's book release attended by the principal, families, and teachers, included this photo essay.

Alina first handwrote her instructions for praying. Then she asked Lauren to type her instructions:

1. Stand up and cross your arms. I am praying.
2. Bend and put your hands on your neck. I am praying.
3. Stand up and put your arms out like this. I am praying.
4. Kneel down and put your head on the rug. I am praying.
5. Sit up and put your hands on your knees. Put your one finger out. I am praying.
6. Criss cross applesauce. Take the beads and prayer on prayer rug. I am praying.
7. Take Quran to read and to make you smart. I am praying.
8. This is what you need to pray with. I am not praying.

Alina writes in direct, clear, and imperative sentences. She directly addresses the reader/viewer by writing in the second person voice and then switches to the first-person voice to repeat, almost in a reverential tone, "I am praying." Displaying an awareness of her audience, Alina's writing is instructional, while also poetic and serene.

Across the photo essay, Alina uses her body to demonstrate the distinctive and precise movements associated with praying. In attending to the visual mode of the photo essay, she also carefully selected and highlighted the essential material aspects that accompany praying, from the rug to the beads to the holy text. She has made evident these prized aspects of her identity and brought them into a school space for a school audience. Importantly, Alina's multiple literacies and cultural identities coexist in the photo essay. For example, she employs a uniquely American directive used to instruct children how to sit in elementary classrooms, "criss cross applesauce." This phrase appears on the same page on which Alina has written the Arabic word for "pray." In this way, the photo essay serves a culturally sustaining function in which Alina is showcasing her multiple languages and identities. Her independence and self-initiative are in evidence as well. Of her own accord, Alina requested to take home *Golden Domes and Silver Lantern: A Muslim Book of Colors* (H. Kahn, 2015). Alina's actions are also revealing of her self-assuredness and sense of purpose in both performing the act of prayer and directing her mother in documenting the process. As noted above, Paris and Alim (2017) assert that CSP exists "wherever education sustains the lifeways of communities" (p. 1). In this instance, it is Alina herself who has created the conditions for her schooling experience to be connected to her home and spiritual lives.

"I Just Didn't Know": Navigating the Expectations of Reading Intervention with a CSP Lens

During the time period in which Alina was crafting her "I Am Praying" photo essay, Lauren and I sat together in another context, with other educators within a network of teacher writers, writing in response to a prompt, "Write about a piece of student writing that was special or challenged you in some way." When her time to share arrived, Lauren spoke of Alina, of the photo essay about praying that she created, of the repetition of the "I am praying" line that she read with such conviction. In her writing, Lauren detailed Alina's singular focus, her strong independence, her determination to create, produce, and perfect the essay. She wrote about how Alina drew on multiple modalities, resources, and individuals in order to meet her self-initiated objective. Lauren also noted how she hadn't set out an assignment or a list of expectations; rather, Alina took this on herself and leveraged the resources available to her to do so. As Lauren read her writing about Alina to this gathering of teacher writers, her voice faltering just a bit with emotion, she recounted her happiness at Alina's writing, but also the feeling of sadness that she had not known all this about Alina before, that there were so many other stories she was unaware of. "I just didn't know," Lauren wrote. "What else have I been missing for all these years?" she asked.

As Lauren read her piece to the other educators gathered in the room, I also thought of all the conversations Lauren and I had engaged in as we reflected on our efforts to bring a culturally sustaining lens to the intervention setting. In these conversations, we often remarked upon the brilliance of the connections the children were making and often marveled at the stories they told in response and the multiple languages in which they did so. At the same time, however, those conversations were also often filled with worry and with concern. Noting the plethora of assessments Lauren needed to administer in her role as a literacy specialist and her concern that some of the students were not making the demonstratable progress the data team and others would like to see, Lauren would often interject, "We gotta move," and "I need to do more to move the kids academically." Within this intervention setting where children would ultimately be assessed through formal assessments not always shown to be responsive to the children's full linguistic and cultural resources, Lauren at times pulled back from the CSP-informed work to focus exclusively on explicit instruction in foundational reading skills. She would exchange interactive read alouds of diverse picture books for leveled texts that would support direct instruction in subskills, for example, or suspend a time for narrative writing in order to complete a task related to progress monitoring. Although Lauren believed in the value and efficacy of teaching foundational reading skills in systematic ways, these choices to pull back from the culturally sustaining work were often difficult for her, especially when she felt there was momentum building with the children's responses to diverse picture books and as she felt her relationships with families to be strengthening.

Lauren's decisions here need to be understood within the context of the implicit and explicit expectations ever-present across intervention settings to demonstrate measurable progress in students' foundational reading skills in English. As a result, Lauren and I often felt stymied by broader institutional constraints and by our own limitations. First, we had difficulties finding pedagogical resources designed specifically to be inclusive of multilingualism while simultaneously targeting foundational reading skills responsive to the reading profiles of emergent bilinguals (Goldenberg, 2020; Hopewell & Escamilla, 2014). These difficulties were enhanced by our own monolingualism, which inhibited a creation of our own multilingual pedagogical resources. Limited hours available for translation services also restricted communication possibilities with multilingual families. Second, at the classroom, school, and district level, we navigated a lack of mandated and informal assessments attuned to the linguistic and cultural strengths of emergent bilinguals. Third, definitions of what constituted growth, progress, or "data" were tied to these assessments, which were not sensitive to linguistic and cultural diversity. As a result, the reading, writing, and meaning-making that the children did in relation to the CSP-informed interactive read alouds and through book-making were not always viewed as markers of growth and proficiency as traditionally understood and measured in the intervention context. Therefore, despite how the above vignettes suggest that rich literacy practices can be cultivated by bringing a CSP lens to one's practice, Lauren also navigated many challenges in doing so that curtailed a fuller integration of CSP into the setting.

DISCUSSION AND IMPLICATIONS

When I first met Alina in the school library, I learned that she was a big sister, a daughter buoyed by her love for her parents, and a girl who delighted in the sparkle of a piece of jewelry held up to the light just so. Over the course of the 2 years of the study, I would also learn that Alina spoke Arabic, that she practiced her Muslim faith daily, and that she was a seeker, writer, reader, and photographer of her world. The vignettes show how Alina fluidly drew on her multiple languages, religion, and lived experiences while building a multidimensional literate identity in creative and agentive ways. They also reveal how Lauren's efforts to cultivate connections across homes, schools, and communities through diverse picture books and family engagement efforts helped to link literacies, languages, and lifeways in ways resonant with a culturally sustaining approach. By bringing a culturally sustaining lens to the intervention setting, I witnessed how the space could shift, from one focused on mastering discrete reading skills in one language, to a space of collaborative meaning-making with multiple languages, with books, with the world, and with families. As I showed in the vignettes, Alina fully and agentively embraced the openings Lauren provided: a book with the word Muslim in the title, a class camera and journal that traveled home to all families, an invitation to speak Arabic in a read aloud. In this way, I believe Alina teaches us that when we make available picture books reflective of students' languages and when we open classrooms to intergenerational family stories and heritage practices, culturally sustaining pedagogy can flourish.

Paris and Alim (2014) have called for "explicitly pluralist outcomes that are not centered on White, middle-class, monolingual, and monocultural norms of educational achievement" (p. 95). What would it mean to work toward "pluralist outcomes" within reading intervention? As a starting point, we would first need to assert that culturally sustaining pedagogical practices are just as foundational to the aims of literacy education as the teaching of foundational reading skills, a daunting prospect given the historic and ongoing lack of attention to the assets of students from diverse cultural and linguistic backgrounds (Klingner & Edwards, 2006) and the disclination to acknowledge racial disproportionalities within RTI (Willis, 2019a). For a fuller integration of CSP-informed practices, a consideration of the primacy of assessments and the goals of reading intervention to include CSP-related outcomes may be necessary. As one step forward in reconsidering the nature and emphases of assessments, we might take guidance from studies like the one conducted by Noguerón-Liu et al. (2020) that provides insight into the roles of parents in shaping reading assessments more reflective of the linguistic and language resources of emergent bilinguals.

In considering the challenges of integrating translingual writing approaches into composition courses, Milson-Whyte (2013) has warned of the danger of "valorizing, but not legitimizing minoritized languages"

(p. 115). This concern resonates with what I learned working with Lauren. Across public statements, ranging from curriculum documents to celebrations of diversity on websites, there was an explicit and implicit valorizing of the linguistic and cultural diversity among students and families. As much as this recognition appeared to be genuine, it also coexisted with monolingual instructional practices and monolingual high-stakes assessments, as well as limited resources for translation services to promote family engagement. While good intentions may have been present, there were a number of structural barriers that prevented a legitimization, let alone a sustaining of, multilingualism and heritage practices.

As I reflect on the vignettes featuring Alina, I am mindful of this distinction between valorization and legitimization. Wider educational discourses often declare commitments to inclusivity and diversity and many schools take sincere pride in the contributions and presence of a diverse teaching staff and students. However, while we may valorize or celebrate diversity, do our instructional and assessment practices legitimize the use of multiple languages, value transnational literacies, and create space for embodied cultural knowledge? In what ways are we still centering monolingual language practices? Are diverse texts the exception and not the norm? Where are children exposed to languages other than English in our classroom materials? Are we building pathways between home and schools with intentionality and with a true sense of reciprocity?

Although making large-scale systemic change related to instantiating culturally sustaining instructional and assessment practices across K–12 spaces may seem out of the reach of individual educators, I offer the following suggestions for what each of us may consider in our own practice:

- Make space for high-quality picture books reflective of children's multilingual worlds. To do so responsibly would mean drawing on a wide range of resources in making decisions about book selection (e.g., consulting lists of award-winning books representing linguistic and cultural diversity, such as the Pura Belpré Award, the Coretta Scott King Book Awards, the Asian/ Pacific American Award, and the Arab American Book Award). Teachers may also wish to select books from publishers who show a commitment to linguistic and cultural diversity in the books they choose to publish and promote, such as Lee & Low Books.

- Build curriculum from family narratives and heritage practices. Inviting children and families to write, draw, and paste pictures into the family journal not only provided Lauren a more textured understanding of her students, but also created texts to read aloud and discuss in class.
- Invite children to compose their own books from the stories and languages of their lives. In crafting their own picture books, the children incorporated multiple languages, rendered heritage practices significant to their families, and drew on multiple modalities to make meaning.
- Reclaim the power of story and narrative in reading intervention. Although there were many challenges in this study, my work with Lauren repeatedly revealed to me the power of picture books and their importance within the intervention setting. They invited children into the world of story, to experience a journey, to feel and dream alongside the characters who spoke multiple languages and who embodied transcultural experiences. It is this recognition of the possibility and the purpose of picture books that was a powerful through line in the study and that can sometimes be lost in a focus on skills, data, and progress monitoring.

To practitioners facing daunting assessment climates and the adopting of commercial reading programs, I would argue that even the most constrained learning environments can be punctuated and enlivened by becoming proximate to children and families through cultivating the very languages and literacies that are already present, if we look intently and if we listen carefully. When Alina came to Lauren's class, speaking multiple languages and embodying transnational experiences, she was illustrative of the growing cultural and linguistic diversity within school spaces. As Alina took up and also created her own opportunities to engage in culturally sustaining literacy practices, I believe she can serve as an inspiration and a call to action for all of us to begin to reimagine educational contexts for emergent bilinguals more worthy of their gifts and more sustaining of their literacies and languages.

Part II

MODELS OF CSLP IN CLASSROOMS FOR ADOLESCENTS AND YOUTH

CHAPTER 3

Disciplinary Literacy and Culturally Sustaining Pedagogies

Tensions and Potentials

Britnie Delinger Kane and Rachelle S. Savitz

Over roughly the last 15 years, work in disciplinary literacy has gained credibility and interest among literacy researchers and practitioners. High profile state and national organizations (e.g., National Council of Teachers of English; Literacy Research Association; Common Core State Standards) have highlighted that students need to develop particular ways of reading, writing, speaking, listening, and thinking in specific disciplines. In addition, disciplinary literacy approaches to instruction have shown promise as a theoretical and practical way to support the deep, conceptual learning that the 21st century will require and as a response to frequently aired concerns about the adolescent literacy "crisis" (Goldman et al., 2016). Concurrently, research on culturally sustaining pedagogies (CSP) has come to prominence. At the heart of CSP is the idea that students of color and other historically marginalized students need educational opportunities that will not simply support students' access to social, economic, and academic power structures, but also will develop language and literacy practices capable of challenging the White-dominated status quo in the United States (Paris, 2012; Alim & Paris, 2017).

In this chapter, we argue that there is both deep alliance and deep tension at the nexus of disciplinary literacy and CSP. Particularly in fields like the English language arts, disciplinary literacy is, if not synonymous with, then at least closely related to the dominant forms of language and literacy use that culturally sustaining pedagogies seek to critique and broaden. Yet, scholars point out that both disciplinary literacy and culturally sustaining literacy pedagogies must rest upon the same central assumption: namely, that literacy cannot be understood apart from the contexts and purposes of its use. Based on this essential similarity, we will bring these two lines of work together to suggest specific instructional practices that middle and high school ELA teachers might draw upon so that teachers can capitalize on the advantages of both.

The main goal of this chapter is to provide vignettes of instructional practices capable of bringing to life the precepts of these important lines of work. We will describe the following practices:

1. Investigating and studying the disciplinary excellence of scholars of color and other marginalized groups.
2. Making students' individual and cultural ways of being substantive, necessary aspects of the curriculum from which disciplinary ideas are constructed.
3. Designing instructional activities that honor the language and literacy practices that have typified the cultural groups represented in classrooms.
4. Encouraging students' critical reflexivity of their own cultural practices.

We will describe how these practices can be mutually supportive of one another, ending with a discussion of what teachers will need to know and be able to do to use these instructional practices to support students' language and literacy development.

UNDERSTANDING THE POTENTIAL—AND TENSION—IN CULTURALLY SUSTAINING DISCIPLINARY LITERACY PEDAGOGIES

Contexts and Positionalities

This chapter comes out of our own experiences teaching and researching content-area and disciplinary literacy, particularly with pre- and inservice English language arts teachers at the middle and high school levels. As teacher educators and researchers, we teach courses on content-area and disciplinary literacy and on culturally responsive and sustaining pedagogies. Teaching these courses has helped us recognize tensions endemic to these two fields.

In this chapter we draw upon examples from our combined 34 years in the field—as teachers, literacy coaches, teacher educators, and educational researchers—to make sense of how, on a practical level, teachers can draw upon both disciplinary literacy and culturally sustaining pedagogies to support all students' learning. Examples from Britnie's classroom come from her time as a 9th-grade English language arts teacher in a deeply segregated Title I school in Charleston, South Carolina, where approximately two-thirds of the students were identified as Black and about one-third were identified as White. Rachelle has been a K–12 literacy interventionist, literacy coach, and reading teacher. The majority of her classroom experience was in Florida, teaching culturally, economically, and linguistically diverse students in Title I schools. Both Rachelle and Britnie currently teach in predominantly White institutions of higher education in South Carolina. It is also important to note that we are both White, cisgender, monolingual women, so we speak from a place of allyship with those from historically marginalized groups, rather than from a place of personal experience. This reminds us, also, to speak from a place of humility: There is much that we have to learn about both disciplinary literacy and culturally relevant and sustaining pedagogies, and this chapter represents just one contribution to these vital lines of research. We look forward, always, to work that will specify, refine, and improve upon what we include here.

What Is Disciplinary Literacy?

A central goal of disciplinary literacy is to support students to become, not disciplinary experts necessarily, but "disciplinary insiders" who can identify and use discipline-specific language and literacy practices so that they can "engage in the cognitive, social, and semiotic processes specific to the discipline" (Spires et al., 2018, p. 1405; see also Shanahan & Shanahan, 2012). Disciplinary literacy assumes that students need to be apprenticed into an understanding of the epistemologies, habits of mind, modes of inquiry, and valued language and literacy practices that characterize work in particular academic disciplines or domains (Goldman et al., 2016; Moje, 2015).

For example, recent research in the English language arts has focused specifically on what it means to teach ELA from the standpoint of disciplinary literacy (Goldman et al., 2016; Rainey, 2016; T. Reynolds et al., 2020). Much of this work has focused on literary reasoning, a branch of work in ELA. It has revealed specific epistemologies, modes of inquiry, and discipline-specific literacy practices, such as the following:

- Epistemologies: ELA is a social and problem-based discipline in which practitioners use specific sets of tools to build interpretations of literature as a means of understanding the human condition.

- Modes of inquiry: Disciplinary practitioners in ELA are focused on using character, setting, plot, structure, genre, text type (e.g., magical realism, Western, mystery), theme, and figurative language to build multiple interpretations of literature.
- Discipline-specific literacy practices for literary reasoning: articulating literary puzzles, identifying strangeness, identifying patterns, recursively building new interpretations, and making claims.

To support students to learn these discipline-specific literacy practices, disciplinary literacy highlights the role of modeling the use of discipline-specific literacy practices and presenting students with authentic opportunities to participate in inquiry (Gabriel & Wenz, 2017).

Affordances of Disciplinary Literacy from the Perspective of CSP

Disciplinary literacy instruction has much to offer in terms of its focus on inquiry, collaboration, authenticity, and relevance, which are also—broadly speaking—interests of CSP and consistent with research on how to support deep, conceptual learning. Disciplinary literacy traces its roots to what Street (1984) called the ideological model of literacy, which is—at its base—the recognition that literacy must be examined as a set of culturally and contextually situated social practices. As Gutiérrez and colleagues (2009) highlighted, "An ideological model posits that literacy is always embedded in social practices, where the consequences of learning a literacy are dependent on its context of development" (p. 213).

Like disciplinary literacy, culturally sustaining pedagogies take as a foundational construct that literacy must be understood in the context of its use. Although both disciplinary literacy and CSP emphasize the importance of context to literacy learning, they see differing contexts as most central. In disciplinary literacy instruction, the focus is on academic disciplines as central contexts/communities that influence the social practices of literacy. In CSP, the focus is on cultural communities and everyday practices that influence the lives of—especially—students of color and students growing up in poverty. This difference, as will be discussed, creates important tensions at the nexus of disciplinary literacy instruction and CSP.

Disciplinary literacy takes as a focus a deeper understanding of the processes through which knowledge is constructed within particular disciplines, which is also a central interest of CSP. In fact, from the perspective of CSP—and its forerunner, culturally relevant pedagogies (Ladson-Billings, 1995b)—students must become deeply aware of the social practices through which knowledge is constructed so that they might become more critically conscious and advocate for change and expansion in the epistemologies, purposes, and literacy practices that typify disciplinary work.

However, here again, differences assert themselves. For instance, an undergirding epistemology about the purpose of ELA—from scholars and theorists who are often, but not always, White—is that interpretations of literature are, ultimately, a means through which practitioners can examine the human condition (Goldman et al., 2016). Yet, as Alim & Paris (2017) point out, Toni Morrison highlights a different epistemology about the purpose of literature: that writing (and, presumably) reading literature is about escape from the White gaze. In this, she is connected to a long line of critical theorists who have seen literacy as the practice of freedom (Freire, 1970). Thus both disciplinary literacy and CSP emphasize that students must understand the processes through which knowledge is built in different disciplines. Importantly, however, culturally sustaining forms of disciplinary literacy take disciplinary literacy's call to allow students access to the epistemological underpinnings of disciplinary work one step further, highlighting the need to include more voices—and especially the voices of marginalized people—to critique and broaden existing definitions of discipline-specific epistemologies, modes of inquiry, and literacy practices.

Tensions Inherent in Disciplinary Literacy and CSP

Importantly, it is too simplistic to say that CSP can be added onto disciplinary literacy pedagogies. Instead, we must take stock of the tensions inherent in these two fields. Thus we must recognize that a central goal of disciplinary literacy is to apprentice students into discipline-specific ways of reading, writing, speaking, listening, viewing, composing, and thinking. However, students—particularly students of color and students from other marginalized communities—often resist such a positioning. The literature is rich with examples of students who refuse to define themselves as mathematicians or writers as a form of resistance to schools which have routinely suggested to students of color that "survival, achievement, and success can happen only if they follow the rules, meet above and beyond the expectations, and perform in specific ways that, ultimately, *other* who they are (e.g., their familial, community, and racial identities, linguistic practices, and cultural and intellectual traditions)" (Kinloch, 2017, pp. 27–28, italics in the original; see also Bucholz et al., 2017; Gutiérrez et al., 2009).

Students' resistance has, in many cases, been warranted. The history of language and literacy instruction in the United States is rife with

examples in which students' use of language and literacy have been ritu-
ally and systematically demeaned—too often in the name of discipline-
specific goals sanctioned by the state and the academy (e.g., see Gutiéerrez
et al., 2009). For example, the idea that there is a "Standard English"
or, as Alim and Smitherman (2012) call it, "White Mainstream English,"
and that one's academic and economic success should be predicated on
it, is an example of the ways in which the expectations of ELA as a discipline have ostracized students from marginalized communities (e.g.,
Smagorinsky, 2015). As Bucholz and colleagues (2017) argue, such a
focus on "Standard" English strips people of their identities and social
agency (p. 44) while overlooking the value of other languages, such as
Black Language, which reflect important "ways of knowing, interpreting, surviving, and being in the world" (Baker-Bell, 2020a, p. 2). In short,
the majority White, female, and monolingual teaching force has failed to
recognize that Black Language, to take just one example, "is systematic
with regular rules at the lexical, phonological, and grammatical level"
(Rickford, 2002, p. 1).

In fact, advocates of students from historically marginalized communities have consistently noted that institutions in the United States have
routinely dismissed the intellectual and creative strengths of many students of color, constructing students of color, instead, as deficient when
set against the White, middle-class norms that pervade most schools in
the United States (Alim & Paris, 2017; Gutiérrez, et al. 2009; Kinloch
et al., 2020; Kirkland, 2013). As Gutiérrez and colleagues (2009) point
out, early research on literacy conceptualized difference as nonnorma-
tive, and nonnormativity as deficient. She argues that, as a field, literacy
research was actually built on the idea of marginalized, non-European
people as deficient.

This history is particularly problematic where disciplinary literacy is
concerned because the language and discipline-specific practices of the
academy have often been identified not only as problematic, but also
as outright racist: "The purpose of state-sanctioned schooling has been
to forward the largely assimilationist and often violent White imperial
project, with students and families being asked to lose or deny their languages, literacies, cultures, and histories in order to achieve in schools"
(Alim & Paris, 2017, p. 1).

Indeed, without thoughtful attention to equity, disciplinary literacy
can be taught in ways that are nothing more than a direct attempt to
reassert the primacy of what Audre Lorde (1984) called "the master's
tools." Lorde famously noted that historically marginalized people will
not be able to dismantle the "master's house" using the "master's tools."
From the standpoint of many scholars writing about CSP, the tools that

disciplinary literacy relies upon include epistemologies, modes of in-quiry, and literacy practices that are informed by "White middle-class norms of knowing and being . . . [which] continue to dominate notions of educational achievement" (Alim & Paris, 2017, p. 2). In short, one way of understanding disciplinary literacy is to assume that its purpose is not to dismantle the master's tools, but rather to insist that all students use them. Indeed, giving students access to the practices of schooling was an initial goal of work on educational equity that blossomed during the 1980s and 1990s (Paris, 2012).

However, Lee (2017) rightly points out that, although academic dis-ciplines have too often been constructed in U.S. schools as the primary province of White colonizers they are not in fact the intellectual property of whiteness. As Lee (2017) powerfully argues, academic domains are not monolithic reinstantiations of White communities of practice, noting:

> The idea that there is a White, middle-class culture is a myth, a myth that has been idealized in an array of norms by which schools and children are evalu-ated. The idea that there is a homogenous standard of what it means to be an American is a myth. The idea that there is a singular dominant academic English is also a myth. Languages evolve. (p. 268)

As she goes on to point out, language, literacy, and social practices as a whole are always improvisations and hybridizations brought about by the multifaceted nature of all students' identities and by the reper-toires of practice in which they participate (see also Gutiérrez & Rogoff, 2003). For example, Lee (2017) points out that American literature is "inherently diverse and hybrid" (p. 268). She notes that magical realism, as a genre, includes authors as varied as Toni Morrison and William Faulkner and Gabriel Garcia Marquez, "who said he couldn't write down the kinds of stories his African-descent grandmother told until he read the German–Jewish writer Franz Kafka" (Lee, 2017, p. 268).

Like Lee (2017), Gutiérrez and her colleagues (2009, 2017) remind us that the literacy practices that individuals use are always, in some senses, hybrid creations that allow individuals and groups to accomplish specific purposes. This foundational assumption of sociocultural theory has major implications for culturally sustaining approaches to disciplin-ary literacy. Specifically, sociocultural theories assert that, as humans participate in communities of practice, they take up the practices that characterize that community, but they also improvise and redefine them, sometimes slightly and sometimes drastically (Holland et al., 1998; Wenger, 1998). Thus literacy practices that occur in the context of com-munities of practice are defined by both stability and change. Academic disciplines are communities of practice, so the disciplinary literacy practices that happen within them are always improvisational and hybrid. Students need to know that, when they participate in the literacy practices of a discipline, their individually, culturally informed engagement also influences the discipline itself.

Remembering that disciplinary literacy practices are improvisational and hybrid is essential if we are to teach disciplinary literacy in ways that are culturally sustaining. Indeed, if we forget that literacy practices are by nature improvisational and hybrid, we run the risk of presenting disciplinary literacy practices as though they are a stable set of inflexible tools which marginalize students' own individual and cultural ways of being. Indeed, Paris (2012) describes the ways that a spate of research, which arose principally in the 1990s, theorized that equitable instruction should provide students with access to dominant literacy practices. Although the authors of this research did not necessarily intend it, researchers and practitioners alike often interpreted this to mean that the teacher's role was to support students to take up a set of literacy practices which students often described as foreign, unfamiliar, inflexible, and inexplicable (Irizarry, 2017).

However, CSP is predicated on the idea that access to a set of supposedly stable literacy practices is not enough. Instead, in CSP, students' own use of individual, cultural, and youth-oriented literacy practices must be engaged as important resources students can use to improvise and construct their own take on disciplinary literacy practices. If students are to do so successfully, they must be able to use the full power of their individually and culturally improvised ways of being, reading, viewing, writing, composing, speaking, listening, and thinking (Kirkland, 2013). If we recognize and encourage students to draw upon their own literacy practices as they make sense of disciplinary work, we are positioning the literacy practices with which students are most familiar as valuable, authentically inviting students' entire selves into the work, and honoring the improvisational nature of all social practice.

Finally, if we assume that disciplinary literacies are reinstantiations of White, middle class culture, we ignore the field-building contributions of people from non-White, non-Eurocentric backgrounds (Lee, 2017). For example, in computer science, *algorithms* are named after the 9th century Islamic scholar and mathematician, astronomer, and geographer Muḥammad ibn Mūsā al-Khwārizmī (Isaacson, 2014). Where ELA is concerned, Muhammad's (2020) recent work on Black literary societies highlights the ways that these societies helped members to define literacy—and the reading of literature—as something that can lead toward "liberation, self-determination, self-reliance, and self-empowerment" (p. 28). Her work also outlines the ways that these Black literary societies provided a platform through which its members collectively advocated for rights on a larger public stage. In short, members of these Black literary societies very literally used disciplinary literacies to dismantle what Audre Lorde called "the master's house." Contributions like these show that disciplinary practitioners—who were not necessarily White—have always defined disciplinary work through improvisation and the use of literacy practices that are hybrid and syncretic, drawing from the many cultural, everyday, and academic literacy practices of people of myriad races, ethnicities, cultures, and backgrounds.

Thus we highlight that culturally sustaining disciplinary literacy represents an opportunity not just to teach students the "master's tools," as Audre Lorde memorably put it, but also to equip students with tools they might use to dismantle the master's house. If disciplinary literacy and CSP are to be mutually informing, disciplinary literacy must be understood as a set of literacy practices to which students should have access, yes, but also with which students will also—inevitably—improvise, depending on the values and goals to which students have committed themselves. By making these literacy practices, and our inbuilt, human ability to improvise in light of them, central to instruction, students have opportunities to question, challenge, critique, redefine, and broaden disciplinary literacy practices as they develop their own personal repertoires of literacy practices which they will use throughout their lives.

INSTRUCTIONAL PRACTICES FOR CULTURALLY SUSTAINING DISCIPLINARY LITERACY INSTRUCTION

Disciplinary literacy is very specific, and it is at times considered the "expert" language, and trying to integrate any type of expert language in a K–12 class, of course, is tricky. Um, I think it can—introducing such specialized language— can do a couple of things that will result in maybe . . . an exclusivity to English language arts that may, well, we may lose students in the process, and I think, one, if we say, "Hey, this is how experts do English language arts, and this is how experts talk in English language arts," then all of those kids who don't necessarily align with English language arts or even wanting to be an expert in English language arts, or wanting to major in English or be a writer, all of those students will sort of take a back seat, or slump in their seats when they hear, "Oh, this is how experts talk," and I think that is one of the main concerns I would have in a K–12 class.

—A preservice ELA teacher studying disciplinary literacy

In this section, we will use English language arts as a site in which to discuss how the tenets of culturally sustaining pedagogies can be used in conjunction with those of disciplinary literacy to leverage the advantages of both. To do so, we recommend and discuss particular pedagogical practices, providing a brief discussion and vignette of each. The goal of this section, as in previous chapters, is to provide thick descriptions of what it might look like to develop and use pedagogical practices in culturally sustaining disciplinary literacy. We define *culturally sustaining disciplinary literacy instruction* as instruction which begins from an asset-based mindset in which students' cultural identities are not only valued but embedded within instruction. Such instruction assumes that *literacy* is a set of culturally and contextually defined practices and explicitly teaches students that reading/viewing, writing/composing, speaking, and listening are practiced in particular, discipline-specific ways, while highlighting that these literacy practices are not synonymous with White-dominated, mainstream culture. Instead, students' cultural, everyday, and youth literacy and language practices are valuable resources from which students might better understand disciplinary work.

We provide descriptions of these pedagogical practices from a standpoint that is ever mindful of the preservice teacher's words above, as she has hit on a central tension for teaching disciplinary literacy in culturally sustaining ways: Disciplinary literacies may appear to students to be exclusive. Indeed, as we have outlined above, the literacy and language practices of historically marginalized students have very much been excluded from disciplinary work, so students may resist or reject efforts to make students speak or read or write like experts. Given that this is a site of potential tension between disciplinary literacy and CSP, we organize our suggested pedagogical practices around the idea that, in disciplinary literacy, students must be positioned as apprentices to a discipline. If students are to take up the position of disciplinary apprentice that disciplinary literacy offers, we must heed the advice of more than 30 years of research on culturally relevant teaching, and now CSP. Specifically, we suggest the following four pedagogical practices for culturally sustaining disciplinary literacy instruction:

1. Investigate and study the disciplinary excellence of disciplinary practitioners of color and other marginalized groups.
2. Make students' individual and cultural ways of being substantive, necessary aspects of the curriculum from which disciplinary ideas are constructed.

3. Design instructional activities that honor the language and literacy practices that have typified the cultural groups represented in your class.
4. Encourage students' critical reflexivity about their own cultural practices.

Instructional Practice 1: Investigate and study the disciplinary excellence of disciplinary practitioners of color

One important way to assign cultural competence at a foundational level is to study the disciplinary excellence of disciplinary practitioners of color. Such studies should go beyond reading *Beloved* in the 12th grade or Martin Luther King Jr.'s "I Have a Dream" speech every year. Although these are both essential to the literary canon of the United States, they do not necessarily show the ways that everyday people have made use of disciplinary language and literacy tools for the betterment of their lives, which should be a goal of culturally sustaining disciplinary literacy instruction (Lee, 2007).

Also, addressing these or a handful of other frequently taught pieces (i.e., MLK Jr.'s "Letter from a Birmingham Jail"), risks presenting the contributions of novelists and rhetors of color—marvelous though these works are—as a version of literary tokenism. Britnie's 9th-grade students, for example, grumbled that they had been asked/forced to read MLK Jr.'s "I Have a Dream" speech every year, typically during Black History Month. Although perhaps well-intentioned, such presentations of Black culture may serve to further marginalize the work of disciplinary practitioners of color, partitioning it off and away from "regular" American literature.

Gholdy Muhammad's (2020) work in culturally and historically responsive literacy, which—like CSP—is predicated on CRP, highlights the importance of showcasing for students the ways in which members of Black literary societies used their study of literature as a set of practices that supported a move toward freedom. Students, then, should be made aware of the disciplinary work that people of color and those from non-Eurocentric backgrounds have contributed to the disciplines. Here in Charleston, South Carolina, for example, Septima P. Clark is the name of a major highway, as well as the name of a school, but Clark's vital work in support of adult literacy and voting rights in Charleston (and beyond) is too rarely understood. From the perspective of culturally sustaining disciplinary literacy, studies of the contributions of literary people of color must raise important questions and critiques about how the discipline of ELA has been defined, by whom, according to what standards, and through what genres. Such inquiry must go to a deeper understanding of the epistemologies, habits of mind, and social practices of knowledge construction that should inform students' use of discipline-specific language and literacy practices.

Instructional Practice 2: Make students' individual, linguistic, and cultural ways of being substantive, necessary aspects of the curriculum from which disciplinary ideas are constructed.

Another foundational idea in the literature on both CSP and its predecessor, culturally relevant pedagogies, as well as substantial related work on cultural modeling (i.e., Lee, 2007) and third spaces (Gutiérrez et al., 2009) is that students' individual and cultural ways of being must become substantive, necessary aspects of the curriculum from which disciplinary ideas are constructed (see Paris & Alim, 2017). As Bucholz and her colleagues (2017) put it, "a pedagogy that truly sustains culture is one that sustains cultural practices too often excluded from classroom learning and leverages these as resources both for achieving institutional access and for challenging structural inequity" (p. 45). To illustrate an example of this, we showcase a vignette from Rachelle's high school reading intervention classroom:

In my previous job as a reading interventionist in Central Florida, I was given wide latitude to teach according to students' interests. There was no set curriculum, so we read and talked, talked and read. The course was not scripted, and I had freedom to get to know my students and to interact with them in authentic ways around authentic texts. However, in my new job—still in Florida—I was handed a strict, scripted curriculum. The first few days were a disaster. The classroom felt like a standoff, not a productive community of learners.

So I stopped. I stopped my lessons. I stopped talking. And I started to listen. I asked them why things were not going well. I asked them what wasn't working for them. I wanted to know what I could do to support their learning. This was ultimately a pivotal moment in my teaching. My students first sat back, quiet. Then, all at once, they had something to say. I will never forget one student in the back of the room. She explained to me that I had waltzed in demanding respect, but that respect needed to be earned. I realized that we had very different cultural norms and expectations around what it meant to show—and earn—respect. Over the next few days, we continued this dialogue. Students shared with me and their classmates norms and expectations that they had for me. We discussed communication preferences, instructional approaches, and instructional materials. Students were open about the harmful narratives that had been attributed to their lives over the years because they "couldn't read." Many highlighted that they were "just not interested" in the district-provided stories, lessons, or materials. I could relate to this. In my own education, I had resented being asked to interpret in the "expected way" and to do what I was told, rather than finding things that interested me.

These conversations led to dialogue and negotiation about the next steps forward—together. We discussed requirements to which I was accountable, such as teaching specific standards and themes. Students shared their desire to use their native and cultural language and norms in our classroom. For instance, when discussing poetry, students asked to bring in poems or lyrics that they wanted to analyze. Another change was that students wanted to investigate topics that related to them and their interests, leading to the use of inquiry-based learning. From a culturally sustaining disciplinary literacy perspective, then, students could "formulate and address authentic questions of interest" (Savitz & Wallace, 2016, p. 92) based on "lived experience [that] connect[ed] this experience to the curriculum and guide[d] students to address real-world issues in a consciously crafted classroom culture" (Wilhelm, Douglas, & Fry, 2014, p. 4).

As a class, then, we centered issues that were important to students' lives, aligning our research and investigations to themes required in the district curriculum—indeed, we even used some of the materials presented in the district-provided curriculum. However, that's not all we used. Through our joint inquiry, students continuously asked questions of one another, brainstorming ways to transform topics into meaningful learning for them. This approach bore rich fruit; for example, in a unit on identity, one group explored how African tribes used tribal art and tattoos to share and communicate their identities. Such critical inquiry can support students' conceptually rich learning, their development in literacy, and their ability to become more resilient in the political and social worlds in which they live (Spires et al., 2020). Thus, to teach disciplinary ways of analyzing a wide variety of texts from the perspective of CSP, students' lives and interests became the center of the curriculum rather than ancillary to it.

Instructional Practice 3: Design instructional activities that valorize the language and literacy practices that have typified the cultural groups represented in your class.

Our third suggested instructional practice builds upon the second one in that it asks not only that students' ways of being and lived experiences become an integral aspect of the official curriculum, but also that students' individual and cultural language use become central to the explicit curriculum. Teaching disciplinary literacy through the lens of cultural sustainability specifically requires the "valorization of language as a central component of culturally sustaining pedagogy" (Bucholz et al., 2017, p. 44), because the teachers' role in ELA instruction in U.S. schools has too often been—implicitly or explicitly—defined as pushing students toward the use of amorphous, underconceptualized views of "Standard" or "White Mainstream" English. It is important to understand that the standard language ideology, which is a bias toward one language (Lippi-Green, 2012), largely goes unquestioned in our schools as a "result of the disinformation and misrepresentation that gets distributed about dominant languages and marginalized languages and dialects" (Baker-Bell, 2020a, p. 15). This causes linguistically marginalized students to be assessed as inadequate because their language practices do not align with White Mainstream English. To explore an example of this, we will go to Britnie's 9th-grade ELA classroom:

In my second year of teaching English I to 9th-grade students, I opened a lesson on denotation and connotation with a reference to the most controversial of animals—the pit bull. In my own tiny, toddling way, I had hoped this would be culturally responsive, since many of my students, most of whom identified as Black, had described either owning or hoping to own a pit bull. I, too, am a bit of a pit bull enthusiast, since they are—in my mind, at least—the underdog of dogs. In my experience, the breed was consistently vilified and blamed and characterized as a dangerous menace. In fact, the state of Colorado, where I grew up, had recently considered making pit bull ownership illegal, and I had been unable to adopt a pit bull while living in Nashville, because my apartment complex prohibited them. My family had owned a pit bull growing up, though, and I remembered the way Max cuddled with me on the couch as I struggled, during a rough junior year of high school, through both walking pneumonia and mononucleosis. He'd been a deep comfort to me through several weeks of illness and frequently got his oversized square head stuck in the box of crackers I kept at my side as I slept. Our veterinarian, though, had advised us to tell others that he was not a pit bull, but an American Staffordshire Terrier.

This example in itself, I thought, would make excellent fodder for a class discussion on connotation, and I busily set about making a Power-Point filled with pictures of pit bulls—my dog Max with his head in a Better Cheddar box; a picture of sad, droopy pit bull eyebrows from the Humane Society; and a picture of a rabid, slathering maniac snarling from behind a chain link fence (posted from a group organized against pit bulls). I included the slathering maniac picture first, because I assumed that my students would begin by describing pit bulls as dangerous, menacing, problematic. From there, we would investigate the other pictures; we would discuss the connotation of the words we might use to describe pit bulls in each situation; we would consider the sources of each image; we would investigate the bias inherent even in visual imagery; we would consider relationships between connotation, stereotypes, and bias. If we were really on point, we might even be able to discuss the ways connotation, bias, and stereotyping could influence public policy. After all, where I'm from, pit bulls were on the verge of being illegal. So I began by asking students about the adjectives they associated with pit bulls.

A collective shrug settled over the class. Because they were used to my seemingly odd entrees into the English language arts, one or two decided to humor me:

"Protective," someone offered.

"Yes," another student agreed. "Loyal."

"Loving."

In my shocked brain, twelve thoughts presented themselves at once, but none of them were particularly helpful. The one that surfaced was this: They aren't right, are they? The connotation of *pit bull* isn't protective . . . is it? My mind flashed to the picture of the snarling monster with glittering eyes I had loaded up, ready to illumine the Smart Board. One thing was certain—if that snarling picture didn't align with students' overarching perceptions of pit bulls, then it wasn't going to help them understand connotation. I pivoted. All these years later, I don't know how. I probably dove into the much safer—but largely useless—territory of the multiple-choice test prep that my district required.

What I do remember is that, that night, students' descriptions of pit bulls forced me to access my inner philosopher. What was connotation, really? It had not occurred to me that my understanding of this breed would differ so substantially from my students'. In retrospect, it should have, given our vast cultural, racial, and regional differences. What I did not understand then is that I was creating and teaching curricula through the prism of my own whiteness. From my own cultural perspective, pit bulls were dangerous. I personally disagreed with this dominant cultural stance, but my students had not—apparently—even heard of it. The one thing that I did right was to ask students for their initial thinking, which uncovered the mistake I was about to make and gave me time to rethink the lesson. If I had dived into a discussion of the ways "everyone" thinks pit bulls are scary, seeking to explain the concept of connotation from there, the lesson would have been deeply confusing from an academic standpoint and (at best) irrelevant and irksome culturally. Who am I to claim deep-rooted knowledge about the nature of pit bulls?

The next day, I tried again. I decided that connotation is a set of value-laden social meanings that are ascribed to words and concepts by particular communities—and, apparently, different communities could come to very different conclusions about the connotations of concrete things. Since I clearly had no way of predicting what students would say, I decided to start with language they knew. Thus I stumbled into one of the clearest and most foundational tenets of CSP. My students' vocabulary was peppered with words with which I was unfamiliar, so I wrote one of them on the board: *jokey*. I asked my students to please explain to me what *jokey* meant. I told them I wanted to know both its denotation and its connotation, and that I would never be able to really use the word correctly unless I understood both. Students giggled, shifted in their seats, crinkled their noses. Finally, someone yelled, "What do you mean, denotation?" Importantly, during the prior lessons in which I had attempted to make this clear, no one had cared to ask this question.

And so it began. Because I honestly did not know what this word meant, I was able to ask a number of authentic questions that led us to a deeper discussion of both the denotation and connotation of words, and the ways that we need both in order to make sense of new vocabulary. By the end of class, we had collaboratively decided that an appropriate definition of *jokey* might be something like *flirtatiously silly*. We had also discussed the ways that the use of words can be gendered (I had almost exclusively heard female students use this word in reference to male students, and it was often accompanied by laughter and giggling, as in "Boy, you so jokey"), and the ways in which words are community and context dependent. That is, it would mean something different for me, a White adult, to use the term *jokey* than it would for a student of color or, for that matter, an adult of color to do so.

From the perspective of disciplinary literacy and CSP, this conversation had a number of benefits: It positioned students as disciplinary experts, capable of using an important set of tools (denotation and connotation) that students would be able to use in order to adopt a critical lens for "reading the world," as Freire (1970) put it. The lesson also provided students with a window into a more expert other's thinking about how to make sense of new vocabulary (i.e., teacher modeling). Importantly, such modeling of problem-solving is central to work in accomplished disciplinary literacy instruction (Gabriel & Wenz, 2017; Goldman et al., 2016) and in CSP (Lee, 2017). In addition, our work enabled students to develop a metaknowledge about words, which Nagy and Scott (2000) have called "word knowledge"—important for vocabulary development. From the perspective of CSP, the lesson design communicated, through the explicit and official curricula, that "[students'] language is a crucial form of sustenance in its own right, providing the basis for young people's complex identities, as well as their social agency" (Bucholz et al., 2017, p. 44). This is especially important where Black Language is concerned, as an anti-Black Language approach can contribute to Black students' despising their native language and can even cause them to view themselves through a White gaze (Baker-Bell, 2020a; hooks, 1992).

Baker (2002) describes how to valorize students' language use in the context of the English language arts. She details the value of providing students with opportunities to investigate their own and others' language differences in ELA. For example, in Baker's (2002) classroom, students made audio recordings of their parents, grandparents, aunts, and other community members, interviewing them about the histories of their speech and what it means to them to speak in the ways that they do. They then analyzed the recordings, finding "patterns of speech, rules of grammar, vocabulary, tonal features, and emotional characteristics of language" (p. 52).

Throughout her unit, Baker (2002) focused on "how different forms of English are appropriate for different contexts, instead of relying on the right/wrong dichotomy students usually face in school" (p. 52). Her rationale is directly in line with the tenets of CSP: "I do this because I want [students'] own usage, vocabulary, modes of expression and their self-esteem to survive the language learning process" (p. 52). From a disciplinary perspective, Baker highlights that, when students' home language(s) are validated and valorized, it "allows them to feel comfortable with language study in general" (p. 56). As she explains, "I am convinced that high school students can achieve a deep and personal understanding of the most academic and formal varieties of English if it is separated from trappings which demean their own cultures" (p. 61).

Of course, in this suggestion for practice, as in others, a few quick cautions are in order. One place where this can go wrong—indeed, where many attempts to instantiate culturally relevant pedagogies and CSP in U.S. classrooms have gone wrong—is if we hold tightly to an idea that cultural practices are a monolith that individuals adopt wholesale. As both Gutiérrez and colleagues (2017, 2009) and Lee (2007; 2017) have consistently pointed out, culture—and, as a corollary, language use—is a tapestry of individual, hybridized improvisations. For this reason, it is important that Baker (2002) gives her students opportunities to study their own language practices and that of people they know and love, for these practices will show the improvisation and hybridization that are a part of each of our identities.

   If we, instead, were to insist that students learn, for instance, grammar rules of African American Language (Baker-Bell, 2020a) or other languages, alongside of grammar rules associated with academic forms of English, we will still have missed the mark. In so doing, we risk essentializing students by making assumptions about their lives and cultures—and whether or not they participate in particular cultural practices (Gutiérrez & Rogoff, 2003). Even the term African American Language has been problematized, as that label, and others such as African American Vernacular or Ebonics, do not provide the needed context for Black speech in an American context (Baker-Bell, 2020a, p. 3). Instead, if we offer students opportunities to make sense of their lives and everyday literacy practices—not just the ones that are widely associated with the heritage of particular cultural groups, but also those that are happening here and now in the worlds of our youth—we are positioning their work and lives as essential to the future of disciplinary work (Alim & Paris, 2017). Thus culturally sustaining disciplinary literacy pedagogies center students' cultural experiences and language uses in the official curriculum, thereby supporting students to study language more broadly—a goal that is central to the English language arts.

Instructional Practice 4: Encouraging students' critical reflexivity about their own cultural practices.

Recent formulations of CSP have highlighted that CSP must not only place students' lives and language use at the center of disciplinary curricula, CSP must also teach students to be critical of both dominant, oppressive narratives and of their own communities' cultural practices. Specifically, Alim & Paris (2017) highlight that an important way forward for CSP is not only to bring students' everyday cultural practices into the classroom, but to support students as they develop critical consciousnesses that allow them to lovingly critique them. In Britnie's classroom, an opportunity to do just that arose. Unfortunately, I was not wise enough to take advantage of it until, years later, I had read more deeply in the field of culturally sustaining pedagogies.

   Excited after our joint success over understanding the denotation and connotation of *jokey*, as was described earlier, students shouted over one another, "Mrs. Kane! Do *tone mixx* now."

   "*Tone mixx*?" I asked.

   "Yes," they said. "Two words. Two x's."

A silence—almost a reverence—passed over the room as I added the extra *x*. "Okay," I said, "what's the denotation of *tone mixx*?"

"To carry a gun," they said.

I nodded, thrilled: Denotation, as a concept, was now making sense to them. "Okay. What's the connotation?"

The room went quiet. I prodded: "Like, connotation has to do with value systems, like what's considered moral or desirable. Like, good. What's the value system behind *tone mixx*?"

Students who had been bodily jumping out of their seats were now stone silent, flat in their chairs.

I waited, floundering. "Um. Is it cool, or it is a bad thing? What would your community say?"

The silence was utter.

At the time, I didn't know how to respond, so I moved on to a different word. In retrospect, however, the tenets of CSP explain that I should have drawn attention to the tension in the room, making public my guess about the reasons for the silence—that the connotation of *tone mixx* was positive and that students were not sure whether they were comfortable valorizing that practice (and were certainly not sure they wanted to talk about it with a White lady).

Following the principles of CSP, I could have asked students to join small groups of their self-selected peers to discuss the connotation of *tone mixx* and to analyze critically whether they thought this connotation was helpful to the larger society. In this way, students could have had this discussion away from my White, authoritative gaze. Of course, I should also note that such an approach can only work in classrooms where substantial work has been done to build an academic community of respect for diverse ideas, and where students have been taught how to disagree constructively. Having sentence stems on the walls is a good instructional practice here: "What I hear you saying is . . .";"One thing your point makes me wonder is. . . ."

Such an approach would be a start toward helping students build a critical consciousness about the world, which CSP requires. This example also highlights that sometimes building critical consciousness forces us all to look inward. As Alim and Paris (2017) have noted, "CSP must work with students to critique regressive practices (e.g., homophobia, misogyny) and raise critical consciousness" (p. 10). Importantly, particularly for me as a White person, but also for any of us who find ourselves in positions of authority, it was not for me to judge what the connotation or moral character of carrying a gun is. Instead, CSP highlights that this is for students to discuss and critique—indeed, equipping students with interpretive and analytical tools is a central goal for both disciplinary literacy and CSP. Yet CSP asks those interested in disciplinary literacy to go a step further: Students must be supported to develop interpretive and analytical tools so that they can build the critical consciousness they will need to challenge existing structural inequities (e.g., Bucholz et al., 2017). Asking students to make judgments about the ways in which carrying a gun is framed within their own youth culture is one example of how this might work in an actual classroom.

DISCUSSION AND IMPLICATIONS

What we have presented thus far, of course, has significant implications for what teachers will need to know and be able to do to support pedagogies in culturally sustaining disciplinary literacy. For example, teachers must recognize the tensions inherent in culturally sustaining disciplinary literacy. Insisting upon "expert" ways of speaking, listening, thinking, reading, writing, and acting can be—and has been—understood as an incursion on students' individual and cultural personhoods. As a corollary, teachers must understand, based upon research coming out of linguistics and literacy studies, that "Standard" English does not exist, and that specific, Eurocentric language and literacy practices are not superior to others. Instead, both literacy and language have deep ties to culture and identity, and both are made meaningful in the context of its use. In addition, individuals are members of cultures only insofar as they identify and take up repertoires of practice from particular communities, and part of the role of members of all communities of practice, both cultural and academic, is to create improvisations and hybridizations that lead to new knowledge.

On this note, teachers must further understand that the language of academic disciplines is not, as Lee (2017) and others have emphasized, synonymous with the language of whiteness. Instead, to teach in ways that are both culturally sustaining and true to the underpinnings of disciplinary literacy, teachers must understand the breadth and range of the domain, how expertise grows in this domain, and how language and literacy practices within the domain are taken up, modified, improvised, hybridized, and enriched by the contributions of multiple people from a variety of backgrounds (Lee & Goldman, 2015). As teacher educators, we must recognize that the largely White, female, monolingual teaching force may not be able to articulate the epistemological underpinnings of their disciplines, nor will they necessarily be able to identify the contributions of disciplinary practitioners of color. Teachers' "apprenticeships of observation"—that is, the ways they were themselves taught in schools—are unlikely to have made this set of epistemological assumptions available to them. Thus teachers are likely to be learning about the contributions of disciplinary practitioners of color, as well as the epistemologies and modes of inquiry and production that undergird their disciplines, along with their students. Given that this is the case, teachers must be taught how to teach for inquiry, becoming comfortable with—and excited about—the ways in which such teaching will open up space to learn alongside their students.

CHAPTER 4

Making Arij Chaj N en Tres Idiomas
A Middle School Language Arts Lesson

Sarah N. Newcomer and Kathleen M. Cowin

Listening to her students chatter excitedly as they rolled corn husk strips into small arms and legs for the dolls they were making, Ms. Cortez knew she had selected the right book for her literacy lesson. She had chosen the book *The Corn Husk Doll* (2016) by Melissa Schiller based on an interview with one of her students, Sachi, who revealed that she often made corn husk dolls at home. In addition to making dolls, the lesson focused on comprehension, finding the main idea, and writing a summary paragraph (all participant names are pseudonyms). We highlight this particular lesson for two reasons. First, several lesson elements strike us as practices which strongly reflect Paris's (2012) definition of culturally sustaining pedagogy, as discussed in the Introduction to this book. This lesson takes a strong asset-based approach to literacy instruction and focuses on maintaining students' linguistic and cultural competencies while developing proficiency in English. Throughout the lesson Ms. Cortez and her students "translanguaged" (see Garcia, 2009a) with one another using English, Spanish, and, at times, Mam, in order to communicate their ideas and accomplish the lesson's goals. Second, we wish to show how this lesson reflects the *development* of a culturally sustaining teacher, a journey that is ongoing. We also share the teacher's reflective commentary upon her lesson after teaching it, wherein she recounts key aspects of the lesson and notes both strengths and aspects she would refine in the future.

CONTEXT AND POSITIONALITIES

The lesson occurred in a literacy methods class, which was also part of the alternative route to teacher certification program, called ELLPARAS[1] at Washington State University Tri-Cities (WSUTC). WSUTC is located in a growing population center in southeastern Washington. The three largest population centers in the Tri-Cities (Richland, Kennewick, and Pasco) have a joint population of over 300,000.

The lesson takes place at Local[2] Middle School in the Pasco School District. Local Middle School's demographics vary somewhat from the district as a whole, with a student population of 94.9% designated as Latinx, which is greater than the 73% noted districtwide. The student population of Local Middle School designated as White is 3.9%, while districtwide the White population is 21.8%. At 93%, the free and reduced-price lunch rate at Local Middle School is substantially higher than the districtwide 68%. The English language learner designation was assigned to 46.1% of students at Local Middle School, as compared to the districtwide percentage of 33.4%. Migrant status designation was given to 11.6% of Local Middle School students, which is also greater than the district at 6.5%. The homeless designation was given to 2% of the students attending Local Middle School, districtwide percentage unknown (Washington Office of Superintendent of Public Instruction, 2021).

Finally, the lesson presented here is connected to a project in which we (Sarah and Kathleen) have been engaging with our teacher and leader candidates (pre-K–8 teacher and pre-K–12 principal certification candidates), called Collaborative Conversations. Sarah is a White woman whose pronouns are she/her and whose cultural background includes a mixture of Western European heritages. She grew up speaking English and started learning Spanish in junior high, continuing to study it throughout her schooling and majoring in Spanish in college. Kathleen is a White woman whose pronouns are she/her and whose cultural background includes a mixture of Western European heritages. She also grew up speaking English and started learning Spanish in the fifth grade, continuing her studies throughout college. We have both spent time studying and/or volunteering in Mexico.

As university instructors, we have been working with teacher and leader candidates in the local school districts, including Pasco, for the past 7 years. In our respective roles, we have been immersed in the local schools and are familiar with the communities they serve. As previous pre-K–12 practitioners, we both have extensive experience working in bilingual communities in various different contexts. During this project, we brought our candidates together four times over the course of the semester to discuss shared readings centered on culturally sustaining, socially just pedagogy (CSSJP) (Newcomer & Cowin, 2021). The leader candidates were enrolled in Kathleen's class focused on communication and community engagement and the teacher candidates were enrolled in Sarah's intermediate literacy methods course.

The purpose of the Collaborative Conversations is to support both teacher and leader candidates in learning about CSSJP as well as to create a space for the candidates to reflect together on CSSJP in an effort to bridge two preparation programs that are often siloed from one another. We hope these conversations foster a mindset for continuing this collaborative work once both groups of candidates assume their professional positions. As part of the literacy methods course, the teacher candidates also complete two key assignments connected with culturally sustaining pedagogy—conducting an interview with a student from a linguistic, cultural, and/or ethnic/racial background different from their own and designing, teaching, and reflecting upon a culturally sustaining lesson developed with insights from the student interview. The Collaborative Conversations influenced the lessons planned by the teacher candidates, where ideas shared among all the candidates, such as: "Kids have to feel valued before learning can happen" and "We really believe that administrators and teachers have the power to empower students into the learning process and become successful," were put into action.

DEVELOPING LITERACY AND AFFIRMING STUDENT IDENTITY THROUGH CREATING CORN HUSK DOLLS

Ms. Cortez taught the following 4-day lesson, which was focused on reading comprehension and writing a summary paragraph, (again, all personal names in this chapter are pseudonyms) in a combined 7th/8th-grade middle school classroom. At the time of the lesson, which took place in March of 2020, Ms. Cortez was a teacher candidate who had already been working with emergent bilingual students as a paraeducator for 2 years. With parents originally from Mexico, she grew up in Pasco and describes herself as Mexican American/Hispanic. Ms. Cortez grew up speaking only Spanish at home and was introduced to English in school. Today, she is fully bilingual and biliterate in both Spanish and English. She currently teaches Spanish and Advisory classes and hopes to secure a permanent teaching position in the future.

Ms. Cortez's lesson was conducted with seven 7th- and 8th-grade students, most of whom had resided in the United States for less than 6 months and were considered to be beginning emergent bilingual students. The lesson was taught in the context of the school's Advisory program. Advisory classes were part of a schoolwide initiative designed to provide students with personalized academic and social support, including through the use of *Character Strong*, a curriculum aimed at teaching values and skills for lifelong success through topics such as empathy, healthy habits, growth mindset, resilience, emotional intelligence, mindfulness, kindness, respect, and acceptance. Advisory classes were also used to provide the school's emergent bilingual students with additional language support. We recognize that this program represents a districtwide effort to provide extra support to students. Yet it is important to acknowledge that students already bring to the classroom rich funds of knowledge, emotional intelligence, and character strengths, which encompass those taught by the *Character Strong* program. As a paraeducator assigned to support the school's emergent bilingual students across the school day, Ms. Cortez worked in a variety of classrooms, including the Advisory classes, as well as ELA/History and Math/Science classrooms. This meant she knew the cross-curricular content and if students needed additional support with this content or with completing an assignment, she would also provide students with assistance.

One of the students participating in the lesson, Sachi, had been in the United States for 4 years. Ms. Cortez knew Sachi from working with her in one of the other Advisory classes and had decided to interview her for her course assignment. In doing so, she learned that Sachi and her mother had sewed traditional Mayan clothing in Guatemala and also made corn husk dolls as a hobby. Knowing that Sachi aspired to become a teacher, Ms. Cortez invited Sachi to help her teach the corn husk doll lesson. In the beginning English level Advisory class in which this lesson was taught, there was one other student from Guatemala, one student from El Salvador, and five students from Mexico. Aside from Sachi and Ian, who spoke different varieties of the Mayan language of Mam, the other students were native Spanish speakers. Ms. Cortez decided to select the text, *The Corn Husk Doll* (2016) by Melissa Schiller based upon her interview with Sachi. Each of the lesson segments lasted approximately 40 minutes. First, we provide an overview of the 4-day lesson and then we present a more detailed description about each day of the lesson.

Lesson Overview

Ms. Cortez's objectives for this lesson were designed to address the following Common Core State Standard for English Language Arts/Literacy (CCSS.ELA-LITERACY.RI.7) focused on Reading: "Cite several pieces of textual evidence to support analysis of what the text says explicitly as well as inferences drawn from the text." Based on this standard, her content objective for the students was: "I can cite several pieces of textual evidence by writing a summary of the main idea and supporting details of the book *The Corn Husk Doll*." Her language objective was: "I can identify the main idea in the text by writing three supporting details." The first day of the lesson was devoted to introducing the book, discussing the idea of brainstorming, predicting what the book would be about, and previewing key vocabulary. These activities were designed to help support students' comprehension of the book before beginning to read. Day 2 of the lesson mainly focused on reading the book, with some time to begin brainstorming possibilities for the book's main idea, as the students would be writing summary paragraphs about the book. On Day 3 the lesson focused on continuing to discuss the main idea as well as supporting details and the students began making their corn husk dolls. Day 4's main activities consisted of decorating the corn husk dolls and completing their paragraphs. Ms. Cortez taught the lesson in both English and Spanish, an approach that aligns with translanguaging. Ms. Cortez often asked the students questions in English first, but would follow up with additional clarification and support in Spanish as needed. The students mainly used Spanish, although they practiced saying the vocabulary words, reading the book, and writing their summary paragraphs in English. A couple of students opted to write their paragraph in Spanish first and then translate it to English. Due to space constraints, we mainly use English to capture the dialogue that transpired; we also use some Spanish to maintain the character of the lesson.

Day One–Brainstorming Predictions and Previewing Key Vocabulary

Brainstorming Predictions. The lesson began by Ms. Cortez inviting her students to sit in small groups of three or four so that they could work collaboratively. Once the students were seated, she showed them the cover of the book, which displays a small doll dressed in a striped yellow shirt and blue pants with brown pigtails fastened with bright red yarn. The doll is pictured between the image of a blank head, torso, and arms, seemingly woven out of something yellow, like straw, and a picture of an ear of corn, with the green husks partially peeled down and a soft brown tassel waving on top. The tassel almost appears to resemble a ponytail waving in the wind. Ms. Cortez explained that she wanted the students to brainstorm ideas about what the book might be about. She wrote both her question, "What do you think the book will be about?" and the word "brainstorm" on the board. Wanting to be sure they understood the concept of a brainstorm, she then guided them through a discussion of this word, asking them, "What type of word is this? *¿Qué tipo de palabra es* *ésto?*" The students had already been learning about the difference between a compound word and contractions, so she felt confident that they would be able to identify that this was a compound word.

Once the students identified that brainstorm was, indeed, "*una palabra compuesta,*" she underlined each of the words, "brain" and "storm."

Pointing at her head, she asked, "What is brain in Spanish?"

She felt this gesture would help the students guess the meaning of the word.

One student suggested, "*¿Pelo?*" (Hair?)

Ms. Cortez pointed again, emphasizing that, "We all have one *inside. Lo temenos adentro de la cabeza.*"

"*¡Cerebro!*" (Brain!) responded another student.

"That's right!" Ms. Cortez affirmed, "Brain is *cerebro.*"

She did the same thing with "storm," making a movement with her hands like rain.

She reminded them, "Remember, we read a book about storms. Do you remember the *storms?*" (emphasizing this word).

"*¡Oh, es una tormenta!*" replied another student.

Although the students had correctly identified the individual words in Spanish, Ms. Cortez wanted to be sure they understood the meaning of the combined words, so she again made a gesture like rain drops falling next to her head and asked them, "Knowing what *cerebro* and *tormenta* are in Spanish, what do you think *tormenta de cerebro* means?"

She asked the students to do a quick "turn-and-talk" in their groups.

When she called them back together, one of the students raised her hand and said, "*Es cuando tienes ideas ó sea cuando tienes cosas en la cabeza que están allí volando.*" (It's when you have ideas or when you have things in your head that are flying around.)

"That's right!" Ms. Cortez affirmed. "It's when you try to think of as many different ideas as you can."

Next, she asked the students to brainstorm ideas for what the book might be about in their small groups.

Reporters from each group shared ideas, such as "*¡Oh, va a ser de una muñeca!*" (Oh, it's going to be about a doll!) and "*Creo que se va a tratar de maíz.*" (I think it is going to have to do with corn.)

After the students shared their ideas, Ms. Cortez proceeded to preview key vocabulary that she thought the students would need to understand the story.

Previewing Key Vocabulary. Ms. Cortez provided each student with a copy of the book and a blank sheet of lined paper. She explained:

Today, we will begin reading this book. After reading the book as a class,
we will brainstorm what we think the main idea is. We will practice
your writing in English by writing a paragraph of the main idea with
three supporting details. So, while we read the book, keep this in mind.
At the end, we will also do a very fun activity with the contents of the
book!

Next, she previewed key vocabulary that the students would en-
counter in the book, stating, "We will begin by first identifying the main
vocabulary you need to know before we begin reading the book. This
will make it easier for you to understand what the book is about."

She began with the word "husk," saying the word as she wrote it
on the board, and asking the students, "What do you think this word
means? *¿Qué piensan que significa esta palabra?*"

Uncertain, the students remained quiet until Ms. Cortez provided
further support, explaining, "*Es lo que tiene afuera en el elote . . .*" (It's
what the corn has on the outside . . .)

One of the students exclaimed, "*¡Oh, es la hoja, la cáscara!*" (Oh,
it's the leaf, the husk!)

"Yes, that's right!" affirmed Ms. Cortez.

She wrote the Spanish translation *cáscara* on the board next to
"husk." Next, she wrote the word "craft" on the board, again asking
them what they thought it meant.

Even though Ms. Cortez provided a clue, "*Es arte que haces con las
manos.*" (It's art that you make with your hands), this word proved particularly challenging. Finally, Ms. Cortez supplied them with the word,
artesanía. They continued in this way, with Ms. Cortez writing and saying each word in English and then guiding the students to decipher the
meaning by providing different clues.

When they came to the word "tear" one of the students said that it
meant *una lágrima* (a tear, that you cry). This provided Ms. Cortez an
opportunity to discuss homonyms:

*Hay muchas palabras que se escribe lo mismo pero que tienen diferentes
significados. Sí, es verdad que esta palabra significa "lágrima" pero también
se puede pronunciar de otra manera y tiene otro significado. Cuando se dice
"t-ear" [here she emphasized the "ear" sound in the word] significa una
lágrima pero cuando se pronuncia "t-air" [emphasizing the "air" sound
in the word] significa cortar ó romper.* (There are many words that you
write the same way but that have different meanings. Yes, it's true that
this word means "tear" [that you cry] but it also can be pronounced

differently and it has a different meaning. When you say "t-ear" it means a tear [that you cry] but when you pronounce it "t-air," it means to cut or to break.)

Another challenge arose from the phrase, "wind them loosely." Ms. Cortez demonstrated this action several times with her hands, acting as if she was winding something very slowly. This still proved difficult to guess and so she told the students that it meant, *enrollarlos sin apretar* (to roll something up without squeezing). See Figure 4.1 for photos from day one of the lesson.

Day Two—Reading the Story and Brainstorming Possible Main Ideas

Reading the Story. The following day, Ms. Cortez and the students read the story together. She reminded the students to keep their list of translated vocabulary words on their desks in front of them so that they could refer to their meanings, and she also asked the students to follow along with their fingers as they listened. Ms. Cortez began by reading the first page aloud and then she paused to ask them what they understood and if they had any questions. Then she summarized the page's contents again in Spanish to be sure the students understood. After she read the first couple of pages this way, she began taking turns with the students in order to provide them with opportunities to practice reading in English. When it was the students' turn to read, she asked them to read the page together in their small groups. She explained that someone could volunteer to read the page aloud, or the group could read the page quietly to themselves. Regardless of how each page was read, she asked for a volunteer to summarize the page in Spanish. She then read the same page aloud again in English in order to model fluency. Throughout the reading, she paused often to see if the students had questions by asking, "Any questions so far? Does this

Figure 4.1. Day One—Brainstorming Predictions and Previewing Vocabulary

make sense?" The book's many illustrations helped to support their meaning-making efforts.

Brainstorming Possible Main Ideas. Once they finished with the book, Ms. Cortez led the students through an initial discussion of what they thought the main idea of the book might be. As they talked, she passed out a graphic organizer which showed a picture of a three-legged stool, stating:

What I just handed out is a paper that will help us write our paragraph. Remember, our paragraph has to specifically say the book's main idea and give three details to support this idea. We also want to make sure to use book citations in our paragraph. Does everyone know what is pictured here?

After the students identified that the picture was *un banquito* or a stool, Ms. Cortez explained how the stool was a visual representation of the task at hand: "The main idea and its supporting details work like a stool. If the seat of the stool is the main idea, we need to support the seat with the three legs which are the three supporting details."

She felt that this visual image would emphasize the idea that one cannot sit on a stool without the three supporting legs, just like we cannot write a paragraph about the main idea of the book without three supporting details.

Next, they brainstormed possible main ideas, suggesting ideas such as, "*se trata de una muñeca*" (it's about a doll), "*se trata de hornear magdalenas*" (it's about baking muffins), "*se cuenta sobre el proyecto de Sue*" (it tells about Sue's project), "*habla de tradiciones*" (it talks about traditions), and "*nos da los pasos para hacer una muñeca*" (it gives us the steps to make a doll). At this point, class ended and Ms. Cortez told them that they would resume the next day. See Figure 4.2 for photos from day two of the lesson.

Figure 4.2. Day Two—Reading the Story and Brainstorming Main Ideas

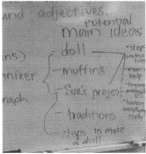

Day Three—Completing Graphic
Organizers and Making Corn Husk Dolls

Completing Graphic Organizers. On Day 3 the lesson continued with determining possible main ideas as well as supporting details and the students also began making their corn husk dolls. Although Ms. Cortez had originally planned for the students to write their summary paragraphs first, and then make the dolls as a final activity, she decided to switch the order of these two activities in order to motivate the students with something "fun and engaging" before diving into the writing. Their conversation began by reviewing the previous day's discussion of possible main ideas. Ms. Cortez had copied down the students' initial ideas from the day before and written them on the board so that they could revisit them. Next, she guided them through a discussion of potential supporting details for each one. She also explained that the supporting details should be taken directly from the book. As they began talking about details for each idea, the students made suggestions such as "*los pasos ó las instrucciones para hacer la muñeca*" (the steps or instructions to make the doll), "*la mamá de Sue le ayuda*" (Sue's mom helps her), "*comprando materiales*" (buying materials), and "*tener todo listo*" (having everything ready).

When they reviewed their original list of main ideas, they came across the suggestion that the story was about making muffins. Ms. Cortez asked them what details they could use to support this. One of the students commented that, except for the beginning of the story when Sue was thinking about making muffins for her school project, there was no other mention of the muffins in the book. Ms. Cortez then asked them if they thought this could be the main idea without any other details. Could the stool be supported without any legs? The students decided that, no, making muffins could not be the main idea without supporting details, and they abandoned this idea. Ms. Cortez asked the students which ideas could be supported by the suggested details and after some discussion, they decided that both the idea that the story was about a doll and that it was about Sue's project could work. Next, Ms. Cortez told the students that they could choose any of the main ideas that had enough details to support it and asked them to write this main idea and supporting details in their graphic organizer. Once their graphic organizers were complete, they moved on to making the dolls.

Making Corn Husk Dolls. To begin the doll-making activity, the students excitedly arranged their tables into one big group while Ms. Cortez placed all of the materials in the middle, explaining:

Here is the fun part of this lesson! We will be creating our own corn husk dolls. I was able to talk to your classmate, Sachi, and she let me know she used to make these dolls in Guatemala. I thought it would be fun for us to learn how to make our own dolls and follow the instructions of how to do so directly from the book and from your classmate and her experience making them.

They began by creating the doll's body. Ms. Cortez explained that she had soaked the corn husks earlier in the day in order for them to be flexible. Recalling the activity later, she commented:

I remember it was fun because we got to do the activity on those two days, so instead of doing the activity in one whole day, it motivated them to write because it was like, okay, well, after the decoration is the writing, and that was kind of like a reward, but backwards.

The students eagerly began rolling the corn husks into the shapes they would need for the torso, head, arms, and lower body, attaching the various parts with pieces of string, talking among themselves as they worked. They followed the illustrated step-by-step directions in the book, but they also watched and listened to Sachi explain how she made hers. Her method was a little different from that outlined in the book, and she would point out these differences as they worked. Some of the students wanted to try her method, so Sachi walked around helping them.

As they worked, the students wondered how to say doll in Sachi's native language of Mam, and so Sachi wrote the word *arij chaj n* (corn doll) on the board for them and modeled how to pronounce it. Ms. Cortez and the students practiced saying it several times. Later, Ms. Cortez explained to us how, in a different math lesson, Sachi had brought in some of the traditional clothing items that she and her mother sewed in Guatemala, leading to a lesson on measurement. Several students making corn husk dolls had also participated in this math lesson, and as they made the dolls, Sachi explained how she would also make traditional clothing for her dolls too, with extra yarn that her mom might have had leftover. Reflecting back on the lesson, Ms. Cortez commented:

While making the dolls, it was also like a nice break, just to get to know each other more, because they all come from different cities or states from Mexico and from Guatemala, so they were kind of comparing, you know, like, "I never played with a doll!" or "I played with mud, not toys, we didn't have money for toys." So, it was nice to just hang-out.

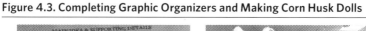

Figure 4.3. Completing Graphic Organizers and Making Corn Husk Dolls

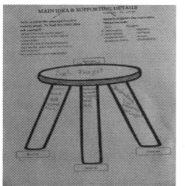

The day concluded as students set their dolls aside to dry with plans to decorate the next day. See Figure 4.3 for photos from day three of the lesson.

Day Four—Decorating the Corn Husk Dolls and Writing Summary Paragraphs

Decorating the Corn Husk Dolls. On the final day of the lesson, Ms. Cortez provided time for the students to decorate their corn husk dolls before writing their summary paragraphs. The students had fun drawing faces on their dolls' heads and adding pieces of fabric to make their clothing. Thinking back on the lesson, Ms. Cortez reflected on how much the students enjoyed this part of the process, creating faces and making hair out of pieces of yarn and felt. They also fashioned clothing out of scraps of fabric and felt. Some of the students embellished their dolls' corn skirts with felt hearts and polka dots as well as belts and shawls. All the while, the students exchanged ideas in a mixture of Spanish and English as they worked. Clearly, this part of the lesson was enjoyed by all, including Ms. Cortez.

Writing Summary Paragraphs. Once they finished making their dolls, they used their graphic organizers to help them write their summary paragraphs. Although this portion of the lesson was completed individually, Ms. Cortez explained that they were welcome to help each other as they wrote. A few students had a hard time writing in English, so Ms. Cortez gave them the option to write in Spanish first and then translate their paragraph into English. The students also had access to a list of high frequency words in English with translations in Spanish, as well as a word wall full of transitional words in English and Spanish. Ms. Cortez walked around the room in case students asked for assistance and that way she could help them translate their thoughts from Spanish to English, if needed. As the students wrote, the newly decorated corn husk dolls were displayed on the table, and they almost appeared as if they were cheering the students on with their work, adding a festive flair to the writing. Once they finished, Ms. Cortez collected the paragraphs in order to check them, but later she returned them and invited the students to share their writing, and their dolls, with their parents.

To bring closure to the lesson, Ms. Cortez gathered the students together once more. She began by reviewing the objectives of the lesson, stating, "You should have been able to identify the main idea in the text with three supporting details. You should have done this by citing several pieces of textual evidence when writing your summary of the book we read."

After reviewing the objectives, she asked the students for their opinions about the lesson. The students thought the lesson was fun, making comments such as, "*¿Podemos hacerlo otra vez?*" (Can we do this again?)

In fact, Ms. Cortez recalled that during the third day of the lesson they had been running late trying to finish their work before the period ended when the time came to switch classes. As some of her students in the following period entered the classroom, they also made comments such as, "*¿Maestra, qué están haciendo?*" (Teacher, what are you making?) and "*¿Oh, yo lo puedo hacer?*" (Oh, can I make one?)

Ms. Cortez commented, "I think the whole crafty part, the whole engaging part, that's what kids, especially middle schoolers enjoy the most, doing something other than just the writing. So that feedback was nice to get from them."

As the students left, they could be overheard admiring each other's creations. One student commented, "*¡Oh, me gusta como pusiste esto!*" (Oh, I love how you put this!) while another, admiring her classmate's doll's hair, said, "*¡Ay, yo espero que yo hubiera hecho así!*" (Ay, I wish that I would have done it like that!). See Figure 4.4 for photos from day four of the lesson.

DISCUSSION AND IMPLICATIONS

As discussed in the Introduction, culturally sustaining pedagogy is asset-based and critically oriented teaching that centers on maintaining students' cultural identities and linguistic proficiency in their home

Figure 4.4. Completed Dolls and Summary Paragraphs

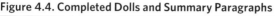

language, supports students in thinking critically and questioning societal inequalities, and ensures that students have access to culturally
dominant competencies. While this particular lesson does not encompass a critical orientation, multiple aspects of Ms. Cortez's lesson reflect
the other dimensions of culturally sustaining teaching.

First, the use of both Spanish and English throughout the lesson
supported students' continued linguistic proficiency in Spanish while simultaneously helping them develop their skills in English, the dominant
language in the United States. Ms. Cortez's modeling of and encouragement for using both languages, interconnectedly, reflects a translanguaging approach to language development and use (Garcia, 2009a), which
views students' various languages holistically, to be utilized as one interconnected resource that supports meaning-making and communication.
In addition, by welcoming Sachi to teach the others how to say "corn
doll" in Mam, Ms. Cortez signaled to Sachi that her native language is
important, and to all of the students that multilingualism is valuable.

Second, the entire lesson revolved around a cultural practice with
which Ms. Cortez knew at least some of her students would be familiar.
Discovering that Sachi knew how to make corn husk dolls and recognizing that corn husk doll–craft is a prominent cultural tradition, with indigenous roots across the Americas, Ms. Cortez saw an opportunity to build
upon Sachi's funds of knowledge (Moll et al., 1992/2005), or accumulated
and culturally developed knowledge and skills. This lesson valued Sachi's
linguistic and cultural identity and mirrored her home world while offering the other students a window into that world. Bishop (1990) asserts
that multicultural literature must be used in the classroom to affirm students' identities and lives while helping them learn about others from backgrounds different from their own. This lesson on reading and writing about

corn husk dolls was purposefully designed to shine a light on Sachi's abilities and knowledge, including the craftwork and artistry that she engaged in with her mom, which also reflected a tradition in her home country of Guatemala. In addition, this lesson opened up space for the other students to share their own backgrounds and lived experiences with one another as they worked together, another means for each student to share their funds of knowledge. In this way, Ms. Cortez's lesson squarely embodied the ideal for teaching set forth by Moll et al. (1992/2005) of learning about and building upon our students' funds of knowledge and bridging the world of students' homes and communities with that of school.

The significance of these practices on the students' biliteracy growth may also be seen throughout this lesson. Across the 4 days, the students expanded their vocabulary in both English and Spanish. The students also practiced their reading comprehension skills, through the structure and support of a shared bilingual reading experience—while the text was in English, there was ample opportunity to discuss the text in Spanish. The lesson also helped the students grow in their writing skills. The graphic organizer of the stool provided the students with a visual metaphor for how the main idea must be supported by key details. The lesson offered a well-scaffolded experience with an authentic reason for reading and writing—the students not only read and wrote about corn husk dolls, they *made* them and shared them with their families.

We also see important effects on the students' identities (Muhammad, 2020). Creating a lesson focused on a shared cultural tradition and doing so in a way that integrated the students' home languages of Spanish and Mam, affirmed their cultural and linguistic identities. Reading about corn husk dolls directly related to Sachi's, as well as the others' cultural heritage. The lesson also provided the students with a venue for talking and sharing about themselves and their backgrounds, another way to affirm their lived experiences. Furthermore, by inviting Sachi to act as a guest teacher during the corn husk doll–making activity, Ms. Cortez affirmed and supported her aspiration to become a teacher, an important part of the identity Sachi is imagining for herself in the future.

This lesson suggests important understandings and practices for educators to consider as they develop as culturally sustaining practitioners. First, teachers need to consider the significance of getting to know their students. Teachers can become acquainted with their students by conducting interviews, as Ms. Cortez did in this case, or by conducting visits to students' homes and communities. Next, teachers must build upon these insights to create meaningful and engaging lessons that maintain students' linguistic and cultural identities while addressing curricular requirements. While this lesson was inspired by Ms. Cortez's interview

with Sachi, it also met a Common Core State Standards (CCSS) require-
ment and provided *all* of the students with a fun and engaging way to
practice reading comprehension and summary writing.

In relation to this last point about the CCSS, we would like to acknowledge points raised in this book's Introduction about how CCSS
and related standardized testing policies have continued to contribute
to curricular standardization across the United States, making it difficult for teachers to find the time and space to enact culturally sustaining practices. We highlight how Ms. Cortez addressed the standard of
identifying the central idea of a text and supporting details while simultaneously utilizing a culturally sustaining approach. Although her
lesson complied with this curricular mandate, importantly, she did not
begin by shaping her lesson around a particular standard, but rather,
she designed it, intentionally, to first build upon her students' cultural
backgrounds and, specifically, to showcase the funds of knowledge of
one of her students, Sachi. Then she aligned her lesson ideas with a cor-
responding standard. We believe this shift of focus in lesson design represents powerful teacher agency and is an important aspect of enacting
culturally sustaining pedagogy.

Continuing our discussion of how the CCSS and standardized testing
often lead to a narrowing of what is taught in school, and by extension,
during literacy instruction, we would also like to point out that finding
the main idea of a text is frequently a primary goal when teaching reading
comprehension. Often, this skill is delivered as a school-based practice
in the sense that finding the main idea and/or summarizing are often assessed through some sort of classroom exercise completed primarily for
the teacher's assessment. This skill may also often be taught in such a
manner that it can appear to students that they must find the "correct"
main idea, as opposed to finding evidence in the text to defend alternative
key ideas (Aukerman & Chambers Schuldt, 2016). We applaud how Ms.
Cortez guided her students in brainstorming multiple possibilities for various main ideas. Encouraging this kind of divergent thinking is important
for helping students to develop critical thinking skills.

In relation to these thoughts about how, and with what outcomes,
culturally sustaining literacy lessons may be carried out, we feel it is
important to highlight some of the many other ways that students can
meaningfully transact with a text like *The Corn Husk Doll*. In the
future, Ms. Cortez and other teachers wishing to design a similar lesson, might invite the students to write different corn husk doll makers
to find out more about their craft. Or, students could post their own
directions for how to make corn husk dolls on the Internet for others
to follow. Likewise, the dolls and accompanying written descriptions

about how they were crafted, could be displayed in a prominent location in the school, such as the front office or library, to spark schoolwide interest in this cultural tradition. Another possibility could be to engage the students in putting on a doll play with their new dolls. Such an endeavor could include creating characters for the dolls, writing scripts, rehearsing, and staging a production. This would involve occasion to learn about writing dialogue (which could be multilingual), including appropriate punctuation, such as quotation marks, and many opportunities to rehearse the dolls' lines. Such drama-inspired practice and repetition would help to support the students' developing oral language production in English as well as their fluency and prosody across all languages incorporated into the play. The students could then share this corn husk doll play with another class, perhaps of younger students who would likely be delighted with such a show, or with their families, who would surely enjoy witnessing their children's burgeoning bi- (and tri-) lingualism.

The students could also engage in research projects related to the history of corn husk dolls (and other kinds of doll-making), including investigating the indigenous roots of this practice and variations in how corn husk dolls are made across North and South America (and how this practice has been adopted and adapted in other parts of the world). For example, in some indigenous doll-making traditions, dolls were not given faces due to a legend that the Spirit of Corn, conceptualized as one of three "sisters" of staple crops of the Americas, along with beans and squash, made a corn husk doll for her daughter. However, she became so taken with the doll's beautiful face that she spent less and less time with her daughter and more time fixating on her own beauty. Due to her vanity, the doll's face was removed. Other corn husk dolls are used in sacred healing ceremonies, such as to carry away the evil of bad dreams.

Such a focus on the doll's native roots could potentially lead to further exploration and critically oriented inquiry into Native American peoples and cultural practices and provide additional opportunities to learn more about the many, too often untaught, contributions of Native Americans to past and present-day American life, traditions, art, science, environmental stewardship, cultural practices, and more. Corn husk doll–making is a practice that was taught by Native Americans to Europeans and, over time, it has spread across the world. This history could be used to talk critically about such concepts as cultural appropriation, settler colonialism, and could be related to other contemporary issues, such as the way countless places across the Americas were renamed by Europeans, or the misuse of Native names and words today, including for sports teams. In fact, such a related study could be connected to *Since*

Time Immemorial, a Native-created curriculum that has been mandated as part of the K–12 curriculum in Washington State. Originally passed in 2005, the law at first only encouraged that this curriculum be taught. However, because so few school districts adopted it, the law was changed in 2015 to require school districts to teach it (Rawlings, 2018). Although it is slowly being taken up across the state, relatively few of the teachers with whom we work are aware of it, likely because this curricular policy has not yet been widely implemented (Rawlings, 2018).

All of the above examples of additional opportunities for students' authentic and purposeful reading, writing, and speaking are activities that may be shared with audiences beyond the teacher, with real purposes such as educating, entertaining, and engaging students and their classmates, peers, families, and community members in activities that are fun and meaningful and that may raise awareness about issues related to social justice, and potentially lead to justice-oriented action steps. These are just a few additional examples of culturally sustaining and meaningful ways to engage with a book like *The Corn Husk Doll*.

In conjunction with these ideas, it is important for teachers to recognize that becoming a culturally sustaining educator is a *journey*. It takes time, trial and error, and a commitment to learning and growth. Teachers—*and school leaders*—must be willing to seek out and reflect upon the many opportunities to learn and grow along the way. We saw these kinds of opportunities being developed across the Collaborative Conversations in which the teacher and leader candidates engaged together. For example, during our second Collaborative Conversation, which focused on discussing Moll et al.'s (1992/2005) article on funds of knowledge, Ms. Cortez's group selected the following quote for the whole class to consider: "Teachers rarely draw on the resources of the 'funds of knowledge' of the child's world outside the context of the classroom" (p. 134). In the ensuing discussion, teacher and leader candidates discussed many ideas related to doing this work. Their thoughts included: concern about the time and energy that designing such lessons might entail; utilizing the strategy of finding cultural topics that energize students from many different backgrounds, such as candy, as mentioned in the Moll et al. (1992/2005) article; and finding shared interests with their students. One leadership candidate mentioned,

It goes along with using their funds of knowledge, like letting the students teach you. So, during my first couple of years, I was in a bilingual flip [classroom] and I didn't speak hardly any Spanish except "please" and "thanks," that was about it, so just letting the students teach me the numbers in Spanish or teach me how to say this or that, kind of like, the same sort of idea, letting them teach you about themselves. . . .

Finally, the reporter for Ms. Cortez's group shared that, at the heart of the funds of knowledge concept was the idea of, "getting to know your students, really getting to know them . . . meeting them at their level, and realizing, hey, we have this in common and now we can build on that." We see these same ideas about getting to know your students and letting them teach you at the heart of Ms. Cortez's lesson.

We also see important moments of learning in Ms. Cortez's lesson and in her subsequent reflection on her lesson. In retrospect, Ms. Cortez identified things she would have done differently. For example, she commented that using visuals during the vocabulary preview would have further supported her students' comprehension. She also mentioned that, if she were to repeat this lesson, she would invite the students to read their summary paragraphs aloud to one another, providing opportunity for fluency practice while affirming their identity as writers. With reflection, additional opportunities like these can be seized in the future. We admire and acknowledge Ms. Cortez's efforts to enact a culturally sustaining lesson so early in her career as well as encourage Sachi's aspirations to become a teacher. We hope that this lesson may lead to further discussion and reflection about enacting culturally sustaining pedagogy in the context of teaching language and literacy.

NOTES

1. ELLPARAS is an alternative route to teacher certification designed for paraeducators seeking to earn their certification and endorsements in both English language learners (ELL) and bilingual education (BLE). It was created by a team of WSU researchers through a grant project supported by the U.S. Department of Education. The research reported here is part of a different study; however, it features a paraeducator's lesson enrolled in ELLPARAS, and we would like to acknowledge the ELLPARAS team: Gisela Ernst-Slavit (PI), Judith Morrison (Co-PI), Yuliya Ardasheva (Co-PI), Kira Carbonneau (Co-PI), Sarah N. Newcomer (Co-PI), and program coordinators: Steve Morrison and Lindsay Lightner. For more information, please see: https://education.wsu.edu/research/projects/ellresearch/#:~:text=ELL%20Impact %20Project,in%20the%20state%20of%20Washington.

2. All names of people and places beyond the use of WSUTC, city names, and Pasco School District are pseudonyms in order to protect the confidentiality of the teacher and students.

CHAPTER 5

Culturally Sustaining Pedagogies

Amplifying Youth Critical Consciousness in Classrooms

Aimee Hendrix-Soto, Erica Holyoke, Heather Dunham,
and Melissa Mosley Wetzel

A key tenet of culturally sustaining pedagogy (CSP) is that students' identities are affirmed by teachers who are also persistently committed to fostering their critical consciousness (Paris & Alim, 2014). Critical consciousness involves the ability to understand, critique, and ultimately transform inequity. Teachers who enact CSP are already transforming the inequitable status quo of education when fostering academic development and cultural affirmation, but to realize the full potential of CSP, youth must be supported in transforming inequities in institutions and structures themselves.

In this chapter, we share a story of how teachers at two schools in one urban district amplified the consciousness of their students. As authors, we utilize the term *amplify* to indicate that the Latinx young people in the classrooms portrayed here were critically, and sometimes personally and painfully, aware of injustices in their local communities. They also understood ways to resist injustice. In 5th- and 12th-grade classrooms, teachers drew from theories of critical literacy (Freire & Macedo, 1987) to build upon students' analyses of power as a way of being and doing in their everyday lives (Vasquez et al., 2019).

CONTEXT AND POSITIONALITIES

In this chapter, we will provide a thick description and analysis of critical literacy-informed approaches for engaging students' critical consciousness and extending it in reading, writing, and inquiry units. We specifically focus on the ways that 5th- and 12th-grade teachers employed a critical pedagogical approach (Freire, 1970), allowing youth concerns to drive the official curriculum, and their methods for centering local community and larger social issues in literacy pedagogies.

Mendez Elementary

Sylvia Mendez Elementary School is located in the northeastern area of a growing city in the U.S. Southwest. Though neighborhood demographics are rapidly shifting due to gentrification, the school served learners who identified as 89.8% Latinx, 4.5% African American, 3.4% Asian and Asian American, 2.1% White, and 0.2% multiracial. Sylvia Mendez Elementary School has a strong partnership with the university, employing the authors at the time of our research, and through that partnership preservice teachers worked with 5th-grade readers and writers who all identified as Latinx and Spanish–English bilingual. The instructional and pedagogical practices of three of those preservice teachers and their students are highlighted in this chapter.

The three teachers—Manny, Genevieve, and Angelica—were in a critical literacy–focused cohort getting their ESL Early Childhood through Grade 6 teaching certifications. Manny identified as a Latinx, male, bilingual (Spanish–English) teacher and was a first-generation college student. Genevieve identified as a White, female, bilingual (Russian–English) teacher. Angelica identified as a Latinx, female, bilingual (Spanish–English) teacher. The teachers worked with 5th-grade learners throughout the school year on a novel study of *Harbor Me* by Jacqueline Woodson (2018) in the fall, and a writing for social change unit in the spring. Across the two units, the curriculum and instruction emphasized community, social change, and literacy identities.

Erica, Heather and Melissa (authors) facilitated the units with preservice teachers and the 5th-graders and simultaneously taught the literacy methods courses, which were held at Sylvia Mendez Elementary. Heather identifies as a White, monolingual, female educator. She previously taught elementary multilingual students in a Title I school. Melissa, a former early childhood teacher, also identifies as White, monolingual, and female, and has been leading these courses for the university for many years. Together, Heather and Melissa led the novel study of *Harbor Me* with the 5th-graders and teachers in the fall semester, by modeling various reading instructional strategies and mentoring the preservice teachers as they embedded these strategies in their one-on-one and small-group work with the 5th-graders. Erica identifies as a White female educator, whose native language is English, though she is also an emergent Spanish bilingual speaker. She worked as a former elementary and special education teacher and administrator. Erica taught minilessons to the 5th-graders and teachers for the writing unit. She supported rising teachers (Manny, Genevieve, Angelica) in their teaching and instruction, serving as a mentor and course instructor across three semesters and five classes.

Community High School

Community High School was located in the neighborhood of East City, several miles away from Silvia Mendez Elementary School (hereafter called Mendez). Although geographically separated, Community and Mendez Elementary served similar demographic populations. Black (15%) and Latinx families (81%) have attended the school since the 1960s, even as the demographics of neighborhoods surrounding it shift to include more White people. Community is both a source of pride and a marker of racial inequity in East City, with award-winning academic and extracurricular programs, but also far fewer course offerings than (whiter and wealthier) West City high schools a few miles away, all factors which became important in the teaching and learning represented here.

The students in the focal class were known as the Youth Equity Agents (YEAs). The majority of the 25 students were in the 12th grade, and all identified as Latinx, Black, or multiracial. The course was led by two White female coteachers. The first was Ms. Morrison, who also taught fine arts at the school and had a long history of supporting youth in resisting local injustice, including a district plan to turn Community over to a charter network rather than address structural inequities. The second was Aimee (author), who was invited by Ms. Morrison to help teach the course. Aimee was a former English teacher at Community, who had maintained her ties to the school as she shifted to teacher education and research at the same university where Erica, Heather, and Melissa were based. During this course, Aimee also acted in a dual role as a researcher, observing 131 hours of class, conducting interviews with the YEAs, and collecting artifacts of teaching and learning.

AMPLIFYING CRITICAL CONSCIOUSNESS WITH 5TH-GRADERS AT MENDEZ ELEMENTARY

Melissa and Heather led rising teachers working with the 5th-graders in an elementary setting to collaborate in a novel study of *Harbor Me* by Jacqueline Woodson (2018), and Erica led the writing for social change purpose unit. *Purpose units* focus on the intent of the writing, rather than a target genre. We (Erica, Heather, and Melissa) observed the three rising teachers through these units. In both of the units, the literacy structures followed a readers' and writers' workshop format where Erica, Heather, and Melissa led the whole-class minilessons with the 5th-graders and teachers together. The teachers then worked with learners in small groups and one-on-one to dive deeper into the reading and writing. While a whole-class format would have learners working more independently, the model in this class allowed for teachers and learners to learn side-by-side together. The teachers often taught additional minilessons, drawing heavily on conferring and iterative and responsive planning. Teachers pedagogically drew from culturally sustaining pedagogy (Paris & Alim, 2014), critical love (Freire, 1970; hooks, 2000), and restorative justice (Winn, 2018).

As part of the course, we (authors) designed the workshops to engage 5th-graders as people, readers, and writers with their local communities as well as broader critical social issues in our country. *Harbor Me*, a middle-grades text, included topics of immigration, the criminal justice system and incarceration, special education, and building a community. In the novel, readers are immersed in critical social issues as six young people discuss issues that impact them personally. Drawing on this text to facilitate in amplifying youth's critical consciousness allowed them to see it modeled as they read along with the youth's journey in the text. We set up the workshop to mirror the workshop community that the youth in the book experienced. The writing unit, which followed the reading experience, explicitly engaged learners to brainstorm what and who they considered to be their community and what mattered to them and their communities, and supported them in the creative design of their genre, purpose, and audience for their published writing pieces. The purpose of the writing unit was to write for social change, and the mentor texts included books by Marley Dias, who as an elementary student launched the #1000BlackGirlBooks campaign, and other young activists. Reading and writing were connected and provided opportunities and space for children to bring their experiences, critical consciousness, and writing abilities into their learning.

The preservice teachers established a literacy community with 5th-graders through their reading unit and drew on the funds of knowledge the learners brought, their interests, passions and critical social issues, their communities, and their families to design writing experiences that fostered a collaborative space for students' critical consciousness to emerge. In the writing unit, Erica appealed to the teachers to design minilessons based on what they knew about the learners, and encouraged responsive modeling and conferring for youth to identify their topics, as well as their strengths as writers in the community. Figure 5.1 shows that youth's existing critical consciousness and daily experiences were funds of knowledge that shaped the classroom space alongside current events. This consciousness and knowledge entered the space through dialogue and in partnership with teachers, who facilitated critical reading

Figure 5.1. Amplifying Critical Consciousness Through Reading and Writing at Sylvia Mendez Elementary School

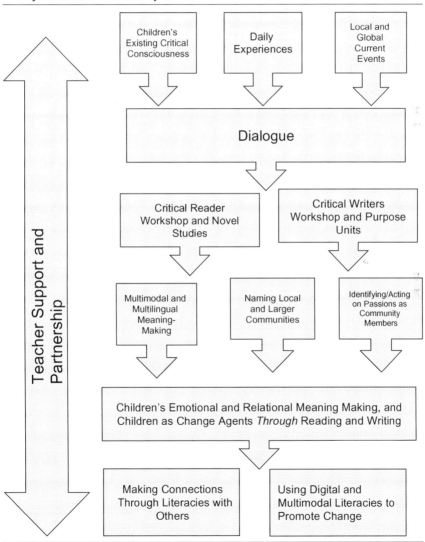

and writing workshops. The class became a literacy community where critical consciousness could be amplified through the literacy learning experiences.

Through these units, we learned with the teachers and youth that culturally sustaining pedagogy manifested through an approach (1) where youth drove the curriculum through the literacy process and (2) where local issues were central in the literacy learning. Rising teachers Manny, Genevieve, and Angelica worked with students Santi, Adrian, and Juan to show how prioritizing critical consciousness through workshop models and learning alongside youth can facilitate culturally sustaining literacies.

Allowing Youth to Drive the Curriculum

Teachers designed learning experiences for comprehension and writing engagement to emphasize the process of engaging in literacies in which youth were driving and directing the day-to-day learning. Together the teachers and students explored critical social issues using multimodal resources the teachers brought to them. They discussed students' interests before and during lessons and facilitated space for youth to join and lead by questioning, engaging in dialogue, and conferring. These strategies were utilized to listen and respond to students while making adjustments in the moment and creating responsive lessons from one day to the next. By prioritizing a workshop model, youth were not only actively engaging in reading and writing but were sharing as leaders and learners in the literacy units. The teachers were able to amplify critical consciousness that students brought into their learning and anticipate making connections to that consciousness through the reading and writing minilessons, mentor texts, and conferences.

Harbor Me Novel Study. The reading unit was designed to engage readers around a text that centered on critical social issues (e.g., immigration, incarceration, equitable learning spaces) through specific reading strategies. One of the most powerful teachers' invitations was a specific reading strategy of inquiry. Within the inquiry, teachers taught a lesson on differentiating between question types, a reading strategy that guided them to ask questions to dive deeper into the text. Working as a group, Manny, Genevieve, and Angelica planned multiple pathways for the group's inquiry using the reading strategy of asking thick questions. Asking thick questions encourages readers to pose open-ended, complex, and critical thinking questions. These questions often extend beyond the literal meaning in the text.

To do this, the three teachers read three chapters before planning their lesson, looking for important themes from the section of the novel that the 5th-graders might want to learn more about. After the class read the three chapters, the teachers modeled asking thick questions around the text, such as "Why do we have to do the Pledge of Allegiance? Why do people get offended with other languages being spoken besides English?" and prompted the 5th-graders to pick a line of inquiry to research and discuss based on these questions. Because the teachers had prepared different potential lines of inquiry, inspired by the text and relevant to the lives of their 5th-graders, they could follow their students' lead. They had multiple resources connected to the thick questions they anticipated the students asking: a website to discuss post-traumatic stress disorder, photographs to illustrate the location of a harbor and how it might connect to immigration, a video to talk about different types of hair, and a news article that discussed a student who was sued for not saying the pledge of allegiance in Texas. Ultimately, the 5th-graders decided to follow an inquiry about immigration.

Thus a key instructional practice was the teachers' preparation. They used their knowledge of the students, the cultural context, and reading strategies to model and then step back—gently guiding the young readers to engage in critical discussions around the text. It required reading the text multiple times, engaging in their own research, and drawing on formal and informal conversations with youth.

Writing for Social Change. The writing unit was designed as a purpose unit that allowed students to select a topic, genre, and audience for their composition. The minilessons were designed as invitations for youth to examine their decision-making as writers. In Table 5.1 we share a sample of the minilesson topics in closer detail. Although they are writing minilessons, the connections between the reading and writing units are evident in this sample. The italicized sentences at the bottom of each minilesson indicate how children's (Eric, Amy, and Maria's) writing and writing strategies were incorporated to the minilessons to honor the children's strengths as writers and amplify those strengths to the writing community.

Manny, Genevieve, and Angelica's conferring, which happened daily during the workshop, became a catalyst for future lessons, ensuring that the minilessons responded to what the teachers were learning about students as people and writers. For example, one of the youths, Adrian, came up with a new writing strategy of "research and fact-checking," and also revised a previously shared strategy to be called "brain emptying with words and pictures." Adrian agreed to teach the class the strategies,

Table 5.1. Key Minilessons from Writing for Social Change

<u>Introducing Writing Group and Writers' Notebooks</u>

- How did they tell their stories? How do we tell our stories? Connect to *Harbor Me* characters.
- What does our writing community need? (i.e., what tools, what resources, how we offer and provide help)
- "Getting started" with writers' notebooks by asking questions
  » What are big ideas that matter to me?
  » What are some things that worry or anger me?
  » What communities am I part of? What do I hope or wish for and with those communities?

<u>Collecting Information and Writing for Social Change</u>

- Anchor Chart: Notice and name writer's strategies.
- Mentor text: Marley Dias and her #1000BlackGirlBooks campaign.
- Invitations to writers:
  » If you are finding a topic, think about what you care about and what you want to change in the world, in your community, and in your country.
  » If you have a topic, ask more questions:
    ○ Why does this topic matter to me?
    ○ What might it mean to "make change" about this topic?
    ○ What are some of the ideas of what I or we could do to make change?

Invite Maria to share about her lists and how she was making decisions as a writer.

<u>Layering Our Writing and Selecting Genre(s) for the Purpose of our Pieces</u>

- Layering multiple modes/genres of writing to communicate our message.
  » Model this with counter arguments, facts/research and personal narrative.
- Invitations of how to layer topics:
  » Using memories that you have of your life.
  » Feelings about topics—the "big" responses we feel in our heads, hearts, and bodies (e.g. Marley Dias' frustrations).
  » Is there history, dates, or science that you might share?
  » Are there visuals that would support your topic?
  » What would the topic look/sound like in a museum/movie?

Connection to children's tools in previous session: Eric's use of facts or Amy's visuals to support her in thinking about and layering her topic. Also, invite children to consider if they used these already to share with the group. Begin recording a collaborative list of tool/strategies.

and Erica started the next minilesson asking the class to generate all of the strategies they had been trying out as writers, and recorded them in a class anchor chart. As a class, including the 5th-grade writers and preservice teachers, the teachers then discussed how to determine the right fit of strategies and how to draw on the community of writers to try something new. Erica provided a summary of previously introduced strategies. She also provided a space for students to engage in multiple turn-and-talks so they could discuss additional tools and strategies they applied in their own writing with peers. Following one turn-and-talk, Adrian led the class in explaining his approach of "research and fact-checking" as well as "brain emptying with words and pictures" and why these strategies were helpful in his writing. Several peers followed his lead in sharing additional self-created and self-named writing strategies. This process of building a shared strategy toolkit driven by learners amplified the youths' process strategies and solidified their connection to the larger class writing community.

After each lesson, the teachers critically reflected on how their teaching moves allowed youth to drive the curriculum. This reflection carved out an intentional space for learning about youth strengths and planning future instructional moves. For instance, Angelica worked closely with Juan, and frequently focused his attention on counterarguments. As she reflected,

> He is really taking the critique about counterarguments and running with it in such a special way. He is learning how to argue why what he believes in is important, which is great. . . . I asked him to think about people who may not agree with him, and from then on he began coming up with realistic counter-arguments for his writing pieces which made it more powerful than it already was. As a writing teacher, this showed me that by asking scaffolding questions I was able to help Juan become a stronger persuasive writer without telling him what to write or do; he came up with it on his own. This also showed me that going over strategies in the beginning helped him establish his writing goals to keep him productive the entire way.

Angelica reflected on her role as a writing teacher to amplify Juan's strategies and tools and used her reflection, and knowledge of him as a writer, to inform her teaching decisions, instructional moves, and scaffolding questions. Her end goal was to scaffold Juan's growth as a writer by offering him reflection questions that emphasized his strength and interest in counterarguments, through brainstorming together. His topic was focused on contributing to "saving the local environment and animals" and he recognized not everyone would be committed to his cause. Similar to the reading unit, the teachers were able to begin with students' strengths in their writing, and design follow-up experiences that expanded their process as a writer.

Across Reading and Writing Experiences. As the facilitators of the units, we designed space for youth to intentionally drive the learning. This meant asking teachers to plan for and anticipate multiple directions the lesson could go, based on what happened in previous lessons and what they knew about the students' interests. In doing so, teachers were able to amplify students' own strategies and processes as readers and writers. Doing this hard work of planning resulted in stronger learning communities. We noticed a great deal of trust and excitement each day as the youth entered the space, wondering what their teachers had planned for them. In enacting the unit plans, the teachers prioritized how youth, their literacy habits, and lived experiences were central to the curriculum, not just a vehicle toward reaching a teacher's agenda or standards.

Supporting Local and Larger Community Connections

Through both of the units, the teachers amplified students' knowledge and critical awareness of their local and larger communities as conduits for literacy learning and shared knowledge. Teachers valued students' linguistic knowledge, views about their communities, and their reading and writing literacies. It was important that the youth defined what community meant to them and discovered their own topics of interest. The priority for the teachers was making writing and reading relevant for youth in their lives and anticipating that they already had strong emotions, passions, and interests related to people and places they cared about. The connections the youth made to their communities were primarily linked to critical social issues and thus amplified their critical consciousness into the literacy learning space.

Harbor Me *Novel Study.* During the novel study, the teachers and 5th-grade students attended to multiple topics and themes such as immigration, gun violence, incarceration and the criminal justice system, and learners with differences. As they read the text together, the teachers and students made connections with these themes that applied to larger communities and national news (i.e., #BLM, U.S. Immigration and Customs Enforcement [ICE]). Throughout the weekly lessons, Manny, Genevieve, and Angelica also found connections between the themes from the text and the 5th-grade students' local communities by layering multimodal sources to foster discussion. Immigration was one of those connections. In *Harbor Me*, the main character's father goes missing and the character infers that ICE has taken him. This event in the text was a mirror for one of the 5th-graders, Santi's, lived experiences. The teachers were careful not to pressure Santi into making the connection aloud for the group, knowing the sensitivity of the topic. Rather than requiring personal connections to the text as a reading strategy, which is often the case in intermediate-grade reading lessons, the teachers chose to focus on the critical social issue from the text and connect to events in the larger community through news articles and videos.

Santi ultimately chose to share his personal connection between the events in the text and his local community (i.e., family) with his group. Manny wrote in his teaching reflection:

> I appreciated him (Santi) sharing openly about his mom because that showed me that he felt safe and could trust us as a group. He would always let me know if he found something confusing in *Harbor Me* or just wanted to fill me in about what was happening at home with him. I am very thankful for having Santi as my reading buddy because I learned that being vulnerable with a student is okay because we learn from our experiences together.

The teachers thoughtfully approached critical social issues with multiple entry points for youth and their meaning-making. By offering space for thoughtful dialogue about the issues, youth felt supported and safe to share their personal connections to the topics as well.

Making connections is an important strategy in reading lessons, but we note here that by creating space for this as an *option* during reading, students were able to discuss sensitive topics with their peers and try on other reading comprehension habits that still allowed for them to engage in discussions as a community. This space allowed students to be heard, to process their emotions, and to see themselves as active in making decisions about how they read the text and their lives.

Writing for Social Change. The writing unit was structured with the understanding that youth were already invested in various communities and had strong critical awareness of actions they might take to improve experiences for themselves, for their families, and for their communities broadly. Importantly, while the unit was focused on social change, we see connecting to activism as a core aspect of culturally sustaining literacy practices in all literacy learning not unique to this writing unit.

Utilizing minilessons (such as those listed earlier in Table 5.1) as invitations for youth to process, share, and explore the people, places, and topics that mattered to them was a strategy that amplified students' critical perspectives. Planning minilessons began with awareness of what and who the youth considered to be their community, the people and places they cared about, and with invitations offered to organize this in the personal, local, and global orientations. Another important strategy was group work. Youth shared their thinking and ideas with peers throughout the unit.

As Genevieve reflected, "Adrian learns best through modeling and conversations about what we are writing about. He also likes working with his friend Santi because they bounce ideas off one another."

Finally, teaching a purpose unit, and not a genre unit, which is common in school (i.e., poetry, "how-to," research essay, personal narrative, and so on), allowed youth the flexibility and autonomy as writers to determine the format and audience for their publication. In our context, the purpose of writing for social change considered the youth, as authors, in charge of using their critical awareness to make and facilitate change. Some learners wrote letters to the principal, and others to the president of the United States, still others created posters for their neighborhoods which we laminated or created public service announcements to hang in the school and share on various media platforms. Most importantly, they saw their writing and publications as a vehicle to make change based on their critical consciousness of topics important to them and their communities.

As they progressed through the unit, the minilessons prioritized strategies to try on as writers, including how to select topics, make their message heard, and consider audience and design. The foundation was to create tools as writers to write about topics of their choosing. In the unit, youth wrote about issues such as immigration, bullying, pollution, and mental health.

Santi, who worked with Manny, wrote about the pollution in the river at his school. He created a digital photo essay to bring awareness to the community and with Manny's support scheduled a meeting with the principal to share his piece. Manny had encouraged Santi to take pictures of the pollution, and he also had done the same, while providing strong mentor texts of photo essays to offer Santi a platform for communicating his message to the school community and administrators. Together they had decided on the audience, and Manny had guided Santi in determining how and where he would communicate. Manny wrote a note to Santi summarizing their learning:

> During our writing times together, I was always struck by how thoughtful you were about your writing. You connected your experience of the trash at the playground to the trash you saw in Guatemala. By using the writing strategy of "writing what we notice" you were able to build connections to other experiences you had with this social issue.

Manny reminded Santi how he approached this topic by first thinking of his family in Guatemala, and also about how much he cared about his school community in determining his topic, and what he should do about it through his writing.

As Santi showed (and as you will see in the vignette later in this chapter), youth were aware of and committed to environmental issues. Using culturally sustaining literacies provided a space to explore these concerns and act upon them. To create space for youth to share connections between themselves and their communities and to see themselves as change agents, we designed learning experiences to name our communities, what we love about our community, and wishes and hopes for various communities we are part of. The central focus of writing as a tool to process and make change provided agency for youth to determine how they wrote, what they wrote, and who they were intending the social change to impact.

Across Reading and Writing Experiences. Across the reading and writing units, the idea of centering local and larger issues with youth-created space for topics that mattered to the learners. These topics and issues became part of the literacy curriculum and the learning within the units. Teachers used small groups, were critical partners in exploring students' selected topics, and focused on amplifying what youth already knew about themselves as people, their communities, and their strengths as readers and writers. Teachers also offered literacy tools, such as making connections and determining a format or audience for writing so the youth had a vehicle to engage in self-selected and text-related topics. Through literacy learning, youth saw themselves as change agents within their communities large and small.

AMPLIFYING CRITICAL CONSCIOUSNESS
AT COMMUNITY HIGH SCHOOL

The Youth Equity Agent Project was situated in a leadership elective course at Community, where coteachers had significant freedom to engage culturally sustaining pedagogies (Paris & Alim, 2014) without navigating official course skills or standards. Like they had at Mendez, the teachers utilized a critical pedagogical approach that allowed students' social concerns, which often focused on racial equity issues in the local community, to drive the curriculum.

Within the YEA project, many overlapping curricular activities facilitated youth engagement with local community issues: developing a school racial climate survey, designing a new high school campus, countering deficit narratives of urban schools, and mentoring at Community feeder schools. In this chapter, however, the examples from Community will focus specifically on how critical inquiry amplified critical consciousness.

Specifically, it will detail the teaching and learning that occurred as youth investigated racial inequity in the local school district, their community, and beyond.

Though this critical inquiry was student-driven and at times very organic, it was cultivated through strategic teaching. Figure 5.2 displays the formation of our inquiry community, which became a place where youth could utilize literacies to explore social issues to understand how these issues were shaped by power, including systemic racism. As at Mendez, youth's existing critical consciousness, lived experiences, and current events entered the space through dialogue. Based on these emerging themes of inquiry, the Community coteachers facilitated exploratory activities where

Figure 5.2 Amplifying Critical Consciousness Through Inquiry at Community High School

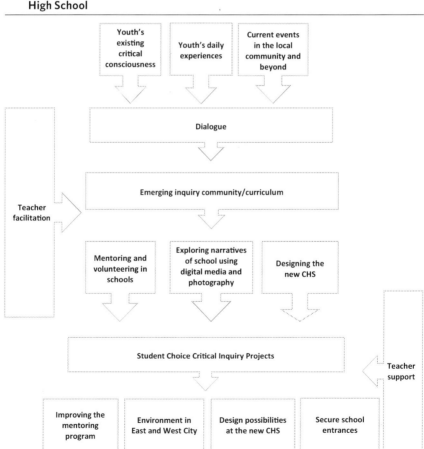

youth could extend their critical consciousness and share this with the classroom community through self-selected critical inquiry projects.

At the onset of the class, the coteachers were aware of some issues that interested students, such as the stark differences between building maintenance, community engagement, and course offerings across East and West City, because these were perennial interests of both teachers and students. Additionally, Ms. Morrison had taught many of the students in other courses and had participated in workshops on dismantling racism with them. However, beyond just knowing youth concerns, creating a curriculum space for inquiry driven by youth requires spaces where those concerns can be shared with the classroom community and made available to be pedagogically engaged. In the YEA project, the coteachers facilitated this by having open spaces for dialogue where youth could share whatever was on their mind freely. During this time youth shared successes and struggles in school, told jokes, and responded to current events like mass shootings or the decision to relocate their school. Teachers also engaged youth in more structured dialogue, such as asking youth to respond to digital media, weigh in on news or particular social issues, or engage with guests, such as a school board member sharing information about the relocation.

Information shared in these spaces became lines of inquiry that the coteachers sought to engage and then extend through particular activities. For instance, because youth were interested in the deficit narratives surrounding their school, coteachers facilitated a series of lessons where youth viewed journalistic media about Community as well as Chimamanda Adichie's (2009) TED Talk, *The Danger of a Single Story*. Through discussion of these texts, youth articulated new understandings of the ways deficit narratives can be created (through essentialized stories), but also countered (through complex narratives).

The youth engaged this concept again in response to news that upset some students, which was that Community's feeder elementary schools were slated for closure due to official district reports of deterioration and underuse. While school district facilities management may not sound like an especially relevant topic for adolescents, the youth were especially aware as young members of the East City communities impacted by these policies. Despite consistent improvement in all official metrics, district policies allowed youth zoned for Community to choose "higher-performing" schools in West City instead, leading to a situation where the school was perpetually underenrolled. Just before the beginning of the school year, the district decided to turn Community's historic campus over to another district school, a disproportionately White and affluent magnet school with swelling enrollment. Many of the students held strong feelings about the move and critically analyzed it as evidence of systemic racism, thus facilities management was a fresh topic. As an aside, the students at Mendez were also reading about and discussing the impact of these school closures in close-by communities.

Ms. Morrison and I (Aimee) facilitated an opportunity to extend this concern with buildings, racial inequity, and deficit narratives as a response to current events. We asked youth to investigate the narrative of despair and underuse with their smartphone cameras as we toured the elementary schools in preparation for mentoring, and then engaged their photos in a series of small classroom activities. In contrast to the official narrative, the students' pictures told a more complex or counterstory (Delgado, 1989) of rich use and value.

The inquiry moves engaged in the investigations of school buildings early in the year shaped the students' ongoing critical inquiry. Youth and teachers repeatedly took up the practice of utilizing their smartphones as a digital literacy tool to investigate material spaces and question narratives of school throughout the project. We (Ms. Morrison and Aimee) drew upon this practice to create activities, and youth used these ways of meaning-making as they engaged in other aspects of the class, such as mentoring work, designing of the new school, and crafting digital inquiry projects for their final course projects.

We asked youth to create and share their final projects with the class. Students were given free choice in the topic. Their projects drew from lines of inquiry around schooling, equity, and current events that they had brought into the space and had explored in depth over time in the supportive context of our inquiry community. The bottom of Figure 5.2 displays examples of the topics youth chose. As at Mendez, this inquiry unit was also guided by a workshop approach.

To further illustrate the relationship between the teaching in the inquiry community and the amplification of youth's existing critical consciousness, we will now focus on the work of Ava, a student whose critical inquiry grew from her interest in environmental justice issues and developed into a critically conscious understanding of how the global issue of environmental destruction manifested in her local community.

Allowing Youth to Drive the Curriculum

Ava was a 12th grader who had attended Community for all of her high school years. Though her family was initially concerned about the school's reputation as a "bad school," Ava embraced the Community's small size and supportive feel. She described herself as someone who "[tries] to work hard," and I (Aimee) observed that she cared deeply about her academic success. In informal chats, she expressed a desire to have a career helping others, such as social work. Though Ava was often quiet in whole-class settings, she talked freely with her friends, and raised her voice when she felt strongly, such as when she talked about the environment or proclaimed "I am a Chicana!" when I asked about her identity. Ava also used the terms Mexican, Mexican-American, Latina, and Hispanic to describe her identity.

Throughout our project, Ava's inquiry consistently focused on environmental issues. This focus first manifested during the activity investigating narratives of elementary schools, which was productive in extending inquiry for many of the students. Youth, including Ava, took pictures of entrances, artwork, classrooms, hallways, and outdoor learning spaces that indicated robust use and value rather than the disrepair. Ava's movements, talk, and photography during this activity focused strongly on two aspects of the schools: the reflection of Latinx culture in the artwork and bilingual signage (Figure 5.3), as well as the environmental education present on the campus, in the form of gardens, animal habits, and conservation (Figure 5.4).

Figure 5.3. Ava's Photo of Bilingual Art

Figure 5.4. Ava's Photo of a Garden

When we asked students to write briefly about the story their photos told, Ava focused on environmental education. She wrote that the garden spaces were important parts of schools because they show the ability to engage students in the "importance of preserving nature" and "taking care of environments on campus." This was an important instance of the youths' collective counterstory (Delgado, 1989) of the value and use of the elementary campuses, through Ava's specific lens focused on the environment. Ava also wrote that the elementary school gardens reminded her how Community "improved in its own eco environmental projects," noting that they were also seeking a "green flag" for their campus, and that "growing a garden is the first step in doing that." Thus her ability to create a counterstory for East City elementary schools that focused on their valuable environmental education was likely drawn from her emic understanding of the school's environmental programs, which repurposed overgrown courtyards into gardens and animal habitats, garnering national praise even as the district narrative focused on underutilization of the campus.

Ava's composing about environmental education was also the beginning of a line of inquiry about environmental justice that Ava would explore throughout the course. Given her enrollment in an environmental science course and her passion for environmental justice, the elementary tours were likely not the first time Ava thought about this issue, but this activity was an entry point where her interest could enter the curriculum space and be amplified by ongoing critical inquiry.

Supporting Local and Larger Community Connections

In the spring semester, Ms. Morrison and I (Aimee) asked youth to create more extensive inquiry projects based on their investigations thus far. Our reasoning was two-fold: First, we genuinely wanted youth to see themselves as critically conscious knowledge holders who were positioned to investigate and alter local community issues in ways that were unique to their identities as Black and Latinx youth in East City. Additionally, Ava and other youth routinely voiced or wrote about wanting to be "pushed more," explaining that a focus on the rigorous academics that would prepare them for college often fell through the cracks. Their thoughts (which were also echoed by many students in our years at the high school) helped us understand that this type of academic success, which is a key tenet of culturally relevant (Ladson-Billings, 1995b) and culturally sustaining (Paris & Alim, 2014) pedagogies, was of value to youth. Youth were signaling that even within a critical and student-driven curriculum, they still desired support and structure from teachers.

A workshop approach provided the structure for teachers to provide key supports while still promoting youth agency and ownership of their work. We supported youth in extending their inquiry into local community issues through minilessons, modeling, and conferences during student work time, culminating in publication and celebration of their projects.

Direct Teaching. This series of workshop days began with a minilesson titled "Moving Complex Stories Forward" (see Figure 5.5). As the teacher of this lesson, I (Aimee) utilized direct teaching about inquiry and modeled how youth could extend their own already critically conscious lines of inquiry. Similar to the teachers at Mendez, I first defined inquiry as a way to "follow your own questions" and as a cyclical act of investigation that we repeat to know more about the world (Slide 1). I extended this explanation by modeling my own inquiry about Community as a teacher and researcher trying to understand how we can simultaneously promote the narrative of Community as a great school, while also raising awareness about systemic racial inequities that manifested as opportunity gaps. Finally, I demonstrated how Ava's existing inquiry into environmental education could be extended to further investigate

Figure 5.5. Slides from Moving Complex Stories Forward Minilesson

the impact of youth involved in ecological justice, simultaneously naming her work as important and inviting her (and other youth) to extend their inquiry (Slide 2).

Side-by-Side Teaching. As at Mendez, side-by-side teaching also supported youth in developing their critical consciousness. Following this first minilesson, Ava was visibly energized and immediately began to develop a project extending her inquiry on the environment as the leader of a small group. At the end of the day, Ava and her group reframed my invitation in their own words, calling upon her photos of elementary environments: "We want to write about how schools are environmentally aware. We can show what schools do to show that to kids." This was followed by a bulleted list that read: "vegetable gardens, planting plants, rain catcher (cistern)."

In the next work session, Ava's group immediately beckoned me for a conference to work out a new idea, focused specifically on environmental education at the school. At times, I was a listener/learner as they explained their ideas to me. At other times, I acted as a consultant, providing information about interview protocols and the recursive nature of research cycles. Over the next few sessions, we worked in this manner, shifting through roles as they crafted a project utilizing interviews and photography to document the history of environmental projects at Community (e.g., chicken habitats, outdoor classroom, and permaculture gardens) as evidence of the value of the school.

Freedom to Explore. For several weeks our collective focus shifted to other aspects of the course (a field trip with mentees, participating in the design of the new high school) and the many activities of the spring semester (college visits, AP testing, state testing). When we came back to critical inquiry work, Ava started our conference by asking, "What is social justice?" a term I had used in my first minilesson. I responded by referencing her own work, explaining that wanting people to re-spect the environment is a form of social justice. At this point, she an-nounced that she was "tired" of the project on environmental education at Community and planned to abandon it despite a successful first in-terview. Instead, she would combine her group with another group of Latinx female students focused on disparities in education across East and West City. Though I was disappointed to not see her project come to fruition, I told her that this was fine, but that I still wanted to chat about the environment as a social justice issue. I offered her the example of environmental racism wherein West City included numerous protective animal habitats, but that these environmental protections did not hap-pen in East City. To illustrate this, I showed her a website about activism against environmental dumping in the green area behind the school. Ava spent time exploring this website and showing me a linked city report before announcing, "I want to do THIS." However, since she was still adamant about working in the new group, I wrapped up the conference by asking her to think about how the project could incorporate all of their interests.

These interests, or lines of inquiry, came together in an unexpected and rather organic way in an extended conference the following week. This conference, which through some lenses would be considered mostly "off-topic," is an example of how centering student agency and freedom served the development of inquiry and critical consciousness. I joined the conversation as a listener while the group was in the midst of roast-ing one another about topics like their ages, ability to take a joke, and being stingy with snacks. The tone remained social overall, but within this there were moments of criticality, such as when the group debated whether the rats infesting their school were mere pests or creatures de-serving respect. The ultimate focus on the intersections of demographic shifts, development, and environmental protections came together dur-ing a debate about luxury apartments and retail development in the neighborhood where they lived. In my role as a critical amplifier, I asked if this displaced the Latinx people who had historically lived there. Some felt that this absolutely did, while others contended that there were Latinx people who could also afford to live and shop there. Ava kept the group focused on the green areas, and the deer habitats within that were destroyed for developments, and the group began to search for images that would reflect how this differed in East and West City.

Publication and Celebration. To publish and celebrate youth's critical inquiry work, the students presented their work to the classroom com-munity instead of taking a traditional final exam. Figure 5.6 displays

Figure 5.6. Slides from Presentation Titled "Social Justice. Environment: East and West (City)"

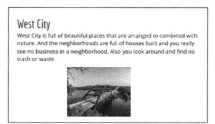

a slide from the presentation titled "Social Justice. Environment: East and West [City]" created by Ava and her new group. In this presentation, they displayed their critical consciousness by identifying rampant development, related displacement of working-class families, and lack of environmental protections in East City as intersecting social justice issues that impacted Latinx people specifically, including themselves.

To provide their peers with insight into this community issue, they provided contrasting pictures of East and West City and drew on their personal experiences. Ava began by explaining that East City is "becoming filled with business" and that as a result her neighborhood has "no neighbors and [developers] keep calling and asking my parents to buy the house."

Other group members explained the impact to wildlife, describing local places where trees were removed for businesses. By utilizing pictures and descriptions of West City locations where development and nature are combined, with plentiful parks for residents and tourists, they illustrated how this is an equity issue disproportionately impacting Latinx people in East City rather than just a general urban density issue. Finally, the presentation ended with a video from a contentious community meeting where Latinx activist groups verbally sparred over how to best address regentrification. When I asked if they could elaborate more on the importance of the video, they connected this issue back to the school district's decision to move the high school, explaining that "this [development and regentrification] is happening, but people in our community feel like they do not have a voice. Like with [the school move], we don't want this and it's unfair."

In doing this, they also engaged in a sophisticated reading of the world (Freire & Macedo, 1987), identifying the existence of a lack of voice for Latinx residents as a pattern manifesting across multiple issues. That was a key critical takeaway of this work and an extension of their existing critical consciousness that manifested only as they published their inquiry to our community.

Students in the YEA project could drive curriculum by exploring local and larger issues that were important to them, but with support from their teachers as facilitators. Ava's inquiry into the environment was supported by space to explore using photography and composition, but also through minilessons and dialogue about extending inquiry, in formal schoolwork, and as a way of thinking about the world. As coteachers, we engaged in culturally sustaining teaching through a mixture of expectations and support, but also freedom. While Ava's work on environmental education and schools was important inquiry even without completing a required project about it, combining this with another group's thinking about disparities across East and West City allowed her, and by extension everyone present, to extend our critically conscious understanding of the intersections between social justice issues faced by Latinx people.

CONCLUSION

Our examples of teaching and learning at Mendez Elementary and Community High School illustrate the possibilities for creating culturally sustaining education by amplifying the existing critical consciousness of Latinx young people across two school settings (elementary and secondary), with multiple age groups (5th- and 12th-graders), as a part of school curriculum. Though this work occurred in a state and local context with a heavy focus on standardized testing and accountability, teachers carefully crafted ways to prioritize the literacies and lives of young people in the classrooms more than official standards.

Above all else, these projects required teachers to be responsive to students in numerous ways. First, our work required teachers to have an agentive vision of literacy education, centering freedom and choice. This agentive vision is strongly connected to an appreciative view of the youth they teach, whose lives are viewed as valuable curriculum. The students developed critical opinions as they moved through their daily lives, such as when Santi encountered pollution in the water near his school, or when Ava repeatedly addressed changes to animal and human habitats near her home. For this critical knowledge of community issues to be centered as meaningful curriculum, teachers must respond to young people in solidarity, joining youth in collective struggle against an unjust status quo. This commitment, however, also requires examinations of positionality and critical reflexivity, which is especially crucial for teachers whose cultures and communities differ from their students, such as the teachers in this article who are White women from nearby but differing communities than the students of Community and Mendez. For instance, though the detainment of immigrants was relevant for Santi, his teachers created conditions (a rich text with many entry points for connection, open discussion, choice in how to respond), offering him a choice about whether to follow that critical thread.

Related is also an appreciative stance toward the literacies of young people. Across the examples, teachers facilitated the use of a wide variety of literacies. At Mendez, teachers facilitated reading of a middle-grades text and respected youth as real authors and activists who could write for important and self-selected purposes. The youth were supported in publishing in multimodal forms as well as drawing on bilingual strengths. At Community, Ava's inquiry made use of her reading of material environments, analyzing them through photography, but also drawing upon her embodied knowledge of elementary schools (through tours), Community's campus, and East City. Ava and her group drew heavily on spoken words and images to illustrate the issues to their peers. Facilitating opportunities for multimodal expressions of literacy is an especially important teacher move in the secondary setting where inquiry is often conceived of as a "research paper" or formal academic essay synthesizing published knowledge from other authors. Though the use of this wide array of literacies is often framed as relevant simply because youth find it engaging, the more culturally sustaining value is that a broad approach, open to youth's entire literate and linguistic repertoires, bends school toward a place where all of their ways of knowing and being can show up.

The final and most important way that teachers were responsive to students was by creating a community to amplify young people's critical consciousness. The freedom within each unit did not mean that youth were alone or that teachers were less active in their teaching. Engaging youth's existing critical consciousness involved balancing an appreciative stance of their literacies with the collective desire to more deeply understand and alter local and larger justice issues. As a result, teachers engaged in extensive preparation to be ready to follow the leads of their students through reading, writing, and inquiry. They thought carefully about how to bring critical and provocative texts to their students, while also responding to youth's in-progress literacy work through minilessons and conferences. They leaned on each other, which we realize is not the norm for teachers in schools, creating a collaborative space that extended beyond the classroom to the community and even the university.

Thus a key capacity of culturally sustaining teachers is an ability to balance freedom with support, with the ultimate goal of youth agency.

Young people must engage, themselves, in critical analysis and design of new, more just futures for themselves and their communities as part of CSP. To realize the goals of CSP, teachers need a robust toolkit of strategies for literacy teaching. With these tools, teachers can practice responsiveness that guides youth to continue to try on new strategies, habits, and innovations. They drive their learning in line with their interests, desires as readers, writers, and inquirers, and toward being and becoming literate in ways that are meaningful to them.

Part III

CONSIDERATIONS, PRACTICES, AND TAKING ACTION FOR CSLP

CHAPTER 6

Collective Diamond Mining

Using Collaborative Curriculum Excavation to Embrace the Educator's Responsibility Toward Culturally Sustaining Literacy Pedagogy

Kelli A. Rushek and Ethan Seylar

In this chapter we examine the reflective practice that Ethan, a preservice English language arts (ELA) teacher, and Kelli, an English education instructor, undertook to critically examine how culturally sustaining literacy pedagogies may be bridged from theory to practice. We used data from the development of one unit of study created in a course in Ethan's teacher education program and our own curricular excavation process of that unit of study. We offer our metacognitive reflections to highlight how we, as two critically informed White teachers at different stages of our educational careers, examined and revised this unit through a culturally sustaining literacy pedagogy (CSLP; Paris, 2012) lens. We argue that this, or similar critical reflective processes, can serve as a reflective framework for preservice teachers, teacher educators, and inservice teachers to excavate (Sealey-Ruiz, 2019) their curriculum and text choices to mine for moments which could be more critically informed and culturally sustaining for ELA students. This reflective, collaborative, critical practice of curricular excavation could inform praxis in English education and teaching. We end this chapter with implications for teacher education and practice with the goal of aiding teachers in developing more culturally sustaining literacy pedagogies.

POSITIONALITIES AND CONTEXT

How we became collaborators on this critically reflective, metacognitive project is notable, as Kelli was Ethan's instructor in an education course during his teacher education program. Ethan, a White man, was a preservice teacher in the Reading and Teaching Adolescent Literature course at a large, research-based Midwestern university. Concurrently, he held a long-term substitute teaching position at a secondary school in a Midwestern district which served a racially, culturally, and religiously diverse group of students. The university course took place in the Fall of 2020 and was delivered as an asynchronous, virtual course during the lockdown phase of the COVID-19 global pandemic. Kelli, a White woman, was the instructor of record of the course in which Ethan was enrolled. A former high school English teacher in Chicago Public Schools and committed to working toward more equitable learning experiences for students of color, Kelli enacted a course curriculum that was collaboratively developed and revised over the years by professors and graduate students. She made sure to hinge this course on her agentive goals as an English educator: to ensure all ELA preservice teachers come to teaching with an orientation that is critically informed, representative, humanistic, and disruptive of the traditional status quo of the dominant hegemonic ways ELA is often taught (e.g., canonical texts, rote learning, skills-based, standards-based, Eurocentric curriculum designed to maintain White supremacy). Ethan was a critically informed social justice advocate who aligned in solidarity with #disruptive goals. From the beginning, Kelli noted that Ethan's orientation toward his future teaching was critical and conscientious and that he displayed traits that this orientation would continue into his teaching practice. Ethan listened intently to his fellow preservice teachers' lived experiences that fell outside of his cultural identities. When a classmate in his teacher education program shared what it was like to live in their community as a queer Black man, or as an immigrant, or as a woman with autism spectrum disorder, Ethan tried to learn from their stories. He believed his classmates when they shared the ways institutions around them—including their university—perpetuated systemic oppression. Ethan learned from his classmates' voices and used their stories to expand his understanding of the complex systems of inequity that surround all of us. While always leaving room for others' voices, Ethan used classroom discussions to question the hegemonic ways institutions intersected to create inequitable schooling experiences for culturally marginalized youth. However, even if we both self-identify as critical and antiracist White educators, we acknowledge that we have shortcomings regarding issues of race and our own potential involvement in perpetuating racism in and outside of schools. Our awareness of these issues is what drove us to this work, as our shortcomings were uncovered further when engaging in this CSLP curricular excavation project.

BACKGROUND FOR BUILDING THE UNIT

In the 5th week of the Reading and Teaching Adolescent Literature course, we explored how hegemonic forces shaped the construction of a "new canon" of young adult literature. For example, we studied how young adult titles are quickly being adopted by school districts in order to fill representative holes in the curriculum (e.g., Alexie's [2012] *The Absolutely True Diary of a Part-Time Indian*, J. Reynolds and Kiely's [2017] *All-American Boys*, or A. Thomas's [2017] *The Hate U Give*). This exploration led to a critical examination of how literature becomes situated in secondary school curricula, and it prompted Ethan to question the role of English teachers in promoting equitable instruction. Figure 6.1 shows Ethan's response to one of his colleagues' discussion board posts.

Ethan noted that in his education courses, his professors framed equitable teaching as a list of what *not* to do rather than offering entry points for preservice ELA teachers to both conceptualize and practice teaching literature in culturally responsive and sustaining ways. As Kelli explained in her lecture recording that week, addressing Ethan's question in how he *"should* teach texts in critically responsive way[s]": the text doesn't do the work, the teacher does. An ELA teacher, in essence, can take a text that is primed for culturally sustaining literacy instruction and teach in nonculturally sustaining ways that recenter White ways of knowing and being; an ELA teacher can also take a text that is not culturally sustaining but teach it in culturally sustaining ways.

Ethan explored these questions in his final project for the course: developing a unit of study based on a text set (a curated collection of multiple texts) on a topic of their choice for a hypothetical ELA classroom. Assigning curation assignments to preservice ELA teachers and preservice school librarians is a common practice in colleges of education. However, text curation assignments often focus on the product or curriculum created rather than on that which is collaborative and

Figure 6.1. Ethan's Discussion Board Post, 9/25/2020

Ethan Seylar
Sep 25, 2020

██████ thank you for your post. It seems like you're grappling with a lot of the same questions I am right now. In all of my English ed courses this semester I have learned about how *not* to teach texts and how to determine if a text is no longer culturally relevant to students. I think that's really important, but I don't know how I *should* teach texts in critically responsive way.

critical in curational processes (Spiering & Lechtenberg, 2020). Kelli wanted the preservice teachers in the course to develop a critically informed unit that would "#disrupt the status quo of English instruction." She expected these final projects to showcase the preservice teachers' criticality of ELA teaching by showing an understanding of multimodality, representation, equity, youth literacies, and young adult literature within ELA teaching practices. These were central themes that had been drawn on throughout the semester.

At the end of the semester, after all of the projects had been graded, Kelli thought Ethan's unit of study and accompanying rationale was a remarkable example of meeting her expectations for the final course project. Ethan had drawn from his own experiences as a long-term substitute teacher, curating a unit of study that asked students to disrupt the dominant and monolithic narrative of Arab culture and the Islamic religion through literature instruction in a 9th-grade ELA classroom. Kelli believed Ethan's project to be a golden nugget that could be considered a framework for other critically informed teachers to use when navigating the tensions of praxis—moving from theory to practice—in creating CSLP and instruction.

Preservice ELA teachers like Ethan often wish for the "answers" to ensure they are not reproducing the status quo in their own ELA classrooms when trying to enact pedagogy that draws on cultural, critical, and asset-based orientations to teaching for a pluralistic society. Searching for "answers" or "methods" on how to be critical and culturally sustaining teachers of students of color from all cultural intersections is a futile goal, as answers and universal methods do not exist within the fluid, ever-changing, and multifaceted nature of culture within a given sociopolitical context (e.g. Brown, 2013; Ladson-Billings, 2017; Paris & Alim, 2017). We offer a way to guide preservice or inservice teachers into embracing the ambiguities and the tensions of curriculum excavation in order to create more critically sustaining literacy practices for students.

EMBRACING THE RESPONSIBILITY, EMBRACING THE PROCESS

By excavating Ethan's unit of study—a diamond, but an uncut one—we were able to identify, question, and revise this curriculum to be more culturally sustaining. While Kelli engaged in process-oriented instruction of the final project (e.g., peer brainstorming and check-ins, draft work, and instructor–student feedback), she discovered, as Spiering and Lechtenberg (2020) found of many text curation projects, that they "fell short in asking learners to critically consider conceptual connections and diverse perspectives" (p. 83). In collaboratively and critically excavating Ethan's final project, a curricular artifact, (here defined as an example of curriculum: unit, mini-unit, assessment, assignment, text set curation, and so on) we looked at each other and thought: is this culturally sustaining *enough*? We realized that this curricular artifact was potentially a culturally *relevant* (Ladson-Billings, 1995b) unit of study, but it was missing elements of culturally *sustaining* pedagogy (Paris, 2012), such as including students' linguistic competencies and making Ethan's critical orientation more transparent. Sealey-Ruiz (2019) suggests that preservice teachers need to critically excavate their identities, looking for places where biases and assumptions are rooted in order to unlearn damaging deficits that would cause harm to their future students of color. It has also been argued that a pedagogy of discomfort (Boler, 1999; Zembylas, 2015; Zembylas & Boler, 2002) is an orientation to teaching that encourages preservice and inservice teachers to wrestle with the tensions of being outside of their comfort zones in order to interrogate their "cherished beliefs and assumptions" (Boler, 1999, p. 176). Here we draw on the concepts of excavation of the teacher's orientation (Sealey-Ruiz, 2019) to speak back to taken-for-granted assumptions about ELA teaching that center the "overwhelming presence of whiteness" in teacher education programs (Sleeter, 2001, p. 94) and in ELA teaching in K–12 schools. This process nudges teachers into a state of discomfort (Boler, 1999; Zembylas and Boler, 2002), in order to analyze and interrogate their own developed curriculum, assignment, or text curation to be more culturally sustaining in literacy teaching (Paris, 2012; Paris & Alim, 2014). Drawing on this scholarship, we suggest, after taking part in this process, that curriculum development should also be critically excavated, a metacognitive and collaborative practice among colleagues (e.g., in-groups such as preservice teachers, inservice teachers, educational faculty, or cross-group) that embraces the tensions, ambiguities, and potential pitfalls of creating a culturally sustaining literacy curricular artifact.

Drawing on Paris's (2012) conceptualization of CSLP as going beyond being "responsive of or relevant to the cultural experiences and practices of young people" to require teachers to "support young people in sustaining the cultural and linguistic competence of their communities while simultaneously offering access to dominant cultural competence" (Paris, 2012, p. 95), we highlight how we embraced our educator's responsibility to engage with collaborative curriculum excavation in order to let the fundamental truths—and limitations—of our teaching practices come to the surface.

THE DIG: METHODS OF EXCAVATION OF CURRICULUM

We present a narrative for the protocol of curricular excavation with a CSLP frame with the goal of embracing the ambiguities of culture—and the practice of teaching—as dynamic and not static (Paris, 2012). In order to do so, we borrow from the metaphor of a multifaceted diamond or prism. Just as there are multiple facets to the face of a diamond, there are many facets to CSLP. Just as each diamond looks different based on light and clarity and a host of other factors, so does the curriculum. So does teaching. Just as the intersections of a diamond create interesting and nuanced patterns of light, cultural and identity intersections create nuanced and pluralistic human beings. A diamond needs all those facets in order to sparkle; an ELA teacher attempting to instruct in solidarity with their orientation to CSLP (Paris, 2012) needs to consider as many facets as possible in order to "reimagine schools as sites where diverse, heterogeneous practices are not only valued, but *sustained*" (Alim & Paris, 2017, p. 3). Figure 6.2 outlines the three facets of the protocol we used to critically deconstruct Ethan's unit.

The facets and cuts of the diamond represent the theoretical tenets that can serve as entry points for critical excavation—analysis and interrogation—of the curricular artifact. We have chosen CSLP as the theoretical lens for excavating the curricula artifact. Figure 6.3 highlights our thinking utilizing the metaphor of the diamond.

The first step of the excavation protocol is to *identify*, to dig into the curricular artifact in order to name and locate what aspects of CSLP are within. The first layer we suggest for critical excavation are the facets of the *teacher's orientation to the curricular artifact* being excavated, such as those that are pluralistic, asset-based, and critical. Therefore, it is best if a rationale, written by the teacher, outlining the metacognitive processes they used in designing or creating the curricular artifact, is provided. This identification step parses out the teacher's orientation

Figure 6.2. Protocol of Curricular Excavation

Culturally Sustaining Literacy Pedagogy in Practice Protocol for Critical and Collaborative Excavation of Curricular Artifact
1) **Identify** (*Mining the Diamond*): Dig into curricular artifact to identify what aspects of CSLP are present.
2) **Question** (*Cutting the Diamond*): Once the facets have been identified, enter into critical and collaborative dialogue surrounding the tenets of CSLP.
3) **Take Action** (*Polishing and Setting the Diamond*): Create action items for praxis— what needs to be included or removed before imparting curricular artifact?

Figure 6.3. Model of Collaborative Excavation of Practice

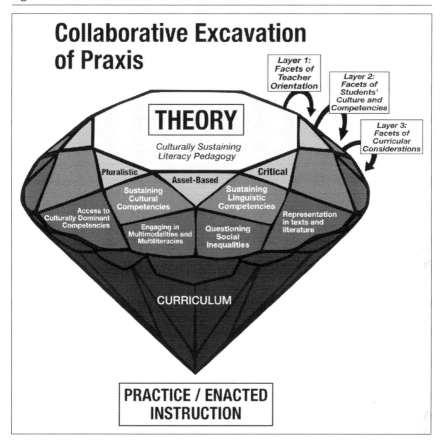

to the curricular artifact they developed—not necessarily their overall teaching orientation. We feel this is important for three reasons. First, we view one's orientation to teaching as always evolving (Brown, 2013); secondly, we know that teachers can feel attacked when their teaching is criticized (Kelchtermans, 1996); and thirdly, we know that most White people—the majority of the teaching force at this time—are emotionally fragile when asked to excavate their long-held biases and assumptions (DiAngelo, 2018). In this identification step of curriculum excavation, we suggest multiple passes through the curricular artifact, focusing on different slices of CSLP. Where is there evidence of a pluralistic outlook, one that embraces cultural multiplicity and cultural equity? Where is there evidence of an asset-based view of culture, students, and students' cultures? Where is there evidence of a critical understanding of how power is wielded in society and how it manifests in everyday societal inequality and oppression? Where is there evidence of intersectionality (Crenshaw, 1991)? Specifically in this case, how did Ethan understand the cultural complexity of the Muslim experience at the intersection of race, gender, sex, and so forth?

The next layer from which to excavate and analyze the curricular artifact would be that which draws on facets of the *students' culture and competencies*. This layer serves to identify where the curricular artifact does or does not give students access to developing culturally dominant competencies (Paris, 2012). Each pass under this facet would excavate where the curriculum is designed to ensure that students maintain cultural and linguistic competencies, question social equalities, and access culturally dominant competencies. The last layer of excavation would be the facet of *curricular considerations*, or where the *how* of ELA curriculum development intersects with CSLPs. Passes through the curriculum may look at the cultural and intersectional (Crenshaw, 1991) representation of characters and authors in the texts chosen—where will students be able to see themselves in textual mirrors, windows, or sliding glass doors (Bishop, 1990)? Where does the curriculum and accompanied instruction ask students to engage with multiple literacies (e.g., visual literacies, racial literacies, or intersectional literacies)? Multiple modes of text (e.g., traditional print, graphic novels, poems, collage, art, or intersections of multiple texts)? In the next section, we share how we collaboratively and critically excavated Ethan's curricular artifact using this multifaceted approach.

CULTURALLY SUSTAINING LITERACY PEDAGOGY IN PRACTICE: EXCAVATION OF CURRICULUM *IN SITU*

Digging in: Identification of CSLP in the Curricular Artifact

As we attempted to revise Ethan's curriculum project so that it better fit the tenets of CSLP, our first goal was to determine where Ethan's critical teaching orientations stood at the time he crafted his text set. Our logic was as follows: we could not attempt to make the text set more culturally sustaining without first determining his pre-existing orientation toward the essential components of CSLP (Paris, 2012; Paris & Alim, 2017). We used the text set as an artifact for study, one we could use to begin digging into Ethan's orientation toward this *specific* curricular artifact. For preservice and inservice educators who wish to critically excavate their own curricula for tenets of CSLP, this is an important distinction, as teachers need to suspend their own beliefs about their orientations toward teaching and instead focus on their orientation as it relates to the individual curricular artifact to be excavated. For example, Kelli may define her own orientation toward teaching as one that advances antiracist and culturally sustaining literacy practices but may produce a curricular artifact that does not necessarily put this orientation into practice. The purpose of this process is to aid the educator in reinscribing what may be lost in the theory-to-practice continuum. This first facet is one of identification and organization, not one of application. The objective is to notice and to categorize what is present in the curricular artifact before questioning and acting on that which is absent.

To start the collaborative and critical excavation process, we independently opened a digital copy of Ethan's text set and set out to probe that which was present. Following Paris's (2012) definition of CSLP, we looked at how it supported an asset-based orientation toward students, maintained students' cultural competencies, and how it engaged students in critical questioning about social inequalities. After coding Ethan's unit of study for these elements, we met to compare our notes. By working independently and then synthesizing notes, we were able to identify various elements of the text set that otherwise would not have been apparent if we had completed the process jointly from the start. This is why the curricular excavation process should be done collaboratively.

Layer 1: Identify Facets of Critical, Asset-Based, and Pluralistic Orientations in the Teacher's Rationale. Our first appraisal of the unit focused on identifying the critical and asset-based orientations that were present in Ethan's rationale, a section in which he explained his intended learning outcomes and why he chose to center his unit on disrupting the monolith of Arab and Muslim experiences in his school's curriculum. Scanning through this first section, we (Ethan and Kelli) independently sought evidence from the rationale that Ethan viewed his students as agentive and full of valuable humanity and knowledge (asset-based orientations). In addition, we looked for evidence that Ethan was approaching this unit with the understanding that power is inherited and exerted in systemic ways (critical orientations). Figure 6.4 shows a brief glimpse into Ethan's introductory passage in which he explained why he chose to develop this text set [location and school names redacted]:

As noted in the final paragraph of his rationale, it is apparent that Ethan is taking a "learner" stance, conveying that his unit of study is "incomplete" and his "only qualification to teach these texts" is his willingness to "listen to the #ownvoices of these authors and of my students." He then highlights the dynamic nature of culture and thus the

Figure 6.4. Ethan's Rationale Opening

Seylar, Ethan
16 December 2020

"And may all our nights be as blessed as this."
Or, a beginner's guide to disrupting the monolith of Arab/Muslim identity in the predominantly white, Christian, American ELA classroom

TEXT SET FOCUS AND RATIONALE
    This year, I had the honor of working with a fantastic group of high school students from the ▓▓▓▓▓▓ area. Together, we studied a short-story unit for ninth-grade English that is tried-and-true, though mostly tried. Many of my students belonged to religious and ethnic backgrounds that were underrepresented in any of our texts. In particular, though, I learned from ▓▓▓ conversation that many of my students were Muslim, immigrants from Arab countries, or the child of Arab immigrants. In fact, a

growing population of students in the ▓▓▓▓▓ School District belong to these three groups. And yet, there was no textual representation for them. In response to this gap in the curriculum, I decided to curate a text set focused on Arab and Muslim identity, particularly as it relates to life in America.
    I have curated a group of works, representing several different types of modalities, that begin to disrupt the monolithic idea of what it means to be Muslim and what it means to be Arab and what it means to be the child of an immigrant from an Arab or Middle Eastern country. To be clear, this text set is incomplete. I am not suggesting that this is the ultimate curation that will disrupt the monolith; I am not even suggesting that I am qualified to disrupt the monolith. Perhaps my only qualification to teach these texts is that I am willing to listen to the #OwnVoices of these authors and of my students. The more I learn, the more my curation will change. So long as teaching is dynamic, this text set will be dynamic.

texts that arise from and respond to said culture, firmly rooting himself as a learner–teacher.

In the curricula excavation process, Ethan learned that he held critical insights that he was not initially conscious of. While he was developing the unit, he found an online resource called the "Riz Test," an analytical framework to measure the portrayal of Muslims in the media, which was inspired by a 2017 House of Commons speech on diversity on screen by Riz Ahmed. Through the discursive process, we learned that Ethan's decision to employ the Riz Test as a framework for his text curation demonstrated an asset-based view of cultures other than his own. He had understood what asset-based teaching was in theory, but he was unaware using the Riz Test was putting that knowledge into action.

There were several guiding questions we found useful to ask as we codified this section of data. Remembering that the purpose of the first layer of curriculum excavation is *identification*, we found these questions served us well when finding moments that demonstrate where the educator's culturally sustaining competencies currently lie: *Where does the curricular artifact draw on asset-based positions toward teaching? Where does the curricular artifact draw on critical orientations toward teaching?* These questions do not serve as complete critical analyses on their own, but we do believe that these questions would be meaningful jumping-off points for discussion between collaborators.

Layer 2: Identify Facets of Students' Culture and Competencies. Next, we sought to question what skills and competencies, both explicit and implicit, were taught through this unit. For a curricular artifact to be culturally sustaining, it must view students as fully agentive and as possessing valuable knowledge regarding their home cultures. At the same time, however, the curriculum must also open a critical discourse about why certain cultures are subjugated in American society. Applying Paris's (2012) framework for CSLP, we used our second pass to search for examples of when the curriculum "center[s] on maintaining students' cultural and linguistic competence." By seeking out these elements of CSLP, we hoped to determine whether Ethan's unit design was truly focused on sustaining students' existing cultural competencies, or if it was interested only in promoting dominant agendas, literacies, and competencies under the guise of a "culture-celebration."

After we finished debriefing the first layer of our dig, we repeated the same process of note synthesis, albeit focused on different criteria from Paris's (2012) framework. We set our documents side-by-side and compared the moments in the text set where Ethan revealed, both explicitly and implicitly, the skills and competencies that he hoped students might gain from the unit of study. We attended to Ethan's curriculum rationale and to his explanatory statements justifying the inclusion of each text. These moments lend insight to the aspects of his students' home cultures that Ethan hoped to sustain and revealed both explicit and implicit goals Ethan had for teaching the poem "Eid Pictures" (Thompkins-Bigelow, 2020). Explicitly, he hoped to introduce poetry into the unit, giving it meaning as a particular literary form. He planned to make this obvious to future students. Implicitly—that is, in a way that may be less obvious to students—Ethan wanted to honor the linguistic tradition that serves as the foundation for many of his students' faith. The holy book of Islam, the Quran, while not entirely a poem, contains many poetic elements. We both noticed that Ethan had an implicit goal of *sustaining his students' linguistic and cultural competence* by teaching poetry in his classroom—particularly poetry that is not centered on Eurocentric traditions.

During this phase of our collaboration, we learned an important lesson about curricular excavation. This type of excavation is essential if preservice and inservice teachers and teacher educators hope to learn the cultural values that the curriculum planner cares about the most. Without excavating the works selected and the justification for those works, the educator's cultural biases remain beneath the surface, influencing the curriculum without the educator's knowledge. When a collaborator attempts to make meaning of the selected texts and the justification for teaching those texts, however, the bias rises to the surface. This process emphasizes the importance of viewing curricula as artifacts and not explicit projections of the curriculum's designer. The separation between the artifact and the creator allows us to examine that which we can measure (the words on the page) and not that which we cannot measure (the internal values of the educator).

We found the following questions useful to guide us as we dug through the text set a second time together: *Where in the curricular artifact is there evidence that the educator views students as capable, agentive, and possessing valuable knowledge?* and *Where in the curricular artifact is there evidence that the educator wants to balance the teaching of dominant cultural competencies and sustaining the cultural competencies the students' already hold?* While exploring these questions alone cannot reveal in what ways the teacher values nondominant competencies and skills, posing these questions in a collaborative space can invite critical and valuable discussions about the potential limitations of the teacher's understanding of CSLP and can draw on the knowledge of those in the collaborative excavation process.

Layer 3: Identify Facets of Curricular Considerations. For the final layer of our curricular "dig," we searched for evidence that the curriculum itself is designed to engage with students' critical literacies and competencies. Drawing on Paris's (2012) CSLP framework, we looked for evidence that the text set or curriculum was supportive for students questioning inequalities. Additionally, we sought evidence of other curricular considerations such as cultural representation in texts and the presence of multiple modalities. These curricular considerations are vital to think about when bridging CSLP theory to practice because these are the elements that constitute the actual content of the unit.

Moments where Ethan offered students access to culturally dominant competencies were relatively easy to find. Ethan often stated his curricular goals explicitly, with rationales like, "As we read this short story, I think I would pair it with activities about conflict. The conflict in this story is mainly character versus self . . ." and "[the short story author] uses clever indirect characterization to teach us about Nadia's mother and her illness, so I want my students to practice articulating those indirect characterization methods." These passages indicate Ethan planned to use his text selection to teach traditional English 9 content regarding literary elements. Additionally, we sought evidence that the curriculum engaged with multiple modalities to increase student learning. Ethan incorporated several modalities of texts, including prose, poetry, videos, podcasts, and sequential art. While these were also easy to identify, they were harder for Kelli and Ethan to categorize. Ethan initially questioned whether teaching nonprint modalities counted as granting access to culturally dominant competencies. To teach cultural criticism and multiple literacies (New London Group, 1996), it is vital that ELA educators allow opportunities for students to make meaning from multiple modes of text, such as podcasts and graphic stories, as these are modalities which are steeped in the counternarratives of the culture and lived experiences of those whose narratives are not included in the dominant narrative (Solórzano & Yosso, 2002).

When looking for moments where Ethan was *supporting students in questioning societal inequalities*, we discovered that these instances were baked into the text set implicitly, rather than explicitly stated. We relied on Kelli and Ethan's in-text comments to find possible moments where students would question social inequalities, and then we talked through how these moments might manifest in the classroom. After discussing a passage from the text set and the accompanying comment, Kelli and Ethan began asking how educators can better *support students in questioning social inequalities*, such as interrogating how Muslim characters are portrayed in texts and advancing critical orientations to literature representation. We realized that transparency must be an essential part of curriculum development, lest the teacher's own critical thought not be shared with the students. Kelli noted that Ethan exhibited critical thought in his rationale but commented that it would have been even more effective had he shared his rationale with students. In other words, by turning the implicit critical goals into explicit critical goals that are shared with the students, teachers can model their critical orientation as they *question social inequalities*. In turn, this becomes yet another way to *support students* as they develop their own critical orientations. Through our dialogue, I (Kelli) gave Ethan ideas for how to make this and future text sets more critical and more culturally sustaining.

In the final pass of our first facet, we looked for evidence that Ethan's text set would encourage critical thought. While the first pass was focused on Ethan's critical orientation as a preservice teacher, this third pass is focused on identifying instances where students may take a similar critical orientation. Using Paris's (2012) framework, we identified particular moments in the text set that "[supported] students in questioning societal inequalities." In our investigation, we looked through Ethan's text set for stories and guiding questions that ask students to consider the weight that cultural difference has on life in America.

During this phase of the excavation process, we discovered that Ethan had not considered entry points for which to explicitly support students in questioning societal inequalities. We found the following questions useful to guide us as we dug through this phase of the curricula artifact together, *Where in the curricular artifact is there evidence that the educator values nontraditional and multiple modalities? Where in the curricular artifact is there evidence that the educator grants students access to culturally dominant competencies? Where in the curricular artifact are there moments for students to question social inequalities?* and *Where in the curricular artifact and subsequent teaching could the educator make their own questioning of inequalities more transparent?*

Cutting the Diamond: Questioning the Binaries, Representative Holes, and Tensions

Once the identification stage of the collaborative and critical excavation process has been completed, it is time for the collaborative partners to embrace the educator's responsibility of interrogating the teacher's tensions, assumptions, or biases as related to creating literacy curriculum that is culturally sustaining. Any time we are teaching outside of our own cultural lived experiences, it is imperative that collaborative conversations shift toward questioning the tensions the teacher may not be aware they hold. Here the collaborator and the curriculum developer have to excavate the curricular artifact from critical lenses to question the binaries and the representative holes within the curricular artifact. This may lead to questioning the tensions the teacher may have in preparing—and thus tensions in potentially imparting—the curricular artifact in order to help guide the teacher through CSLP praxis.

Layer 4: Question the Binaries. Kelli does not remember the use of the word *binary* conceptually being used when she created her curriculum as an English teacher in Chicago. In fact, she's embarrassed to admit she did not know what a binary was until she was well into her graduate studies. While Kelli believed she was creating and imparting culturally sustaining literacy instruction for her students, in retrospect, she knows it was littered with presentation of binary thought: White vs. Black, right vs. wrong, heterosexual vs. homosexual, even gendered binary thought. Kelli believes now that setting up any binary in a classroom is extremely narrowing and leads to erasure of people and lived experiences that fall outside of those binaries, as binaries are just socially constructed generalizations. Therefore, the main question for collaborative pairs to consider at this layer of excavation are: What binaries have been inadvertently relied upon?

While Ethan and Kelli were critically excavating his curricular artifact, Kelli paid careful attention to the binaries that Ethan was inadvertently setting up. For example, Ethan, in his curricular artifact, was setting up a binary between anti-Western and Western ideologies without realizing it and, in doing so, was implicating and conflating devout Muslim faith with anti-Western ideology. For example, Ethan seemed to have tensions in presenting literature content that dealt with a religious faith that he had never practiced. Kelli also noted that Ethan seemed to hold tensions in silencing #ownvoices texts that didn't pass the Riz Test, such as a moment of tension when Ethan did not know if he should include a scene from Kumail Nanjiani's movie *The Big Sick* (Showalter, 2017), as the mother was presented in anti-Western ways. He held tensions because the Riz Test told him to refrain from presenting texts that utilized stereotypes of non-Western leanings. This then led to a tension that Ethan felt, going back to binary thought, of pitting Western versus non-Western ideologies against one another. In fleshing out this binary in collaborative discourse, we realized that any questions Ethan could not answer because he did not have the sociocultural knowledge or lived experiences could potentially be answered in discourse with his students. As a White, non-Muslim man attempting to develop culturally sustaining literacy practices with his Arab and Muslim students, Ethan realized through this process that he did not need to have all of the answers because he could draw on his students' sociocultural knowledge during instruction.

Layer 5: Question the Representative Holes. Once the collaborative pair has identified any binary thought that has been inadvertently presented within the curricular artifact, the teachers can then embrace the in-between of those binaries. At this stage of the excavation dig, collaborators can question: what cultural identity markers are not represented in the curricular artifact? Does the curricular artifact contain mirror texts for students to see themselves and facets of their identities? Does it contain window texts from which to develop empathy across cultural identity markers, as Rudine Sims Bishop (Bishop, 1990) has suggested for three decades? Are there places where multiple facets and intersections of cultural identity markers are represented? Are different racial, ethnic, religious, cultural, romantic, linguistic, and social classes included in the curricular artifact? What ways of knowing and being are represented? In collaborative groups, it is important to question the representative holes that may be present in the curricular artifact in order to offer an educational experience that advances pluralism and disrupts hegemonic dominant narratives. Will the teacher use an intersectionality framework when analyzing the text in order to explicitly address differences rooted in social issues like homophobia and Islamophobia, as Gill (2016) suggests?

For example, in Ethan's curricular artifact, through our discussion of what representative holes there were within his curated text set, we realized that there was not any representation of queer characters or discussion of homophobia at the intersection of Muslim faith. Upon realizing this, Ethan discussed adding texts from *The Love and Lies of Rukhsana Ali* (S. Khan, 2019), a young adult novel which features a fearless Muslim queer female, and pairing it with *The Guardian* article "My whole life I have been looking for fearless queer Muslim heroes" (Joarder, 2019).

Layer 6: Question Teacher Tensions. In this aspect of the curricular excavation, the collaborators should really suspend their ownership over their curricular artifact, for at this layer, collaborators should question the teacher's tensions that arise from analyzing the curricular artifact's rationale and its subsequent curricular product. It is the curriculum developer/educator's responsibility to begin to embrace the messiness, the tensions, and the ambiguities that arise when trying to bridge critical pedagogical theory and actual teaching practice. Kelli admits that as a secondary teacher, she did not often take constructive criticism well when engaging in discussions of the curriculum she created for her ELA students. This is where the individualistic nature of White culture (Katz, 1985) needs to be suspended for collective knowledge that benefits the greater good. We discovered the need to reframe the idea of "constructive criticism," which often seems to exist within a hierarchical, top-down power relationship toward a critical and collaborative excavation of curriculum, of which it is the educator's responsibility to be willing to cut, polish, and set the "diamond" of curriculum they've mined.

As part of the questioning layer of curriculum excavation, collaborators should identify tensions that seem to be under the surface in the educator's curriculum development. This, again, is why a rationale should be written by the educator detailing the reflexive processes they underwent while developing the curricular artifact. We realized that teachers may need to give up the control of knowledge when constructing curricular artifacts that portray individuals outside of their culture. In order to fully excavate a curricular artifact, the educator has to thus examine places where they can be transparent with their students and use these opportunities for the students to gather the knowledge and information—especially those students who have the full knowledge of the representational content because of their own lived experiences outside of their teacher's culture.

Polishing and Setting the Diamond: Praxis and Action

Layer 7: Inviting Critical Questioning and Teacher Transparency. In order to welcome students into conversations about how culture is dynamic and not static and to embrace the nuances, ambiguities, and messiness of culture and identity in American society, the collaborators in the curricular excavation need to examine areas where the teachers can be transparent about their critical orientations and/or lack of sociocultural knowledge in reference to the culture being presented through the curricular content. In this layer of curricular excavation, collaborators should examine places where the teacher's critical orientation can become explicit instruction for students to create their own critical and asset-based worldviews.

   Layer 8: Delineate Specific Action Items for Instruction. In this layer, the collaborators identify specific action items for praxis—in engulfing themselves in the CSLP theory through the curricular excavation, what have they realized they need to include in their curriculum moving forward? What action items would be included in the re-vision of this curricular artifact in order to place the mined, cut, and polished diamond into its setting, or putting it into the world, into practice? Ethan decided to take the following next steps after engaging in the collaborative curricular excavation process: (1) Open up space in the unit of study for developing and sustaining the linguistic competencies of his students by centering the Quran as poetry, teaching about the different languages of Islam, and focusing student attention on Arabic as a liturgical language; (2) bring in more intersectional representation in texts by pairing *Rukhasana Ali* with *The Guardian* article about intersectionality of the queer Muslim experience; and (3) being transparent and explicit about instruction for culturally sustaining literacy practices with the students by having the students take the Riz Test for the texts, explicitly teaching Islamophobia as a critical orientation at the beginning of the unit, and inviting students to disrupt the monolithic binary of Western and anti-Western ideologies. After the excavation and critical collaborative discourse, Ethan concluded that his curricular artifact needed to have a clearer focus on raising students' linguistic competencies, identified and questioned representative holes within the curriculum, and pinpointed exact moments in practice where he could explicitly engage students in developing their own asset-based and pluralistic worldviews.

DISCUSSION AND IMPLICATIONS

Teachers often have trouble moving theory to practice because it is not a straightforward, linear, or static process. Because culturally sustaining pedagogy (Paris, 2012) is a critical and culturally responsive orientation to teaching, the nuances and dynamics of culture coalesce with the nuanced and dynamic nature of culturally sustaining teaching. Bridging theory and practice for teachers can be difficult because it is messy. We have to give up control of the flow of knowledge when it exists outside of what we know, and that makes us vulnerable. In creating a space in teacher education or inservice professional development where the purpose of the excavation is to embrace the messiness, embrace the ambiguities of culture and society, and embrace the collective nature of knowledge development, we may begin to decenter the whiteness of curriculum and make it more culturally sustaining in literacy instruction.

Understanding the embracement of the messiness of curriculum development as an educator's responsibility may take time, but it is our goal that the practice of curriculum excavation, like the practice of preservice teacher self-excavation (Sealey-Ruiz, 2019) is a process—not a product—that could help advance educational equity and pluralistic worldviews of both teachers and pre-K–20 students. Embracing the ambiguity and the tensions in the messiness of culture and society are an educator's responsibility in curriculum creation from critical pedagogical theory. However, teachers are human. Human beings naturally wish to self-preserve, and oftentimes, being purposefully placed into a situation in which they will be uncomfortable, in which they will have to wrestle with difficult ideas, potential cultural conflicts, and allow their shortcomings to be made visible is often not one's first choice on how to spend a class period or a professional development meeting. However, we grow and learn in the tensions, in the in-between spaces, and in the ambiguous lack of answers. Therefore, embracing a pedagogy of discomfort (Boler, 1999) through critical and collaborative curriculum excavation may be a tool to aid teachers in excavating their own biases and assumptions that are showing through to their curricular artifacts. In addition, a curricular excavation protocol such as this may help preservice and inservice teachers connect critical educational theories such as CSLP to their practice.

CHAPTER 7

Five Frames

A Multicultural Curricular Approach to Culturally Sustaining Literacy Practices

Susan V. Bennett, AnnMarie Alberton Gunn, Alexandra Panos,
Steven M. Hart, and Jenifer Jasinski Schneider

In a 1st-grade classroom, Jamie (pseudonym) reads many multicultural books to her students, such as *Knock Knock: My Father's Dream for Me* (Beaty, 2013), a heartwarming story of a boy who misses his father and deals with difficulties while his father is incarcerated. Jamie works in a Title I school that mainly serves students from low socioeconomic backgrounds in a predominately Black community. She selectively choses books, "where it was not only children who looked like them and lived in life situations like them, but experienced problems that they experience." Jamie shares how these multicultural books become worn and torn, a true illustration of how often children read books in her classroom. For example, she witnesses rich conversations around the texts that fill the classroom. Most importantly, when the students read, "you could hear a pin drop in the classroom."

This scenario provides an example of how a teacher implemented culturally sustaining literacy pedagogy (CSLP) into her teaching practice through strategic text selection (i.e., multicultural) and by creating an environment to reflect the identities and experiences of the students in her class. As a result, the teacher established "brave spaces" (Palfrey, 2018) where the students read intently (e.g., "you could hear a pin drop") from textual examples that reflected multiple identities and cultures.

According to the U.S. Census (Jensen et al., 2021), the United States has become more racially and ethnically diverse than ever before, and K–12 classrooms reflect these trends. Alim and Paris (2017) suggested:

Continued social and educational inequality coupled with massive demographic changes sweeping the Unites States and Europe, among other regions, have
brought to the fore an urgent, more pressing iteration of this age-old question:
What is the purpose of schooling in a pluralistic society? (p. 1)

Therefore, as classrooms continue to expand with students who hold
a rich abundance of cultural and personal experiences, it is essential we
"change in stance and terminology in pedagogical theory and practice"
(Alim & Paris, 2017, p. 1). Teachers can support current and future students by adopting culturally sustaining literacy through a multicultural
curricular approach aimed at building bridges of understanding regarding diverse linguistic, socioeconomic, and cultural backgrounds (Gunn,
2016). Scholars have examined diversity as a crucial issue within curriculum; this chapter presents research-based examples of how teachers apply CSLP into curricular and pedagogical practice in K–12 classrooms.

POSITIONALITIES AND CONTEXT

It is important to share our positionality as authors as well as the context of the study. Collectively, we are literacy teacher educators and
researchers who embrace CSLP. Susan (first author), who grew up in
the Midwest, is of English–Irish–Scottish descent. Susan identified as a
select mute (an individual who would not speak at school) while in kin-
dergarten through second grade; together with her mutism, her work in
prisons, and as an elementary school teacher on the Diné Reservation
and in urban schools impact her commitment to support diverse learners. AnnMarie (second author) comes from a second-generation Polish
immigrant background. Her experiences, raised in a cultural enclave in
an urban setting, influenced how she has lived and taught in culturally
and linguistically diverse settings. She taught for over 9 years in K–12th-
grade settings in schools that serve students from Haitian, Puerto Rican,
and Cuban backgrounds. Alexandra's (third author) positionalities are
shaped by her life as a White Midwesterner and Southerner and as the
daughter of working people in a union home. Following Lensmire and
Kinloch (2019), she works to recognize the role White people need to
play in addressing justice and privilege in educational and research spaces. Steven (fourth author) experienced unique opportunities to live in diverse urban centers and rural mobile home communities throughout his
childhood. These childhood experiences helped him navigate his interactions with youth from diverse racial and geographical contexts during

this study. Jenifer (fifth author) is a White, cisgendered female who grew up in a middle-class, English-speaking home; her parents and grandparents spoke Italian and Polish. As the daughter of first-generation college graduates who became teachers, she lived with multiple languages across her immigrant families.

Our positionalities and experiences provide a lens on how we see the world. As literacy scholars and educators, we consider it our responsibility to advocate for and improve literacy outcomes for Black, Brown, Indigenous, Asian, LGBTQIA+, immigrant, multilingual, and other long-marginalized populations, in particular children, as well as eradicate all forms of racism and oppression (Schneider, Smith, & Jones, 2020).

U.S. classrooms represent a mosaic of racial, ethnic, cultural, linguistic, and religious diversity; therefore, classrooms require multifaceted and continually evolving curricula that are not unidimensional or unidirectional (Paris & Alim, 2017). CSLP can address many students' needs because CSLP, in practice, is nuanced and thus requires a variety of strategies to adapt to multiple contexts. Our educational systems are not serving students in culturally sustaining ways that embrace social and academic success for students and their families. We need to bring not only CSLP research but also practices to the forefront where teachers can embrace and use these practices to promote academic and personal success of students (Au, 2011; Gay, 2010; Ladson-Billings, 1995b) and "perpetuate and foster–to sustain–linguistic, literate, and cultural pluralism as part of the democratic project of schooling" (Paris, 2012, p. 95).

In this chapter, we seek to illuminate specific culturally sustaining literacy elements, which evolved from our collective research and expertise, for teachers to utilize in their K–12 classrooms. We present five elements of literacy practice that could be implemented to support and promote CSLP in these classrooms: (1) connecting with students' identity, (2) empowering critical literacies, (3) participating in service-learning and community engagement, (4) reconceptualizing standards, and (5) exploring multimodal composing. We chose to highlight these elements, based on a previous study by Gunn (2016) in which preservice and inservice teachers adopted CSLP orientation after participating in activities such as the critical analysis of multicultural literature (MCLit), teacher inquiry, and a civic engagement project in which students completed literature-based activities related to the Holocaust and culminated in a visit to the Florida Holocaust Museum (FHM). Findings suggested teachers brought the theoretical basis of CSLP into practice through these literacy elements.

FRAMING ELEMENTS FOR CULTURALLY SUSTAINING
LITERACY PEDAGOGY AND PRACTICE

Although CSLP cannot be distilled into a set of formulaic practices, certain elements can have the potential to alter the teachers' frames of reference through the process of targeting more pluralistic outcomes. For instance, identity is an important part of one's culture as well as one's community, and CSLP requires centering on students' identities by re-envisioning the curriculum toward student-centered approaches for learning and demonstrating knowledge, such as multimodal composing (Irizarry, 2017). Critical literacy and service-learning are central elements as well, whereby students take a stand and share their voice to "challenge and change the systems of oppression" (Irizarry, 2017, p. 83). Attempts to enact culturally responsive education have focused on assets of culture, which is important, but these efforts have played out within the traditional White, Eurocentric system. Thus it is essential to re-envision both traditional standards and ways in which students compose to demonstrate their knowledge and express their learning. In the following sections, we share our perspectives on each of these elements of CSLP.

Element 1: Connecting with Student Identity

An essential element of CSLP is understanding student identity and culture and integrating it into classrooms (Au, 2011; Muhammad, 2020). Culturally sustaining teachers create classrooms that value, honor, and sustain cultural identities (Paris, 2012); "our identities are continually being (re)defined and revised while we reconsider who we are within our sociocultural and sociopolitical environment . . . as well as by literacy practice. Examples may include racial, ethnic, cultural, gender, kinship, and community identities" (Muhammad, 2020, p. 67). Teachers must develop relationships with their students, build classroom communities, and provide youth opportunities in school to explore selfhood. Central to the notion of CSLP is seeking to address educational inequities for youth from nondominant communities. Pedagogies and practices that should be used in the classroom "work towards reclamation of the histories, contributions and possibilities of cultural communities, particularly those who have been and continue to be racially, linguistically, and otherwise marginalized" (Gutiérrez & Johnson, 2017, p. 249). In this section, we offer tools to learn about students' culture and identity so that teachers can draw from, build on, and sustain students' cultural knowledge in K–12 classrooms.

As teachers draw on their experiences with colleagues, parents, and community members to learn about the students they serve, they also must continually learn about their students' individual culture and identity. Consistent with Alim and Paris (2017), we conceptualize CSLP as moving away from practices that are closely aligned with linguistic and cultural hegemony and consider how our practices would look if the "kindred patriarchal, cisheteronormative, English-monolingual, ableist, classist, xenophobic, Judeo-Christian," were not the dominant form of educational expectations (Alim & Paris, 2017, p. 2). It's through CSLP that we can implement these pedagogical practices to support students instead of deficit approaches.

Names. One important way for teachers to honor and sustain students' identities is through attention to students' names. Student's names often reflect their family, culture, gender, religion, and language (Botelho & Rudman, 2009). Use of students' names has the power to positively affirm students' identity and foster a sense of belonging to the classroom community. However, naming practices in the classroom also have the power to exclude, stereotype, or humiliate students, especially when a student's name is unfamiliar in sound or spelling (Kim & Lee, 2011; Nash et al., 2018; Souto-Manning, 2011). Often, teachers rename students to help say their names with more ease; and in many cases, students suggest a simpler name to make it easier for others, to not be humiliated, or to conform to the norm. These "renaming practices" are potentially detrimental to a child's self-identify and further contribute to a deficient model.

One way to approach conversations about students' names is through multicultural literature (Nash et al., 2018), such as *René Has Two Last Names* (Colato Laínez, 1996) or *The Name Jar* (Choi, 2013) in elementary school, *Drita, My Homegirl* (Lombard, 2008) in middle school, or *My Name Is Not Easy* (Edwardson, 2011) in high school. These books represent a small sample of literature that highlights characters' names. The books can also be used to navigate important conversations and open discussions focused on the characters or students' names, culture, and identity in classrooms. Teachers can also use "snapshot autobiographies" (Gunn et al., 2013) in their classrooms to learn about their students and then further build classroom communities. Gunn and colleagues (2013) found autobiographies about cultural identities (including but not limited to race, culture, language, religion, sexuality, ability/disability) that provided an opportunity to learn about each student's cultural identity and cultural markers that the students wanted their teacher to learn about. Teachers must create an environment that fosters relationships with students, as well as helps their students develop relationships with each other through learning about one another with practices built upon respect, care, empathy, and trust (Au, 2011; Gunn & King, 2015).

The Power of Literature. Rychly and Graves (2012) stated that the images, posters, awards, bulletin board items, and holiday celebrations used in the classroom create the hidden curriculum that teaches students what and who is valued in school. It is essential for children and youth to engage with literature and materials that are age appropriate and relevant to their lives and interests, in order to increase literacy achievement and motivation (White et al., 2014). One way to accomplish this is to provide children and youth with multicultural literature. In a book distribution project conducted by Bennett, Gunn, and Peterson (2021), parents and children commented on the importance of their children and youth receiving books that reflected their identities. One child cradled *Something Beautiful* (Wyeth, 1998) and then presented it to her mother. She exclaimed, "She looks like me!" and commented on how pretty the girl on the cover was. For over 2 decades, research has demonstrated the significance of multicultural literature in connection with children and youth's reading motivation, engagement, and success, yet there has been an astounding lack of diversity in literature available to children in schools and in their communities (Crisp et al., 2016). Teachers can build classroom libraries, use students' backgrounds, and cultural identities as the foundation for materials they use to teach curriculum.

This subsequent example illustrates how an upper elementary teacher decided to integrate content area literacy practices embracing a CSLP pedagogical practice. In a 4th-grade classroom, Ms. Johnny selected *One Green Apple* (Bunting, 2006) to integrate social studies standards focused on global connections and language arts standards concentrated on how a character's feelings can change after time (Gunn et al., 2020). Ms. Johnny remarked that students used illustrations and text to ask relevant questions about differences and similarities (see Figure 7.1). She stated that utilizing this book fostered conversations of empathy and question-generating because the students wanted to learn more. Most of her students were from Christian backgrounds who had many questions about Muslim immigrants as portrayed in the story. Through names, building relationships, and using multicultural literature, teachers can connect to students' identity.

Element 2: Empowering Critical Literacies

Critical literacies serve as a foundational pillar of CSLP; yet, we have found that teachers struggle with how to enact and understand this practice within the classroom. Through CSLP, teachers embrace assets of students'

Figure 7.1. Class Discussion of *One Green Apple*

evolving language and cultures, resist a deficit stance regarding diverse students, and facilitate discussions that raise critical consciousness, which is directly related to critical literacy (Alim & Paris, 2017; Paris & Alim, 2014). With critical literacy, children approach reading texts in active and reflective ways (Bennett et al., 2018). Children explore, analyze attitudes and values, and construct knowledge to understand and challenge unequal societal relationships. Critical literacy allows children to read and write the "word and world" as it relates to power, identities, and differences, while also providing access to self-empowerment, care, and change (Janks, 2013). When teachers use critical literacy, they can facilitate discussions that challenge biases and societal power relations ultimately leading to social justice change (Bennett et al., 2018; Freire, 1970; Gunn, 2016). Furthermore, "youth with strong literacy skills are able to articulate vital questions about themselves. They can investigate important issues, make decisions, and take action" (International Literacy Association [ILA], 2017, p. 2).

Text Selection. One way that teachers can develop students' critical literacy is through the texts that they select for students to examine. Teachers should find a variety of texts that show multiple perspectives or relations of power; these texts can also offer space to challenge assumptions and values (Bennett et al., 2018). Texts that present opportunities for children and youth to analyze, question, and solve problems provide rich springboards for exploring their identities and developing consciousness about inequities. For critical literacy, teachers can use multicultural literature, but they can also expose students to everyday conversations, media, technology, illustrations, and written and oral texts.

Text Exploration. As one way to promote critical literacy, teachers might offer higher-order thinking questions and opportunities to hold rich discussions about societal issues. It is necessary for the teacher to create a community environment with students where they feel respected and comfortable sharing their opinions. For example, in one classroom in which we worked, an elementary teacher displayed a poster that read, "Can a female do the job of president? Why or why not?" In addition, another poster in her classroom stated, "Panthers' quarterback Cam Newton is being criticized for walking out of a press conference after his team lost the Super Bowl. Do you think that is fair?" The students respectfully discussed the questions with partners. Then as a whole group, the students offered different opinions. Some even changed their minds. The teacher placed the posters on the walls, and some students chose to write about their opinions during their writing block.

Text-Inspired Action. Another way to incorporate critical literacy is by encouraging students to reflect and take action on a social justice issue, such as letter writing to government officials or school board members or, as we describe later in this chapter, service-learning. Referring again to the importance of multicultural literature during a pandemic in a 4th/5th-grade class, a teacher used *Germs Make Me Sick!* (Berger, 2016), an informational multicultural text, and paired it with a news article about COVID-19. The teacher led a discussion and asked, "Should we be required to wear masks?" Students responded utilizing evidence from the book and article, then individual students decided they wanted to write letters to the school board members telling them why they should wear masks. Utilizing multicultural literacy, a teacher can develop critical literacy and CSLP in their classroom.

Element 3: Participating in Service-Learning and Community Engagement

Literacy scholars have proposed that effective culturally sustaining literacy education should be grounded in inquiry-based explorations through which students develop and apply literacy skills to "investigate important issues, make decisions, and take action . . . [to] benefit local and global communities" (ILA, 2017, pp. 2–3). *Service-learning*, a form of experiential learning, offers teachers a structure to meet these proposed culturally sustaining literacy education goals. Service-learning is intentionally designed to link *academic content* and *social action* to support *community transformation* (Billig, 2011; Furco & Root, 2010). Service-learning centers on a process of inquiry, throughout which students use literacy skills to analyze and discuss diverse perspectives and inequities around community concerns. Through this inquiry and community action, service-learning reflects the key goals of culturally sustaining instruction by drawing upon students' cultural knowledge and practices; facilitating students' cultural competence; and developing students' abilities to understand, critique, and address social inequities (Hart, 2006; King et al., 2020).

The International Literacy Association (2017) extended Bishop's (1990) metaphorical framework of multicultural literature to identify characteristics of culturally sustaining classrooms as mirrors, windows, and doorways [Bishop's "sliding glass doors"]. We employ these metaphors to highlight the value of service-learning as a culturally sustaining practice.

Mirrors. Service-learning starts with students *seeing themselves* in their school academic experiences. Ideally, service-learning projects begin with a problem-posing/decision-making process, where students generate ideas through brainstorming sessions, community interviews, or investigations of social issues situated within their lived experiences and concerns. For example, a 1st-grade class located in an urban center used photovoice (photography) to identify concerns they had in areas around their school (Jason & Glenwick, 2016). Fifth-graders from a rural agricultural community initiated a class discussion about drought and water allocation based on dinner conversations they had with their families, who primarily worked in various sectors of agriculture.

Transitioning from these initial brainstorming sessions to the investigation phase can take a number of forms. The 1st-grade teacher curated textual resources about community action, such as *The Great Trash Bash* (Leedy, 1991) and *Recycle! A Handbook for Kids* (Gibbons, 1992), to guide students through developing ideas for action. The 5th-grade teacher opted to allow students to group together in teams to conduct further research and develop more knowledge to determine action options. Engagement in this investigation phase creates a space for students to continue *seeing themselves* in the literacy activities of the classroom. The texts they are examining are purposefully connected to issues they find meaningful and provide insights into their own personal and cultural identities, not only gaining a deeper self-understanding but also a sense of their interconnectedness within broader communities (Kahne & Sporte, 2008; Rubin et al., 2009), which leads to windows.

Windows. The hyphen in the term service-learning denotes how academic and community contexts are interconnected and interdependent. By intersecting community and school contexts, service-learning expands upon typical classroom-based peer and student-teacher interactions to encourage students to *see into* and engage with members of other social, cultural, and civic spheres. Through such interactions, students are provided opportunities to develop cultural competence.

For example, the 1st-graders identified that much of the trash around their school was recyclable, yet there were no recycling bins in or around the school. They wrote letters to the local waste management service and the principal to learn about recycling and to hear their perspectives. Students visited the recycling facility, spoke with a manager, and then organized a community event at the school to deliberate about establishing a recycling program at the school and the immediate borders. Similarly, the 5th-graders used the news articles, documentary films, and podcasts they examined to identify water resource stakeholders and wrote letters requesting their perspectives. This led to a field trip to the local wastewater treatment facility to meet with the lead engineer and a classroom debate between the local farm workers coalition leader and an environmental science professor/activist. CSLP involves developing the competence to navigate diverse cultural spaces. Through experiences like this debate, service-learning creates opportunities for students to engage with diverse perspectives within and across different communities.

Sliding Glass Doors. Most importantly, the action phase of service-learning presents students with an *entryway* into enacting their imagined possibilities for transforming their communities. When students become emotionally invested in a problem, they are compelled to take action. Actions can take a variety of forms. For example, the 1st-graders engaged in direct action—removing trash and establishing a recycling program. The 5th-graders engaged in advocacy—creating and distributing flyers about water conservation throughout their communities. By providing students an *entryway* to enacting change, service-learning facilitates students' sense of empowerment as agents of change.

As described above, educators using service-learning are creating learning experiences for students that provide the mirrors for self-understanding and personal skill development, to understand others and develop the cultural competence to navigate diverse spaces, and *entries* into imagined possibilities (Bishop, 1990). Too often these experiences are not afforded to younger and marginalized students, but as Sofia (1st-grader) emphasized at a community showcase event, "We hope our project shows you that just because we're kids, doesn't mean we can't make a difference!"

Sofia's words show us that service-learning can be used to draw on children's cultural knowledge and expertise about their own lives and use literacy in personally and socially meaningful ways. As an approach to CSLP, service-learning provides teachers a way to link community action with academic content and literacy standards (i.e., Common Core State Standards). However, these standards need to be interrogated and expanded for CSLP.

Element 4: Reconceptualizing the Standards

Culturally sustaining pedagogies can be supported through equity and justice-focused practices in the form of flexible heuristics or guideposts and also be aligned with traditional curricular standards (Dover, 2016). Assessment- and standards-driven pedagogical choices often damage children, in particular minoritized children (Knoester & Au, 2017; Kohn, 2000). For instance, the standard for identifying the "main idea" in texts can work against minoritized children, as children bring their background knowledge and experiences as well as interpretations (see Aukerman & Chambers Schuldt, 2016). Teachers tend to understand that rigid and formulaic instruction is damaging (Comber & Nixon, 2009), although many struggle with a mismatch in how they conceptualize what social justice and/or culturally responsive pedagogy means and what they do or have "permission" to do in classrooms (K. Miller & Weilbacher, 2020; Schneider, 2001). With demands across the United States to do assessment-driven pedagogy, teachers are often at odds with their administrations and the political context of their work. They are pushed to focus on benchmarks in classrooms and through professional development, relegating to the sidelines necessary work they must do that focuses on equity and justice.

Most recently, there has been a concerted effort across conservative states in the United States to legislate away culturally sustaining pedagogies ("Map," 2021). For example, in Florida, legislative bans on critical race theory and the expectation of both SEL (social–emotional learning) and CSLP being removed from curriculum has been the focus of state standards and benchmark updating (DeSantis, 2021; Oliva, 2021). As Ladson-Billings (2021) shared in a video on the banning of critical race theory from K–12 contexts, teachers do not *teach* children critical race theory. Rather, understanding the scope and scale of issues of equity and racial justice informs *how* we teach and demonstrates *what* we value in the content we bring to classrooms. Teachers are understandably uncertain and concerned with their own vulnerabilities and tenable employment if they resist such policies (Walsh, 2021). Teachers must engage in praxis in the face of built-in barriers to cultivating just and equitable classrooms and curricula. Literacy teachers at times can be supported in this work through the advocacy of their professional organizations, such as the National Council for Teachers of English and the International Literacy Association. Both organizations have joined the National Coalition Against Censorship (2021) opposing legislative bans on critical race theory, culturally responsive pedagogies, and social emotional learning. Their shared statement outlines the damage of these legislative actions, identifying how these bans work against "well-established requirements that students be exposed to different interpretations of history and learn to think critically about them" and "directly threaten the teaching and encouragement of critical thinking in public school classrooms." We have found that teachers agree with these concerns, and they are angry. Teachers and their students, in particular BIPOC students, teachers, and their communities, are under intellectual, academic, and financial threat, and they are vulnerable when standards and legislation ignore best practices that are intended to sustain the lives and futures of BIPOC and other minoritized children (Strauss, 2021).

We recognize in this section on standards that enacting pedagogy with children is praxis: the basic understandings of equity and justice we might hope for children to understand and act on are those which we ourselves as teachers and teacher educators must also understand and act upon often in the face of restrictive environments. Thus enacting practices in classrooms when it comes to culturally sustaining pedagogies is inevitably also about our own work expanding beyond state and nationally imposed standards on literacy education. We outline two sets of standards, using the term loosely, as we defined above, as heuristics and guideposts, that support educators and their students in working toward the understandings and actions necessary to build a culturally sustaining literacy space in which to learn, beyond traditional notions of standards and benchmarks.

Equity Literacy. Part of enacting culturally sustaining pedagogies is the interrelated work of understanding and action on issues of equity. The term was first used by Swalwell (2011) to talk about how educators might develop *literacy practices* (meaning the combination of understanding and actions) that promote equity in their spheres of influence. This is to directly counter the *illiteracies* that perpetuate damaging pedagogies and practices (Norton & Ariely, 2011; J. Reynolds & Kendi, 2020) such as those that restrict teaching about the history of racism in the United States or censoring materials in classrooms. As a heuristic, equity literacy has been used to support community-focused literacies (T. L. Green, 2017), educational leadership initiatives (T. L. Green, 2018), and work toward more equitable schools (Wessel-Powell et al., 2021).

When we think about what it means to understand equity and then act toward it, we recognize that linear, but recursive, guideposts might be helpful. With these ideas in mind, Gorski and Swalwell (2015) refined this idea into a series of guiding practices. These include:

1. *Recognizing* bias, meaning that we focus energies in classrooms on the work of recognizing the limits of our own understandings as people (educators included).
2. *Responding* to inequity immediately, meaning that in classrooms and schools if we recognize something is wrong, we work to respond and acknowledge it immediately.
3. *Redressing* inequalities in the long term, meaning that once we recognize something is wrong, we begin to plan on how to redress that inequity for the long term.
4. Seeking actionable products that help in *creating and sustaining equity,* meaning that we recognize that the development of tools to communicate about and sustain equity is part of the expectation of doing culturally sustaining work.

Typically, standards are about curricular content: equity literacy as a heuristic is a layer of school life that sits alongside and above traditional curricular standards. Indeed, we argue that these practices are perhaps most important, if not essential, to the practice of teachers and school staff themselves, in particular when working in damaging policy contexts such as those driven by standardized assessment or by racist laws and policies. We find they are exceptionally helpful when thinking through what might guide a culturally sustaining literacy classroom, when driven by concepts from critical literacy where localized injustices often guide curricular content (e.g., Comber, 2015; Lewison et al., 2015).

Social Justice Standards. In order to create CSLP in a classroom, teachers must incorporate social justice standards with curricular standards.

In a similar, and more detailed and student-driven way, the website Learning for Justice (formerly Teaching Tolerance) outlines explicit social justice standards for use in classrooms. These standards also easily operate alongside traditional curricular standards and interconnect with the content focus of other sections of this chapter (e.g., critical literacy and multimodal literacy). Learning for Justice centers their social justice standards around four anchors: identity, diversity, justice, and action. Their website offers teachers in-depth professional development, texts, and resources that align with each of the anchors, grade levels, and curricular content. Simply put, these kinds of standards are the backbone on which to develop resources and activities for a classroom.

1. *Identity*: This set of standards focuses on intersectional understandings related to what shapes who we are.
2. *Diversity*: This set of standards focuses on becoming comfortable with difference and with naming and expressing ourselves related to our differences across different times, scales, and places.
3. *Justice*: This set of standards focuses on recognizing and analyzing unfairness at different times, scales, and places.
4. *Action*: This set of standards focuses on developing empathy and actionable practices and plans for addressing unfairness and inequity.

Equity literacy standards and the Learning for Justice social justice standards have much in common. There are still other ways one might approach culturally sustaining work and other heuristics to draw on. For example, Muhammad (2020) identifies a four-part framework that includes the pursuit of identity, skills, intellect, and criticality in teaching and learning. Equity literacy standards such as these would provide the guideposts that teachers need to engage in CSLP. Detailed guidance for how to work with students, as Learning for Justice lays out, can easily sit alongside our curricular goals (Dover, 2016). Indeed, the Learning for Justice site not only outlines the kinds of standards that can be guideposts to a culturally sustaining classroom, but they also offer support in thinking about how the texts we select align, or not, with these kinds of standards and have a robust set of resources to explore. Sustaining a classroom that sustains its students and their communities can never be done in isolation (Ritchie, 2012), as such these kinds of standards and guideposts connect teachers to resources and to one another.

Element 5: Inviting Cultural Relevance of Multimodal Composing

For the fifth framing element of CSLP, we suggest recognizing how multimodal composing can provide spaces for students to create relevant content through a student-centered approach. Multimodal theories are rooted in the basic assumption that meaning is created across a range of *modes* that are defined as an organized grouping and cultural shaping of semiotic resources for making signs (Jewitt, 2008). We must take the next step and offer students the opportunities to compose diverse cultural content in the modal formats within which youth are likely to engage and to express their voices. Teaching the structure and construction of culturally popular and powerful genres, such as memes or TikToks, is a sustainable approach to cultural responsiveness (Schneider & Frier, 2020).

"Assigning" Cultural Relevance vs. Seeking Student Relevance. Across educational contexts, students often create or interact with multimodal texts (e.g., presentation software, video games, websites, performance scripts). These semiotically complex structures are inclusive of print, images, sounds, music, graphics and/or video. And, often, these pop-culture texts are increasingly appropriated for school purposes and smuggled into lessons that may be inconsistent with their communicative power. For example, in a previous study, Schneider & Frier (2020) interviewed a high-school student who was required to create 15 memes to sum up different theories of childhood development for an assignment in an AP Psychology course.

Do assigned memes "count" as actual memes? Technically, they are memes; but, then again, they are not. The 15 assigned memes were quick messages in the form of images, videos, and fragments of text; they were not youth-oriented or youth-originated. *Assigned* memes are less likely to represent students' culture. Further, the 15 assigned memes were not shared with the student's peer audiences and did not gain their creator any social influence. These curricular memes met the teacher's goals and were graded. Yet, they lacked the communicative purposes that propel the rapid sharing of memes and their creators' intents.

Audiences, Access, and Social Responsibility. Teaching students how to enter global and networked conversations using multimodal texts can give them social and cultural access to audiences within and beyond classroom walls. Yet access itself is not neutral, and machines are biased by human history and data (Buolamwini, 2018). We must investigate with students how digital machines influence and impact the subscreen aspects of what they see, read, understand, and create. As de Roock (2021) stated, "Everything I write here, on other tabs (such as email, social media, and shopping sites) . . . is read, indexed, and analyzed by algorithms that then shape what Google searches or websites present me with the purpose of driving me to spend money" (p. 183). Spellcheck and grammar advice are not neutral. They are programmed along "intersectional lines that are gendered, racialized, and ableist" (p. 187).

Similarly, youth-composed texts can contain images and words that capture a range of sentiments and experiences familiar to that particular age group. Sometimes youth-composed texts include racist and misogynistic themes (Yoon, 2016), graphic comic book culture (Szablewicz, 2020), explicit musical references (Barrett, 2003), and mental health issues (Burton, 2019). And rather than silencing their voices (Schneider, 2001), students can be guided to understand how to transport messages across space, time, cultures, and social groups.

Furthermore, as students begin grasping the concepts of *register* or *code-switching,* understanding how "dominant discourses" are accommodated and leveraged (Freire & Macedo, 1987, p. 3), they can gain access to the language of power and learn how to manipulate it for their own communicative purposes. Thereby, building their own discourses of success (Schneider, 2001).

Motivating Influence Through Authentic Communication. Meaningful composing tasks increase motivation because students see the value of the task (Daniels & Arapostathis, 2005; Hidi & Harackiewicz, 2000). And, more directly, content creation through multimodal texts results in students learning how to read critically and compose multimodally with the option to influence. According to digital, social, and economic trends, what it means to achieve is to obtain capital skills. As Ladson-Billings stated, "no matter how good a fit develops between home and school culture, students must achieve. No theory of pedagogy can escape this reality" (1995b, p. 475).

DISCUSSION AND IMPLICATIONS

In this chapter, we defined and described five framing elements that need to be considered in order to advance CSLP in literacy classrooms. We have offered concrete examples of implementation of these elements into the classroom. In order to successfully implement CSLP, teachers have to create an environment of care, respect, and self-empowerment.

In service-learning and critical literacies, we discussed social change and action within the larger community or society, not just the school or classroom community. We addressed how multicultural literature, multimodal composing, and justice-based curriculum standards can open spaces for CSLP.

When teachers understand the theoretical and research-based practices that frame CSLP, they can cultivate and implement CSLP into their classroom practices in their own ways. Teachers impact the larger society, and "literacy educators foster exploration through academically rigorous investigations that benefit local and global communities" (ILA, 2017, p. 3). As we move forward, we need to think and act on how we can implement culturally sustaining pedagogy, so students can "survive and thrive" (Alim & Paris, 2017, p. 13). By highlighting these five elements that can support CSLP, we hope to support frameworks and pathways for teachers as they develop classrooms that value youth and their culture and language, while "resisting, revitalizing, and reimagining" (Alim & Paris, 2017, p. 12).

CHAPTER 8

Enacting Culturally Sustaining Literacy Practices

Toward More Socially Just Teaching

Susan Chambers Cantrell, Doris Walker-Dalhouse,
and Althier M. Lazar

This edited book stems from efforts of researchers and teacher educators who formed a study group, under the umbrella of the Literacy Research Association, with the goal of learning more about culturally sustaining literacy pedagogy (CSLP). As we noted in the Introduction, the study group meets annually to share experiences and to explore the ways in which we as researchers and teacher educators can help create more antiracist and socially just classrooms. The study group is part of a larger effort among literacy researchers to create organizational spaces for LRA members to build relationships across difference with the goal of exchanging perspectives, building understanding, and creating equity, as outlined in LRA's strategic plan emphasis on diversity, equity, and inclusion.

As editors, we approached this book as learners, seeking to gather models of CSLP that illuminate the ways in which teachers in K–12 settings are rooting curriculum and instruction within students' language, cultural knowledge, and experiences with the goal of sustaining students' identities and raising their social consciousness. The authors of the chapters that comprise this book provide rich examples of the ways in which teachers honored and sustained students' racial, ethnic, cultural, and familial identities, while empowering students by developing their academic competence. They challenged us to interrogate existing systems and practices to identify the ways in which inequities are perpetuated in schools and classrooms and to make fundamental changes toward more equitable teaching.

In this final chapter we pull together the ideas expressed in the previous chapters into a cohesive model of CSLP that can inform educators about how to advance antiracist and socially just teaching practices. We start by reviewing the insights provided by the authors of the chapters in this book. We draw themes across the chapters that we hope will be useful to educators who want to enact CSLP in their classrooms and for teacher educators who prepare and support teachers' implementation of CSLP. Next, we reiterate and expand on why we think CSLP is challenging, especially in today's political climate. We end with a call to action and explore the ways in which educators can be advocates for antiracist and culturally sustaining pedagogies.

In presenting the models in this text, we acknowledge the complexity of CSLP and reject the notion that CSLP is a set of literacy teaching practices that teachers can systematically implement. Instead, we believe that CSLP is a stance, a mindset, and a way of being that involves valuing the knowledge traditions of practices of students, families, and their communities and centers the curriculum around this knowledge. As the book's chapters illustrate, CSLP requires self-examination, grappling with tensions, and departing from long-held educational processes and practices that serve to reproduce the status quo in classrooms and schools.

START WITH THE INTERNAL WORK

One of the major takeaways that we hope readers will glean from this book is that, as educators, we must do the work to see how our own identities, biases, and assumptions impact our teaching. In Chapter 6 Kelli A. Rushek and Ethan Seylar present a model for collaborative meta-cognitive conversations that draws on a foundation of self-examination and personal reflection including investigation of one's biases, racial beliefs, and practices to consider how those ways of knowing and being perpetuate classroom inequities. Rushek and Seylar draw on the work of Sealey-Ruiz (2019), who presents a technique titled Archaeology of Self as a means of growth as a socially just and antiracist teacher. Rushek and Seylar use an excavation metaphor to show how both authors dug into their own sets of assumptions and beliefs to interrogate a curriculum unit designed to disrupt students' conceptualizations of Islamic culture. Through their collaboration, Rushek and Seylar show how the first step toward a more culturally sustaining curriculum involves excavating the teacher's orientation and committing to asset-based and critically informed teaching. Becoming more culturally sustaining requires that educators begin with interrogations of their own identities, beliefs, and behaviors before they can examine and adjust their curricular and instructional practices to sustain the cultures of their students.

Identity is a central theme across the chapters in this book, and in each model presented, teachers' own identities influenced the ways in which they sustained the identities of their students. W.E.B. Du Bois wrote that "identity is not separate from equity and goals for social justice" (Muhammad & Mosley, 2021, p. 189). Drawing on Du Bois's idea, Muhammad and Mosley argue that a Eurocentric, skills-only approach has fallen short of serving all students in U.S. classrooms, and it is critical to begin centering equity and students' multiple identities in language and literacy teaching. As educators, we must first think about the ways in which we are embodying White Eurocentrism in what and how we are teaching, and what we expect students to learn. How do our own identities influence our interactions with our students? How do our identities influence our literacy expectations for our students?

Answering these questions requires that educators look within to assess and develop their own racial literacy. Price-Dennis and Sealey-Ruiz (2021) describe racial literacy as "a skill practiced when individuals are able to probe the existence of racism and examine the effects of race as it intersects with institutionalized systems" (p. 14). It requires an understanding of the ways in which individuals exist within and contribute to those systems in terms of their own experiences and representation. As Willis (2015) contends, our nation has failed to discuss race and its influence on our lives for centuries, yet such conversations are critical to address inequities. Indeed, Price-Dennis and Sealey-Ruiz (2021) point out that racial literacy requires addressing the "elephant in the room":

> Acknowledging the "elephant" for White people often means they have to interrogate their privilege, face the guilt that comes with unfair skin color advantage, and listen to why Indigenous, Black, Latinx, and Asian people are often so frustrated with White people and the systematic structures that secure and ensure their advantage over others. For people of color, and Black people in particular, facing the "elephant in the room" is dealing with the anger they hold toward Whites and the systematic structures that assure the advantages of Whites at the cost of stifling opportunities for others. (p. 19)

Teachers, as a group, are generally unaccustomed to thinking about how systemic structures inherently privilege some groups over others and contribute to continued inequities in school and classroom settings (Sensoy & DiAngelo, 2017). Moving toward more CSLP requires self-reflection and critical conversations about tightly held assumptions, beliefs, and expectations.

INTERROGATE TENSIONS IN CURRICULUM AND INSTRUCTION

Another theme that emerged across the chapters in this book is that CSLP requires that educators recognize and interrogate tensions in the systems, including what children and youth learn and how they are assessed in school. CSLP begins with an understanding that "allows us to see the fallacy of measuring ourselves and the young people in our communities solely against the White middle-class norms of knowing and being that continue to dominate notions of educational achievement" (Paris & Alim, 2014, p. 86). There is a tendency to view curriculum as neutral; yet a careful examination of what children and youth learn in schools reveals a curriculum that serves to reproduce notions of White superiority and ignores the contributions of Black, Indigenous, and other people of color (BIPOC). These curricular and instructional systems influence the ways in which children and youth view themselves and others within society.

Muhammad and Mosley (2021) point out the need for students to learn about their multiple identities and the identities of others in the areas of state learning standards, school curriculum, state assessments, and teacher evaluation. These four areas control what is taught in classrooms, yet they are rooted in Eurocentricity and not informed by students' literacies or histories. For example, centering whiteness and the perpetuation of White supremacy is evident in remediation practices such as Response to Intervention (RTI). Willis (2019a, 2019b) points out the ways in which RTI policies are rooted in a long history that has positioned Black students and other students of color as deficient and in need of remediation. RTI policies perpetuate the disproportionate number of Black students identified for special education, and the deficit language and assumptions embedded in the policies contributed to the long-held narrative of White superiority.

In Chapter 2 Kelly K. Wissman confronts the tensions between intervening to support students who are having difficulty with school reading and CSLP. In her chapter Wissman notes challenges inherent in intervention settings that can serve to block CSLP, such as lack of assessments that measure students' linguistic and cultural strengths, narrow definitions of progress, and scarcity of multicultural and multilingual resources. Still, Wissman provides an excellent example of the ways in which an intervention teacher honored and sustained a student's cultural ways of being through family collaboration, journaling, and photography around family and faith traditions. Despite the tensions that the teacher felt between "moving" through the skills curriculum and working toward more pluralistic outcomes, she exhibited a stance consistent with Paris & Alim (2014):

> Not filtered through a lens of contempt and pity (e.g., the "achievement gap") but, rather, are centered on contending in complex ways with rich and innovative linguistic, literate and cultural practices of Indigenous American, African American, Latina/o, Asian American, Pacific Islander, and other youth and communities of color. (p. 86)

In Chapter 3, Britnie Delinger Kane and Rachelle S. Savitz provide another example of the ways in which White supremacy is inherent in common literacy pedagogies such as disciplinary literacy. Kane and Savitz point out how positioning students as "disciplinary insiders," without considering the ways in which whiteness pervades the disciplines, does students a disservice. Disciplinary literacy requires a critical analysis on the ways in which knowledge is valued within the discipline and whose knowledge and ways of knowing has been historically elevated and whose has been historically marginalized. As Kane and Savitz note, ignoring the way in which racism, sexism, ableism, and other systemic issues have influenced the disciplines risks alienating students and demotivating them to engage in disciplinary work. Kane provides an illustration from her own secondary English classroom in which she recognized how her own White, middle-class identity caused her to make assumptions about what her students knew and valued. She pivoted in a way that repositioned her as a learner who honored and centered her students' cultural knowledge and expertise.

RETHINK THE HEGEMONIC PROCESSES AND PRACTICES

A third takeaway from the chapters in this volume is the urgent need to re-envision and actively change content, routines, processes, and practices to support students' expressions of learning, show their knowledge, and affirm their languages. A theme across the models presented in this book is that teachers rooted what students learned in their identities, lives, languages, and cultures. It is not enough for teachers to simply acknowledge inequities in the system and think about the ways in which those inequities are perpetuated. They must also commit to changing their own practices while engaging students in identifying and transforming the inequities. As Paris and Alim (2014) point out, sustaining students' cultures must transcend the constraints of White, middle-class, monolingual, and multicultural norms of educational achievement, including those embodied in traditional sets of standards and assessments. Pedagogies must shift to embrace how multiculturalism and multilingualism position students to gain power in a pluralistic society:

> As we reposition our pedagogies to focus on the practices and knowledges of communities of color, we must do so with the understanding that fostering linguistic and cultural flexibility has become an educational imperative, as multilingualism and multiculturalism are increasingly linked to access and power. (Paris & Alim, 2014, p. 90)

In shifting toward more CSLP, teachers can critically analyze their own practices and processes to assess the extent to which the practices support and promote multiculturalism, multilingualism, and student empowerment. In Chapter 7, Susan V. Bennett and colleagues identify elements of literacy practice that help to sustain students' cultural and linguistic expertise. The authors point out the ways in which identity, criticality, service-learning, equity-oriented standards, and multimodal composing can be embedded in classroom curriculum and instruction for more pluralistic outcomes. Each of these elements can be infused into classroom practices as a way of operationalizing CSLP.

In Chapter 4, Sarah N. Newcomer and Kathleen Cowin illustrate how one middle-level teacher affirmed a student's identity by grounding an entire lesson sequence in the student's knowledge and cultural practices while positioning the student as an expert. In the model the authors present, the teacher capitalized on the cultural knowledge and expertise of one student, Sachi, who taught her classmates how to make corn husk dolls, a practice of her family who had immigrated from Guatemala. Through the lessons, the teacher addressed ELA standards while supporting Sachi's developing bilingualism and affirming her Mayan cultural heritage and Mam language. Still, Newcomer and Cowin acknowledge the constraints that the standards may have placed on the ways in which students showed what they knew in interpreting and analyzing texts. They suggest alternative ways in which students might have demonstrated their learning, and how possibilities for CSLP may be extended.

In Chapter 5, Aimee Hendrix-Soto and colleagues provide models at two grade levels—with early adolescents and older youth—in which students drove the curriculum, taught one another strategies, and enacted critical consciousness. In the first model, the teacher used a study of a novel to engage 5th-grade students in studying issues such as immigration, the criminal justice system and incarceration, special education, and building a community, and engaged students in writing for social change. Using a workshop approach, students wrote letters to decision-makers and made posters on student-selected topics such as immigration, bullying, pollution, and mental health. In the second model, teachers engaged high school students in critical inquiry to investigate systemic racial inequities in the local school district, their community, and beyond. The teachers created both open spaces for student sharing and more structured dialogues to explore digital media, current events, and social issues. Students tackled the issue of urban school disrepair and the racial inequities perpetuated by deficit narratives. Students chose their own specific topics for inquiry and used photography to document inequities and raise consciousness. Hendrix-Soto and colleagues showed how teachers prioritized youths' literacies and lives even under the pressures of standardized testing and accountability.

A focus on assessment and accountability from a White, middle-class hegemonic perspective has long contributed to deficit narratives around the "achievement gap" (Smagorinsky et al., 2020). Generally, assessments reflect what knowledge is valued and prioritized from the perspective of the cultural mainstream, teachers develop curriculum around what is assessed, and students are given opportunities to show what they know through traditional classroom assessments. Shifting to CSLP requires a broadening of value for students' ways of knowing and showing what they know.

In Chapter 1 Olivia Murphy and colleagues show how multimodal composition creates space for students to demonstrate their rich knowledge, cultural practices, and ways of being through drawings, photography, family storytelling, and producing picture books. Using a writer's workshop approach (Calkins, 2020), the chapter authors provide examples of the ways in which students can compose multimodal stories of their lives, experiences, and understandings using traditional and nontraditional tools and digital platforms. Centering writing activities in students' lives and experiences and giving students freedom around mode of expression demonstrates a high value for what students bring into the classroom and counteracts deficit narratives.

WHY IS CSLP CHALLENGING?

The models presented in this book show that CSLP is possible and promising for creating more equitable classroom spaces. Yet we acknowledge that adopting CSLP can be challenging. In the current political climate, educators are experiencing fear of backlash as they develop expertise in enacting teaching that is antiracist and culturally sustaining. Recently, teachers in one of our graduate classes posted the following statements on an online discussion board in response to readings about developing critical consciousness as part of CSP:

- I'm always worried about being let go if I dive into topics that are uncomfortable for my admin or parents.
- I can be scared of what parents will think if I talk about "hot topics."
- I worry with some of my coworkers that they are not as open to discussing these topics, and then it causes arguments.
- There are some topics that parents and staff don't want to hear
- Many adults are not willing or even open to having discussions about many of these topics.
- I have experienced very public personal attacks by [other] teachers [when advocating for LGBTQ+ students in school].

As part of the discussion, teachers were expressing their fears about engaging students in conversations and action around topics that are central to students' identities, families, and communities. They were afraid of repercussions from parents, from their colleagues, and from administrators if they implemented pedagogies that addressed the issues that impact students' lives and the larger society.

Racism, xenophobia, White supremacy, and anti–critical race theory rhetoric has emboldened those who promote the status quo and has threatened teachers' autonomy and sense of security in their jobs. At the time of this writing, eight states have passed laws banning the discussion of "divisive concepts" such as race and sex, and many more states are considering the adoption of similar legislation. Implications of the legislation include increased surveillance of teaching, through observation, recording, and reporting (Kumashiro, 2021). Stories in the media of teachers dismissed for teaching and assigning readings on issues such as racism and white privilege—like that of Tennessee teacher Matt Hawn, who was fired after having students read a Ta-Nehisi Coates essay in *The Atlantic* on how racism impacted the 2016 election (E. Green, 2021)—create fear and consternation among teachers.

In addition to external attacks that threaten teachers' abilities to directly teach about systemic racism, White supremacy, sexism, and LGBTQ+ issues, teachers must contend with their own internal resistance to discussing issues that they or others find uncomfortable. Scholars have discussed the resistance among teacher candidates and teachers to discussing issues of race and White supremacy. Sadly, teacher education is not a space in which conversations about race are prevalent (Price-Dennis & Sealey-Ruiz, 2021). Price-Dennis has articulated her own experiences in working with preservice teachers who indicated they would not address race-related issues in their future schools:

1. The majority of them were using highly politicized ideas as a means to argue for neutrality in public education.
2. The majority of them did not see themselves as educators who were responsible for advocating for their students, especially when it involved race.
3. The majority of them viewed race as a negative political construct rooted in deficit ideology.
4. The preservice education program still had a lot of work to do to support the racial literacy development in novice teachers.
5. None of the preservice teachers seemed aware that middle school students spend time talking about issues of race and how race impacts their educational experience. (p. 2)

Ohito (2016) suggests that conversations about race can be challenging in teacher education programs because "when we are cocooned in the familiarity of comfort, we are often either unable or unwilling to jeopardize our sense of equilibrium by tackling emotional risks" (p. 455). The pervasiveness of whiteness in teacher education and in the teaching force has led to the perpetuation of Eurocentric norms in teacher education programs (Sleeter, 2001), yet silence around White supremacy intensifies its impact. Still, issues of emotionality that accompany conversations about race can block effective discussions and education about perpetual inequities in schools (Matias et al., 2016; Ohito, 2016).

In teacher education, it is essential to embrace a pedagogy of discomfort (Boler, 1999; Zembylas & Boler, 2002) in which individuals must grapple with contradictions and emotionally charged issues involving what they have always known or what they have been taught. Learning to teach through discomfort requires the unpacking of emotions and critical reflection that allows the changing of beliefs and harmful behaviors and teaching practices. As Rushck and Seylar remind us in Chapter 6 of this book, discomfort is a normal part of deconstructing curriculum and instruction that occurs as teachers reflect on how the very practices they (we) have enacted to elevate our students have actually perpetuated their marginalization.

A CALL TO ACTION

As our society has experienced a racial reckoning in the wake of a wave of racially motivated violence and murder of people of color, the spotlight is on how White supremacy has impacted our systems and institutions, including schools. Achieving the goal of equity in classrooms and schools requires that educators enact CSLP to create environments that honor diversity and embrace pluralism. The political pressures that stem from a desire on the part of many to maintain current power structures, privatize education, and censor public education pose real challenges for CSLP (Kumashiro, 2021). Still, the chapters in this book illustrate the ways in which individual teachers have taken up CSLP, and we hope that these models inspire other teachers to enact socially just and antiracist teaching. In fact, we believe that these very challenges are what makes embracing CSLP an imperative for our time.

We also believe that literacy professional organizations, teacher educators, and researchers can play a key role in supporting teachers and other educators in enacting CSLP in classrooms and schools. The International Literacy Association has demonstrated a strong commitment to recognizing diversity as a key component in the preparation of literacy professionals as reflected in the 2017 *Standards for the Preparation for Literacy Professionals.* The 2017 standards not only broadened the definition of diversity, ranging from race and ethnicity to political affiliations and other ideologies (ILA, 2018, p. 5), but also included more explicit guidance for teachers to follow in working with diverse students. The 2017 standard on diversity also recognized the need for a key shift in thinking that would lead to an emphasis on equity for diverse students. Thus Standard 4: *Diversity and Equity* was created and "grounded in a set of principles and understandings that reflect a vision for a democratic and socially just society" (ILA, 2018, p. 14). To enact the needed social changes, the standards emphasized the need for literacy professionals to be informed about diversity and to use their knowledge to advocate for the diversity of students in classrooms in different school and community contexts.

Toward that end, Standard 4: *Diversity and Equity* specifies the knowledge, understandings, and classroom environments espoused in the principles of CSP. To achieve these objectives, teachers must demonstrate knowledge of foundational theories about diverse learners, equity, and culturally responsive instruction. They must also demonstrate that they have an understanding of themselves as cultural beings.

This understanding emanates from teachers' self-examination of their belief systems and culture. It requires that they recognize how their own cultural experiences affect instruction and emphasizes the need to learn about and appreciate the diversity of their students, families, and communities (ILA, 2018, p. 80). Such efforts are essential if teachers are to establish high expectations for students, promote their identities as literate beings, and create learning environments that are affirming and inclusive and therefore enhance students' learning by responding to the diversity of the students they teach.

ILA believes that advocacy efforts should be viewed as transpiring within class and school contexts and in the larger community outside of school settings. By creating collaborative and reciprocal relationships among family, school personnel, and community, ILA through its publications and programming encourages teachers to advocate for culturally responsive school policies, practices, and structures, as well as for culturally responsive materials and assessments, and for access to digital tools and spaces (ILA, 2019).

Now let us turn to what professional organizations and groups can do to advance CSLP in all schools and for all students. Organizations such as the Literacy Research Association (LRA), International Literacy Association (ILA), National Council of Teachers of English (NCTE), and the Association of Literacy Educators and Researchers (ALER) are influential in shaping literacy research, teacher education, and literacy instruction in classrooms. Members of these organizations recognize that CSLP is entwined with literacy work. NCTE's statement for elementary teachers is unequivocal: "We believe that it is essential that we resist any attempt that is made to separate school-based language arts programs from the sociocultural realities of children's everyday lives." ILA calls for literacy professionals to know relevant theories related to diversity and equity. LRA has issued reports about the centrality of race and racism in literacy scholarship and practice (Willis et al., 2021). Behind all of these efforts is a recognition that a singular focus on literacy instruction and assessment is insufficient toward the goal of helping all students reach their fullest literacy potential.

Advancing CSLP is predicated on our efforts to interrogate how issues of race, racism, and decolonization live within each of us. We must also recognize the limitations of the Black–White binary, how BIPOC students' schooling opportunities have been historically shaped by systemic racism, how White supremacy functions to perpetuate racial injustices, and the need to interrogate the meritocratic myth that simply teaching students linguistic codes of power will solve systemic racism. Literacy researchers are called to intentionally engage in antiracist scholarship: "Each literacy researcher must make a personal commitment to oppose racism: from how literacy research is conceptualized and conducted; to how it is taught, assessed, written-up, published, and disseminated" (Willis et al., 2021, p. 4). Superficial address of race in literacy scholarship will only serve to perpetuate White supremacy.

The CSLP work described in this book centers literacy instruction and curriculum planning on the lives and experiences of BIPOC students and is therefore a vital part of the campaign toward racial justice. The authors draw from students' worlds to strengthen their literacy skills, and preserve their identities, intellect, and critical abilities (Muhammad, 2020). We recognize, however, that not all teachers are empowered to do this work. There will be limited room for centering instruction on students' experiences if standardized curricula and testing dominate in schools, especially those that serve large numbers of BIPOC students. In addition, educators in several states are now up against legislation that seeks to ban and/or restrict how they talk about racism. This is why the call for racial justice in literacy instruction and curriculum work must extend to policymakers, community leaders, and citizens. We call on LRA and affiliated literacy research organizations such as the International Literacy Association, the National Council of Teachers of English, and the Association of Literacy Educators and Researchers to issue policy statements that clarify what it means to center literacy instruction on the lives and experiences of BIPOC students as a vital component of racial justice. CSLP also needs to be on the tongues of school leaders and teachers, and so we also call on these organizations to engage more intentionally with practitioners working in schools and communities. We also urge LRA and its affiliate organizations to support the need to reconceptualize teacher and school leader preparation around the self-excavation work that is so necessary for student advocacy (Sealey-Ruiz, 2021).

By making transparent what antiracist, culturally sustaining literacy teaching looks like in this book, we have contributed an important component to the campaign for racial justice. We humbly recognize, however, that many more vivid examples of practice are needed in order to bring about the kind of educational changes that are needed to lift every student's literate capacity.

References

Adichie, C. N. (2009, July). *The danger of a single story* [Video]. TEDGlobal . https://www.ted.com/talks/chimamanda_ngozi_adichie_the_danger_of_a_single_story ?language=en

Adichie, C. N. (2009, July). *The danger of a single story* [Speech Transcript]. TEDGlobal. https://www.ted.com/talks/chimamanda_ngozi_adichie_the_danger_of_a _single_story/transcript

Albro, J. J. & Turner, J. D. (2019). Six key principles: Bridging students' career dreams with literacy standards. *Reading Teacher, 73*(2), 161–172.

Alexie, S. (2012). *The absolutely true diary of a part-time Indian*. Little, Brown Books for Young Readers.

Alim, H. S. (2007). "The Whig Party don't exist in my hood": Knowledge, reality, and education in the Hip Hop Nation. In H. S. Alim & J. Baugh (Eds.), *Talkin Black talk: Language, education, and social change* (pp. 15–29). Teachers College Press.

Alim, H. S., & Smitherman, G. (2012). *Articulate while Black: Barack Obama, language, and race in the U.S.* Oxford University Press.

Allington, R. (2013). *What really matters for struggling readers: Designing research-based programs*. Pearson.

Arizpe, E., Colomer, T., & Martínez-Roldán, C. (2014). *Visual journeys through wordless narratives: An international inquiry with immigrant children and* The Arrival. Bloomsbury.

Ascenzi-Moreno, L., & Quiñones, R. (2020). Bringing bilingualism to the center of guided reading instruction. *The Reading Teacher, 74*(2), 137–146. https://doi .org/10.1002/trtr.1922

Au, K. H. (1980). Participation structures in a reading lesson with Hawaiian children: Analysis of a culturally appropriate instructional event. *Anthropology & Education Quarterly, 11*(2), 91–115. https://www.jstor.org/stable/3216582

Au, K. H. (2011). *Literacy achievement and diversity: Keys to success for students, teachers, and schools*. Teachers College Press.

Au, K. H., & Jordan, C. (1981). Teaching reading to Hawaiian children: Finding a culturally appropriate solution. In H. T. Trueba, G. P. Guthrie, & K. H. Au (Eds.), *Culture and the bilingual classroom: Studies in classroom ethnography* (pp. 139–152). Newbury House.

Au, K. H., & Kawakami, A. (1994). Cultural congruence in instruction. In E. Hollins, J. King, & W. Hayman (Eds.), *Teaching diverse populations: Formulating a knowledge base* (pp. 5–23). State University of New York [SUNY] Press.

Aukerman, M., & Chambers Schuldt, L. (2016). Closely reading "Reading closely." *Language Arts, 93*(4), 286–299.

Aukerman, M., Grovet, K., & Belfatti, M. (2019). Race, ideology, and cultural representation in Raz-Kids. *Language Arts, 96*(5), 286–299.

Baker, J. (2002). Trilingualism. In L. Delpit & J. K. Dowdy. *The skin that we speak: Thoughts on language and culture in the classroom.* The New Press.

Baker-Bell, A. (2020a). *Linguistic justice: Black language, literacy, identity, and pedagogy.* Routledge.

Baker-Bell, A. (2020b). We been knowin: Toward an antiracist language & literacy education. *Journal of Language and Literacy Education, 16*(1), 1–12.

Ball, A. F. (1995). Text design patterns in the writing of urban African American students: Teaching to the cultural strengths of students in multicultural settings. *Urban Education, 30*(3), 253–289. https://doi.org/10.1177/0042085995030003002

Barrett, M. (2003). Meme engineers: Children as producers of musical culture. *International Journal of Early Years Education, 11*(3), 195–212. https://doi.org/10.1080/0966976032000147325

Beaty, D. (2013). *Knock: My father's dream for me.* Little, Brown Books for Young Readers.

Bennett, S. V., Gunn, A. A., Gayle-Evans, G., Barrera, E. S., & Leung, C. (2018). Culturally responsive literacy practices in an early childhood community. *Early Childhood Education Journal, 46*(2), 241–248. doi: 10.1007/s10643-017-0839-9

Bennett, S. V. Gunn, A. A., & Peterson, B. (2021). Access to multicultural children's literature during COVID-19. *The Reading Teacher, 74*(6), 785–796.

Berger, M. (2016). *Germs make me sick!* HarperCollins.

Billig, S. H. (2011). Making the most of your time: Implementing the K–12 service-learning standards for quality practice. *The Prevention Researcher, 18*(1), 8–14.

Bishop, R. S. (1990). Mirrors, windows, and sliding glass doors. *Perspectives: Choosing and Using Books for the Classroom, 6*(3), 9–12.

Bogard, J. M., & McMackin, M. C. (2012). Combining traditional and new literacies in a 21st-century writing workshop. *The Reading Teacher, 65*(5), 313–323.

Boler, M. (1999). *Feeling power: Emotions and education.* Routledge.

Botelho, M. J., & Rudman, M. K. (2009). *Critical multicultural analysis of children's literature: Mirrors, windows, and doors.* Routledge.

Bristol, T. J. & Mentor, M. (2018). "Policing and teaching: The positioning of Black male teachers as agents in the universal carceral apparatus." *The Urban Review, 50*(2), 1–17.

Brochin, C., & Medina, C. L. (2017). Critical fictions of transnationalism in Latinx children's literature. *Bookbird: A Journal of International Children's Literature, 55*(3), 4–11.

Brown, K. D. (2013). Trouble on my mind: Toward a framework of humanizing critical sociocultural knowledge for teaching and teacher education. *Race Ethnicity and Education, 16*(3), 316–338.

Bucholz, M., Casillas, D. I., & Lee, J. S. (2017). Language and culture as sustenance. In D. Paris & H. S. Alim (Eds.), *Culturally sustaining pedagogies: Teaching and learning for justice in a changing world* (pp. 43–60). Teachers College Press.

Bunting, E. (2006). *One green apple.* Clarion Books.

Buolamwini, J. (2018, June 21). When the robot doesn't see dark skin [Op-Ed]. *New York Times*. https://www.nytimes.com/2018/06/21/opinion/facial-analysis -technology-bias.html?referringSource=articleShare

Burton, J. (2019). Look at us, we have anxiety: Youth, memes, and the power of online cultural politics. *Journal of Childhood Studies*, *44*(3), 3–17. https://doi .org/10.18357/jcs00019171

Calkins, L. (2020). *Teaching writing*. Heinemann.

Cappello, M., & Hollingsworth, S. (2008). Literacy inquiry and pedagogy through a photographic lens. *Language Arts*, *85*(6), 442–449.

Cappello, M., Wiseman, A. M., & Turner, J. D. (2019). Framing equitable classroom practices: Potentials of critical multimodal literacy research. *Literacy Research: Theory, Method, and Practice*, *69*(1), 205–225. https://doi.org/10.1177 /2381336919870274

Center for Documentary Studies at Duke University. (n.d.). Literacy through Photography. https://documentarystudies.duke.edu/literacy-through-photography

Choi, Y. (2013). *The name jar*. Random House Children's Books.

Colato Laínez, R. (1996). *Rene has two last names / Rene tiene dos apellidos*. Arte Publico.

Comber, B. (2015). Critical literacy and social justice. *Journal of Adolescent & Adult Literacy*, *58*(5), 362–367.

Comber, B., & Nixon, H. (2009). Teachers' work and pedagogy in an era of accountability. *Discourse: Studies in the cultural politics of education*, *30*(3), 333–345.

Crenshaw, K. (1991). Mapping the margins: Intersectionality, identity politics, and violence against women of color. *Stanford Law Review*, *43*(6), 1241–1299. https://doi.org/10.2307/1229039

Crisp, T., Knezek, S. M., Quinn, M., Bingham, G. E., Girardeau, K., & Starks, F. (2016). What's on our bookshelves? The diversity of children's literature in early childhood classroom libraries. *Journal of Children's Literature*, *42*(2), 29–42.

Daniels, E., & Arapostathis, M. (2005). What do they really want? Student voices and motivation research. *Urban Education*, *40*(1), 34–59. https://doi.org/10 .1177/0042085904270421

Day, D., & Ward, B. A. (2019). Yuyi Morales: Dreamweaver and teller of tales. *Journal of Children's Literature*, *45*(2), 82–87.

Delgado, R. (1989). Storytelling for oppositionists and others: A plea for narrative. *Michigan Law Review*, *87*(8), 2411–2441.

De Roock, R. S. (2021). On the material consequences of (digital) literacy: Digital writing with, for, and against racial capitalism. *Theory Into Practice*, *60*(2), 183–193.

DeSantis, R. (2021, June 10). Governor DeSantis emphasizes importance of keeping critical race theory out of schools at state board of education meeting [Press Release]. https://www.flgov.com/2021/06/10/governor-desantis-emphasizes-impor tance-of-keeping-critical-race-theory-out-of-schools-at-state-board-of-education -meeting/.

DiAngelo, R. (2018). *White fragility: Why it's so hard for White people to talk about race*. Beacon Press

Dover, A. G. (2016). Teaching for social justice and the Common Core: Justice-oriented curriculum for language arts and literacy. *Journal of Adolescent & Adult Literacy*, *59*(5), 517–527.

Dyson, A. H. (2003). "Welcome to the jam": Popular culture, school literacy, and the making of childhoods. *Harvard Educational Review, 73*(3), 328–361.

Edwardson, D. D. (2011). *My name is not easy.* Marshall.

Erickson, F. (1987). Transformation and school success: The politics and culture of educational achievement. *Anthropology & Education Quarterly, 18*(1), 335–356.

Erickson, F. (2006). Studying side by side: Collaborative action ethnography in educational research. In G. Spindler & L. Hammond (Eds.), *New horizons for ethnography in education* (pp. 235–257). Lawrence Erlbaum.

Ewald, W. (2002). *The best part of me: Children talk about their bodies in pictures and words.* Little, Brown Books for Young Readers.

Freire, P. (1970). *Pedagogy of the oppressed.* New York, NY: Seabury Press.

Freire, P., & Macedo, D. (1987). *Literacy: Reading the word and the world.* Routledge.

Furco, A., & Root, S. (2010). Research demonstrates the value of service learning. *Phi Delta Kappan, 91*(5), 16–20.

Gabriel, R., & Wenz, C. (2017). Three directions for disciplinary literacy. *Educational Leadership, 74*(5), 8–14.

Garcia, E. E. (1993). Language, culture, and education. *Review of Research in Education, 19*(1), 51–98.

García, O. (2009a). Education, multilingualism and translanguaging in the 21st century. In A. Mohanty, M. Panda, R. Phillipson, & T. Skutnabb-Kangas (Eds.), *Multilingual education for social justice: Globalising the local* (pp. 128–145). Orient Blackswan.

García, O. (2009b). Emergent bilinguals: What's in a name? *TESOL Quarterly, 43*(2), 322–326. https://www.jstor.org/stable/27785009

Garcia, O., & Kleifgen, J. (2018). *Educating emergent bilinguals: Policies, programs, and practices for English learners.* Teachers College Press.

Gay, G. (2010). *Culturally responsive teaching: Theory, research, and practice* (2nd ed.). Teachers College Press.

Gibbons, G. (1992). *Recycle!: A handbook for kids.* Little, Brown.

Gill, V. S. (2016). Everybody else gets to be normal: Using intersectionality and Ms. Marvel to challenge "normal identity." *The ALAN Review, 44*(1), 68–78.

Goldenberg, C. (2020). Reading wars, reading science, and English learners. *Reading Research Quarterly, 55*(S1), S131–S144.

Goldman, S. R., Britt, M. A., Brown, W., Cribb, G., George, M., Greenleaf, C., Lee, C. D., Shanahan, C., & Project READI. (2016). Disciplinary literacies and learning to read for understanding: A conceptual framework for disciplinary literacy. *Educational Psychologist, 51*(2), 219–246. https://doi.org/10.1080/00461520.2016.1168741

González, N., Moll, L. C., & Amanti, C. (2005). *Funds of knowledge: Theorizing practices in households, communities, and classrooms.* Routledge.

Gorski, P. C., & Swalwell, K. (2015). Equity literacy for all. *Educational Leadership, 72*(6), 34–40.

Green, E. (2021, August 17). He taught a Ta-Nehisi Coates essay. Then he was fired. *The Atlantic.* https://www.theatlantic.com/politics/archive/2021/08/matt-hawn-tennessee-teacher-fired-white-privilege/619770/

Green, T. L. (2017). From positivism to critical theory: School–community relations toward community equity literacy. *International Journal of Qualitative Studies in Education, 30*(4), 370–387.

Green, T. L. (2018). Enriching educational leadership through community equity literacy: A conceptual foundation. *Leadership and Policy in Schools, 17*(4), 487–515.

Griffin, A. A., & Turner, J. D. (2021, August 3). Toward a pedagogy of Black livingness: Black students' creative multimodal renderings of resistance to anti-Blackness. *English Teaching Practice & Critique.* Advance online publication. https://doi.org/10.1108/ETPC-09-2020-0123

Gunn, A. A. (2016). Teachers moving forward on a cultural self-awareness spectrum: Diverse children, museums, and young adult literature. *Multicultural Perspectives, 18*(4), 1–7.

Gunn, A. A., Bennett, S. V., Evans, L., Peterson, B., & Welsh, J. (March, 2013). Autobiographies in preservice teacher education: A snapshot tool for building culturally responsive pedagogy. *International Journal of Multicultural Education, 15*(1), 1–20.

Gunn, A. A., & Bennett, S. V., & van Beynen, K. (2020). Teaching about religion with conversations and multicultural literature in K–6 classrooms. *Social Studies and the Young Learner, 33*(1), 10–16.

Gunn, A. A., & King, J. (2015). Using empathetic identification as a literacy tool for building culturally responsive teaching with preservice teachers. *Teacher Development, 19*(2), 1–15.

Gutiérrez, K. D. ,& Johnson, P. (2017). Understanding identity sampling and cultural repertoires: Advancing a historicizing and syncretic system of teaching and learning in justice pedagogies. In D. Paris & H. S. Alim (Eds.), *Culturally sustaining pedagogies: Teaching and learning for justice in a changing world* (pp. 247–260). Teachers College Press.

Gutiérrez, K. D., Morales, P. Z., & Martinez, D. (2009). Re-mediating literacy: Culture, difference, and learning for students from nondominant communities. *Review of Research in Education, 33*(1), 212–245.

Gutiérrez, K. D., & Rogoff, B. (2003). Cultural ways of learning: Individual traits or repertoires of practice. *Educational Researcher, 32*(5), 19–25.

Haddix, M. M. (2017). Diversifying teaching and teacher education: Beyond rhetoric and toward real change. *Journal of Literacy Research, 49*(1), 141–149.

Hart, S. (2006). Breaking literacy boundaries through critical service-learning: Education for the silenced and marginalized. *Mentoring & Tutoring, 14*(1), 17–32.

Heath, S. B. (1983). *Ways with words: Language, life, and work in communities and classrooms.* Cambridge University Press.

Hidi, S., & Harackiewicz, J. (2000). Motivating the academically unmotivated: A critical issue for the 21st century. *Review of Educational Research, 70,* 151–179.

Holland, D., Lachichotte, W., Skinner, D., & Cain, C. (1998). *Identity and agency in cultural worlds.* Harvard University Press.

hooks, b. (1992). *Black looks: Race and representation.* South End Press.

hooks, b. (2000). *Feminist theory: From margin to center.* Pluto Press.

Hopewell, S., & Escamilla, K. (2014). Struggling reader or emerging biliterate student? Reevaluating the criteria for labeling emerging bilingual students as low achieving. *Journal of Literacy Research, 46*(1), 68–89.

International Literacy Association (ILA). (2017). *Characteristics of culturally sustaining and academically rigorous classrooms* [Literacy leadership brief]. https://www.literacyworldwide.org/docs/default-source/where-we-stand/ila-culturally-sustaining-classrooms-brief.pdf?sfvrsn=7b80a68e_10&sfvrsn=7b80a68e_10

International Literacy Association (ILA). (2018). *Standards for the preparation of literacy professionals 2017.* https://www.literacyworldwide.org/get-resources/standards/standards-2017

International Literacy Association (ILA). (2019). *Right to supportive learning environments and high-quality resources* [Research brief].

Irizarry, J. G. (2017). "For us, by us": A vision for culturally sustaining pedagogies forwarded by Latinx youth. In D. Paris & H. S. Alim (Eds.), *Culturally sustaining pedagogies: Teaching and learning for justice in a changing world* (pp. 83–98). Teachers College Press.

Irvine, J. J. (1991). *Black students and school failure: Policies, practices, and prescriptions.* Praeger.

Isaacson, W. (2014). *The innovators: How a group of hackers, geniuses, and geeks created the digital revolution.* Simon and Shuster.

Janks, H. (2013) Critical literacy in teaching and research. *Education Inquiry, 4*(2), 225–242.

Jason, L., & Glenwick, D. (2016). *Handbook of methodological approaches to community-based research: Qualitative, quantitative, and mixed methods.* Oxford University Press.

Jensen, E., Jones, N., Rabe, M., Pratt, B., Medina, L., Orozco, K., & Spell, L. (2021). *The chance that two people chosen at random are of different race or ethnicity groups has increased since 2010.* https://www.census.gov/library/stories/2021/08/2020-united-states-population-more-racially-ethnically-diverse-than-2010.html

Jewitt, C. (2008). Multimodality and literacy in school classrooms. *Review of Research in Education, 32*(1), 241–267.

Joarder, M. (2019, October 25). My whole life I have been looking for fearless queer Muslim heroes. *The Guardian.* http://www.theguardian.com/commentisfree/2019/oct/25/my-whole-life-i-have-been-looking-for-fearless-queer-muslim-heroes

Kahne, J. E., & Sporte, S. E. (2008). Developing citizens: The impact of civic learning opportunities on students' commitment to civic participation. *American Educational Research Journal, 45*(3), 738–766.

Katz, J. H. (1985). The sociopolitical nature of counseling. *The Counseling Psychologist, 13*(4), 615–624.

Keehne, C. N. K., Sarsona, M. W., Kawakami, A. J., & Au, K. N. (2018). Culturally responsive instruction and literacy learning. *Journal of Literacy Research, 50,* 141–166.

Kelchtermans, G. (1996). Teacher vulnerability: Understanding its moral and political roots. *Cambridge Journal of Education, 26*(3), 307–323.

Khalil, A. (2020). *The Arabic quilt: An immigrant story.* Tilbury House.

Khan, H. (2015). *Golden domes and silver lanterns: A Muslim book of colors* (M. Amini, Illus.). Chronicle Books.

Khan, S. (2019). *The love and lies of Rukhsana Ali.* Scholastic.

Kim, J., & Lee, K. (2011). "What's your name?": Names, naming practices, and contextualized selves of young Korean American children. *Journal of Research in Childhood Education, 25*(3), 211–227.

King, J. E., & Mitchell, C. A. (1995). *Black mothers to sons: Juxtaposing African American literature with social practice.* Peter Lang.

King, J. R., Hart, S., & Kozdras, D. (2020). Identity matters in service-learning literacies: Becoming authentic and agentic within role affordance. In L. A. Henry & N. Stahl (Eds.), *Literacy across the community: Research, praxis, and trends* (pp. 211–222). Routledge.

Kinloch, V. (2017). "You ain't making me write": Culturally sustaining pedagogies and Black youths' performances of resistance. In D. Paris & H. S. Alim (Eds.), *Culturally sustaining pedagogies: Teaching and learning for justice in a changing world* (pp. 25–44). Teachers College Press.

Kinloch, V., Burkhard, T., & Penn, C. (2020). *Race, justice, and activism in literacy instruction.* Teachers College Press.

Kirkland, D. E. (2013). *A search past silence: The literacy of young Black men.* Teachers College Press.

Klingner, J. K., & Edwards, P. A. (2006). Cultural considerations with Response to Intervention models. *Reading Research Quarterly, 41*(1), 108–117.

Knoester, M., & Au, W. (2017). Standardized testing and school segregation: Like tinder for fire? *Race Ethnicity and Education, 20*(1), 1–14.

Kohli, R., & Pizzaro, M. (2016). Fighting to educate our own: Teachers of color, relational accountability, and the struggle for racial justice. *Equity & Excellence in Education, 49*(1), 72–84.

Kohli, R., & Solórzano, D. G. (2012). Teachers, please learn our names! Racial microaggressions and the K–12 classroom. *Race Ethnicity and Education, 15*(4), 441–462.

Kohn, A. (2000). *The case against standardized testing: Raising the scores, ruining the schools.* Heinemann.

Kress, G., & Jewitt, C. (2003). Introduction. In J. Jewitt & G. Kress (Eds.), *Multimodal literacy* (pp. 1–18). Peter Lang.

Kumashiro, K. (2021). *Understanding the attacks on teaching: A background brief for educators and leaders.* https://www.kevinkumashiro.com/attackson teaching

Ladson-Billings, G. (1994). *The dreamkeepers: Successful teachers of African American children.* (1st ed.). Jossey-Bass.

Ladson-Billings, G. (1995a). But that's just good teaching! The case for culturally relevant pedagogy. *Theory Into Practice, 34*(3), 159–165.

Ladson-Billings, G. (1995b). Toward a theory of culturally relevant pedagogy. *American Educational Research Journal, 32*(3), 465–491.

Ladson-Billings, G. (2017). The (r)evolution will not be standardized: Teacher education, hip hop pedagogy, and culturally relevant pedagogy 2.0. In D. Paris & H. S. Alim (Eds.), *Culturally Sustaining Pedagogies: Teaching and learning for justice in a changing world* (pp. 141–156). Teachers College Press.

Ladson-Billings, G. (2021, August 21). *Gloria Ladson-Billings: Critical race theory* [Video]. *The Brain-Waves Video Anthology.* YouTube. https://www.youtube.com/watch?v=ufKusK6dQI8

Laman, T. T., & Henderson, J. W. (2018). Using photography in a culturally responsive curriculum: Invitations to read, write, and think. *The Reading Teacher, 72*(5), 643–647.

Lee, C. D. (1995). A culturally based cognitive apprenticeship: Teaching African American high school students skills in literary interpretation. *Reading Research Quarterly, 30*(4), 608–630.

Lee, C. D. (2007). *Culture, literacy, and learning: Taking bloom in the midst of the whirlwind.* Teachers College Press.

Lee, C. D. (2017). An ecological framework for enacting culturally sustaining pedagogy. In D. Paris & H. S. Alim (ds.), *Culturally sustaining pedagogies: Teaching and learning for justice in a changing world* (pp. 261–274). Teachers College Press.

Lee, C. D., & Goldman, S. R. (2015). Assessing literary reasoning: Text and task complexities. *Theory Into Practice, 54*(3), 213–227.

Leedy, L. (1991). *The great trash bash.* Holiday House.

Lensmire, T. J., & Kinloch, V. (2019). A dialogue on reace, reacism, white privilege, and white supremacy in English education. *English Education, 51*(2), 116–125.

Lewison, M., Flint, A. S., Van Sluys, K. (2002). Taking on critical literacy: The journey of newcomers and novices. *Critical Literacy, 79*(5), 382–392.

Lewison, M., Leland, C., & Harste, J. C. (2015). *Creating critical classrooms: Reading and writing with an edge.* Routledge.

Lippi-Green, R. (2012). *English with an accent: Language, ideology, and discrimination in the United States.* Routledge.

Lombard, J. (2008). *Drita, my homegirl.* Penguin Young Readers Group.

Lorde, A. (1984). "The master's tools will never dismantle the master's house." In A. Lorde (Ed.), *Sister outsider: Essays and speeches* (pp. 110–114). Crossing Press.

Love, B. L. (2015). What is hip-hop-based education doing in nice fields such as early childhood and elementary education? *Urban Education, 50*(1), 106–131.

Love, B. (2019). *We want to do more than survive: Abolitionist teaching and the pursuit of educational freedom.* Beacon Press.

Machado, E., & Flores, T. T. (2021). Picturebook creators as translingual writing mentors. *Language Arts, 98*(5), 235–245.

Maniates, H., & Mahiri, J. (2011). Post-scripts: Teaching reading in the aftermath of prescriptive curriculum policies. *Language Arts, 89*(1), 10–21.

Matias, C. E., Montoya, R., & Nishi, N. W. (2016). Blocking CRT: How the emotionality of whiteness blocks CRT in urban teacher education. *Educational Studies, 52*(1), 1–19.

McCarty, T. L., & Zepeda, O. (1995). Indigenous language education and literacy: Introduction to the theme issue. *Bilingual Research Journal, 19*(1), 1–4.

McClung, N. A. (2018). Learning to queer text: Epiphanies from a family critical literacy perspective. *The Reading Teacher, 71*(4), 401–410. https://doi.org/10.1002/trtr.1640

Miller, K., & Weilbacher, G. (2020). Examining the intersection of social justice and state standards with elementary preservice teachers. *Action in Teacher Education, 42*(4), 368–386.

Miller, S. M., & McVee, M. B. (2013). Multimodal composing: The essential 21st century literacy. In S. M. Miller & M. B. McVee (Eds.), *Multimodal composing in classrooms: learning and teaching for the digital world.* Routledge.

Milson-Whyte, V. (2013). Pedagogical and socio-political implications of code-meshing in classrooms: Some considerations for a translingual orientation to writing. In A. S. Canagarajah (Ed.), *Literacy as translingual practice: Between communities and classrooms* (pp. 115–127). Routledge.

Mohatt, G. V., & Erickson, F. (1981). Cultural differences in teaching styles in an Odawa school: A sociolinguistic approach. In H. T. Trueba, G. P. Guthrie, K. H. Au, & W.S. Hall (Eds.), *Culture and the bilingual classroom: Studies in classroom ethnography* (pp. 105–119). Newbury House.

Moje, E. B. (2015). Doing and teaching disciplinary literacy with adolescent learners: A social and cultural enterprise. *Harvard Educational Review, 85*(2), 254–278.

Moll, L., Amanti, C., Neff, D., & González, N. (1992). Funds of knowledge for teaching: Using a qualitative approach to connect homes and classrooms. *Theory Into Practice, 31*(2), 132–141. https://doi.org/10.1080/00405849209543534)

Moll, L., Amanti, C., Neff, D., & González, N. (2005). Funds of knowledge for teaching: Using a qualitative approach to connect homes and classrooms. In N. González, L. C. Moll, & C. Amanti (Eds.), *Funds of knowledge: Theorizing practices in households, communities, and classrooms* (pp. 71–88). Routledge. (Original work published 1992)

Moll, L. C., & González, N. (1994). Lessons from research with language-minority children. *Journal of Reading Behavior, 26*(4) 439–456.

Moore, B. A., & Klingner, J. K. (2014). Considering the needs of English language learner populations: An examination of the population validity of reading intervention research. *Journal of Learning Disabilities, 47*(5), 391–408.

Morales, Y. (2018). *Dreamers.* Neal Porter.

Muhammad, G. (2020). *Cultivating genius: An equity framework for culturally and historically responsive literacy.* Scholastic.

Muhammad, G., & Mosley, L. (2021). Why we need identity and equity learning in literacy practices: Moving research, practice, and policy forward. *Language Arts, 98*(4), 189–196.

Nagy, W. E., & Scott, J. A. (2000). Vocabulary processes. In M. L. Kamil, P. B. Mosenthal, P. D. Pearson, & R. Barr (Eds.), *Handbook of reading research* (Vol. 3, pp. 269–284). Lawrence Erlbaum.

Nash, K., Panther, L., & Arce-Boardman, A. (2018). La historia de mi nombre: A culturally sustaining early literacy practice. *The Reading Teacher, 71*(5), 605–609. https://doi.org/10.1002/trtr.1665

National Coalition Against Censorship. (2021, June 23). Non-partisan coalition statement opposing "divisive concepts" legislation. https://ncac.org/news/divisive-concepts-statement-2021.

Newcomer, S. N., & Cowin, K. M. (2021). The power and possibility of stories: Learning to become culturally sustaining and socially just educators, *Review of Education, Pedagogy, and Cultural Studies,* 1–29. https://doi.org/10.1080/10714413.2020.1860407

New London Group. (1996). A pedagogy of multiliteracies: Designing social futures. *Harvard Educational Review, 66*(1), 60–92.

Noguerón-Liu, S., Shimek, C. H., & Bahlmann Bollinger, C. (2020). "Dime de que se trató/Tell me what it was about": Exploring emergent bilinguals' linguistic resources in reading assessments with parent participation. *Journal of Early Childhood Literacy, 20*(2), 411–433.

Norton, M. I., & Ariely, D. (2011). Building a better America—One wealth quintile at a time. *Perspectives on Psychological Science, 6*(1), 9–12.

Ohito, E. O. (2016). Making the emperor's new clothes visible in anti-racist teacher education: Enacting a pedagogy of discomfort with white preservice teachers. *Equity & Excellence in Education, 49*(4), 454–467.

Oliva, J. (2021, June 9). Addendum to mathematics bid specification [Memorandum]. https://www.fldoe.org/core/fileparse.php/5574/urlt/AddendMath.pdf.

Orosco, J. M., & Klingner, J. (2010). One school's implementation of RTI with English language leaners: "Referring into RTI." *Journal of Learning Disabilities, 43*(3), 269–288.

Palfrey, J. (2018). *Safe spaces, brave spaces: Diversity and free expression in education.* MIT Press.

Paris, D. (2012). Culturally sustaining pedagogy: A needed change in stance, terminology, and practice. *Educational Researcher, 41*(3), 93–97. https://www.jstor.org/stable/41477769

Paris, D., & Alim, H. S. (2014). What are we seeking to sustain through culturally sustaining pedagogy? A loving critique forward. *Harvard Educational Review, 84*(1), 85–100.

Paris, D., & Alim, H. S. (Eds.). (2017). *Culturally sustaining pedagogies: Teaching and learning for justice in a changing world.* Teachers College Press.

PBS Learning Media. (n.d.). *Storytelling: writer's workshop* [Lesson plan]. https://www.pbslearningmedia.org/resource/echo07.lan.stories.lpwritework/storytelling-writers-workshop/

Philips, S. U. (1983). *The invisible culture: Communication in classroom and community on the warm springs Indian reservation.* Longman.

Powell, R., Cantrell, S. C., & Correll, P. (2017). Power and agency in a high poverty elementary school: How teachers experienced a scripted reading program. *Journal of Language and Literacy Education, 13*(1), 93–124.

Price-Dennis, D., & Sealey-Ruz, Y. (2021). *Advancing racial literacies in teacher education.* Teachers College Press.

Purcell-Gates, V. (1995). *Other people's words: The cycle of low literacy.* Harvard University Press.

Rainey, E. C. (2016). Disciplinary literacy in English language arts: Exploring the social and problem-based nature of literary reading and reasoning. *Reading Research Quarterly, 52*(1), 53–71.

Ravitch, D. (2016). The Common Core cost billions and hurts students. *The New York Times.* https://www.nytimes.com/2016/07/24/opinion/sunday/the-common-core-costs-billions-and-hurts-students.html

Rawlings, A. (2018, November 15). Since time immemorial: Tribal sovereignty in Washington State. *Harvard Law & Policy Review.* https://harvardlpr.com/2018/11/15/since-time-immemorial-tribal-sovereignty-education-in-washington-state/

Reid, S. F., & Moses, L. (2019). Students become comic book author-illustrators: Composing with words and images in a fourth-grade comics writers' workshop. *The Reading Teacher, 73*(4), 461–472.

Reynolds, J., & Kendi, I. X. (2020). *Stamped: Racism, antiracism, and you: A remix of the National Book Award–winning Stamped from the beginning.* Little, Brown Books for Young Readers.

Reynolds, J., & Kiely, B. (2017). *All American boys* (Reprint edition). Atheneum Books for Young Readers.

Reynolds, T., Rush, L. S., Lampi, J. P., & Holschuh, J. P. (2020). English disciplinary literacy: Enhancing students' literary interpretive moves. *Journal of Adolescent & Adult Literacy, 64*(2), 201–209.

Rickford, J. R. (2002). *How linguists approach the study of language and dialect (ms. January 2002, for students in Ling 73, AAVE, Stanford).* Available for download from https://web.stanford.edu/~rickford/papers/

Ritchie, S. (2012). Incubating and sustaining: How teacher networks enable and support social justice education. *Journal of Teacher Education, 63*(2), 120–131

Robin, B. R. (2008). Digital storytelling: A powerful technology tool for the 21st century classroom. *Theory into Practice, 47*(3), 220–228.

Rolón-Dow, R. (2005). Critical care: A color(full) analysis of care narratives in the schooling experiences of Puerto Rican girls. *American Educational Research Journal, 42*(1), 77–111.

Rowe, D., & Fain, J. G. (2013). The family backpack project: Responding to dual-language texts through family journals. *Language Arts, 90*(6), 402–416.

Rubin, B. C., Hayes, B., & Benson, K. (2009). "It's the worst place to live": Urban youth and the challenge of school-based civic learning. *Theory Into Practice, 48*(3), 213–221.

Rychly, L., & Graves, E. (2012). Teacher characteristics for culturally responsive pedagogy. *Multicultural Perspectives, 14*(1), 44–49.

Salazar, M. d. C. (2013). A humanizing pedagogy: Reinventing the principles and practice of education as a journey toward liberation. *Review of Research in Education, 37(1)*, 121–148.

Savitz, R. S., & Wallace, K. (2016). Using the inquiry process to motivate and engage all (including struggling) readers. *The Clearing House: A Journal of Educational Strategies, Issues and Ideas, 89*(3), 91–96. https://doi.org/10.1080/00098655.2016.1184923

Schiller, M. (2016). *The corn husk doll.* Scholastic.

Schneider, J. J. (2001). No blood, guns, or gays allowed! The silencing of the elementary writer. *Language Arts, 78(5)*, 415–425.

Schneider, J. J., & Frier, A. D. (2020). *On deficits, dominance, and the eradication of culture: Toward imaginative, access-promoting pedagogies.* Paper presentation at Journal of Language and Literacy Education Conference, Athens, GA.

Schneider, J. J., Smith, P., & Jones, M. (2020). *Deficits, dominance, and the eradication of culture: Toward imaginative, access-promoting pedagogies* [Paper presentation Journal of Language and Literacy Education Conference, Athens, GA.

Sealey-Ruiz, Y. (2019). *Archeology of self.* https://www.yolandasealeyruiz.com/archaeology-of-self

Sealey-Ruiz, Y. (2021). The critical literacy of race: Toward racial literacy in urban teacher education. In *Handbook of Urban Education* (pp. 281–295). Routledge.

Sensoy, Ö., & DiAngelo, R. (2017). *Is everyone really equal?: An introduction to key concepts in social justice education* (2nd ed.). Teachers College Press.

Shanahan, T., & Shanahan, C. (2012). What is disciplinary literacy and why does it matter? *Topics in Language Disorders, 32*(1), 7–18.

Sherman, C.W. (2020) *Brown sugar babe* (Akem, Illus.). Astra Publishing House.

Showalter, M. (Director). (2017). *The big sick [Film]*. FilmNation Entertainment.

Sleeter, C. E. (2001). Preparing teachers for culturally diverse schools: Research and the overwhelming presence of whiteness. *Journal of Teacher Education, 52*(2), 94–106.

Smagorinsky, P. (2015). Disciplinary literacy in English language arts. *Journal of Adolescent & Adult Literacy, 59*(2), 141–146.

Smagorinsky, P., Guay, M., Ellison, T. L., & Willis, A. I. (2020). A sociocultural perspective on readers, reading, reading instruction and assessment, reading policy, and reading research. In E. Moje, P. Afflerbach, P. Enciso, & N. Lesaux (Eds.), *Handbook of Reading Research* (Vol. 5, pp. 57–75). Routledge.

Solórzano, D. G., & Yosso, T. J. (2002). Critical race methodology: Counter-storytelling as an analytical framework for education research. *Qualitative Inquiry, 8*(1), 23–44.

Souto-Manning, M. (2011). Challenging the text and context of (re)naming immigrant children: Children's literature as tools for change. In B. S. Fennimore & L. N. Goodwin (Eds.), *Promoting social justice for young children* (pp. 111–124). Springer.

Souto-Manning, M., & Martell, J. (2016). *Reading, writing, and talk: Inclusive teaching strategies for diverse learners, K–2*. Teachers College Press.

Souto-Manning, M., & Rabadi-Raol, A. (2018). (Re)Centering quality in early childhood education: Toward intersectional justice for minoritized children. *Review of Research in Education, 42*(1), 203–225.

Spiering, J., & Lechtenberg, K. L. (2020). Rethinking curation in school libraries and school library education: Critical, conceptual, collaborative. *School Libraries Worldwide, 26*(1), 83–98.

Spires, H. A., Kerkhoff, S. N., Graham, A. C. K. et al. (2018). Operationalizing and validating disciplinary literacy in secondary education. *Reading and Writing (31)*, 1401–1434. https://doi.org/10.1007/s11145-018-9839-4

Spires, H. A., Kerkhoff, S. N., Medlock Paul, C. (2020). *Read, write, inquire: Disciplinary literacy in grades 6–12*. Teachers College Press.

Stewart, M. A. (2017). "I love this book because that's like me!" A multilingual refugee/adolescent girl responds from her homeplace. *International Multilingual Research Journal, 11*(4), 239–254.

Strauss, V. (2021, August 28). Educators across the country protest laws limiting lessons on racism, vow to teach the truth. *The Washington Post*. https://www.washingtonpost.com/education/2021/08/28/critical-race-theory-teachers-protest/

Street, B. (1984). *Literacy in theory and practice*. Cambridge University Press.

Strickland, M. J., Keat, J. B., & Marinak, B. A. (2010). Connecting worlds: Using photo narrations to connect immigrant children, preschool teachers, and immigrant families. *School Community Journal, 20*(1), 81–102.

Swalwell, K. (2011, December 21). Why our students need "equity literacy." *Learning for Justice* (formerly *Teaching Tolerance Blog*). https://www.tolerance.org/magazine/why-our-students-need-equity-literacy

Szablewicz, M. (2020). *Mapping digital game culture in China*. Springer International.

Thomas, A. (2017). *The hate u give*. Harper Collins.

Thomas, D., & Dyches, J. (2019). The hidden curriculum of reading intervention: A critical content analysis of Fountas & Pinnell's leveled literacy intervention. *Journal of Curriculum Studies, 51*(5), 1–15.

Thomas, E. E. (2016). Stories still matter: Rethinking the role of diverse children's literature today. *Language Arts, 94*(2), 112–119.

Thompkins-Bigelow, J. (2020). Eid Pictures. In S. K. Ali & A. Saeed (Eds.), *Once upon an Eid: Stories of hope and joy by 15 Muslim Voices* (pp. 197–202). Abrams.

Turner, J. D. (2020). Freedom to aspire: Black children's career dreams, perceived aspirational supports, and Africentric values. *Race Ethnicity and Education*. Advance online publication. https://doi.org/10.1080/13613324.2020.1718074

Vasquez, V. M., Janks, H., & Comber, B. (2019). Critical literacy as a way of being and doing. *Language Arts, 96*(5), 300–311.

Vasudevan, L., Schultz, K., & Bateman, J. (2010). Rethinking composing in a digital age: Authoring literate identities through multimodal storytelling. *Written Communication, 27*(4) 442–468.

Walsh, M. (2021, June 10). If critical race theory is banned, are teachers protected by the first amendment? *Education Week*. https://www.edweek.org/policy-politics/does-academic-freedom-shield-teachers-as-states-take-aim-at-critical-race-theory/2021/06

Washington Office of Superintendent of Public Instruction. (2021). *Report card: Pasco School District*. https://washingtonstatereportcard.ospi.k12.wa.us/ReportCard/ViewSchoolOrDistrict/100195

Wenger, E. (1998). *Communities of practice: Learning, meaning, and identity*. Cambridge University Press.

Wessel-Powell, C., Panos, A., & Weir, R. (2021). A year of equity literacy: Community actions and invitations. *Literacy, 55*(1), 62–76.

Whipp, J. (2013). Developing socially just teachers: The interaction of experiences before, during, and after teacher preparation in beginning urban teachers. *Journal of Teacher Education, 64*(5), 454–467.

Whipp, J., & Buck, B. (2014, April 3). *Developing caring with political clarity in high-poverty schools* [Paper presentation]. American Educational Research Association Annual Meeting, Philadelphia, PA. https://convention2.allacademic.com/one/aera/aera14/index.php?PHPSESSID=spe6bdjqike0371td27fgn6ber&cmd=Online+Program+Search&program_focus=fulltext_search&search_mode=content&offset=0&search_text=Whipp

White, T. G., Kim, J. S., Kingston, H. C., & Foster, L. F. (2014). Replicating the effects of a teacher-scaffolded voluntary summer reading program: The role of poverty. *Reading Research Quarterly, 49*(1), 5–30.

Wilhelm, J. D., Douglas, W., & Fry, S. W. (2014). *The activist learner: Inquiry, literacy, and service to make learning better*. Teachers College Press.

Willis, A. I. (2015). Literacy, race, access, and freedom. *Literacy Research: Theory, Method, and Practice, 64*, 23–55.

Willis, A. I. (2019a). Race, response to intervention, and reading research. *Journal of Literacy Research*, 51(4), 394–419.

Willis, A. I. (2019b). Response to intervention: An illusion of equity. *Language Arts*, 97(2), 83–96.

Willis, A. I., Smith, P., Kim, J., & Hsieh, B. (2021). *Racial justice in literacy research* [Literacy Research Report]. Literacy Research Association.

Winn, M. T. (2018). Building a "lifetime circle": English education in the age of #BlackLivesMatter. *Urban Education*, 53(2), 248–264.

Wisconsin Department of Public Instruction. (2011). Wisconsin's Guiding Principles for Teaching and Learning. https://dpi.wi.gov/standards/guiding-principles

Wiseman, A. M., Mäkinen, M., & Kupiainen, R. (2016). Literacy through photography: Multimodal and visual literacy in a third grade classroom. *Early Childhood Education Journal*, 44(5), 537–544.

Woodson, J. (2018). *Harbor me*. Penguin.

Wu, C., & Coady, M. R. (2010). 'The United States is America?': A cultural perspective on READ 180 materials. *Language, Culture and Curriculum*, 23(2), 153–165.

Wyeth, S. D. (1998). *Something beautiful*. Dragonfly.

Yoon, I. (2016). Why is it not just a joke? Analysis of Internet memes associated with racism and hidden ideology of colorblindness. *Journal of Cultural Research in Art Education*, 33, 92–123.

Zapata, A. (2020). Cultivating a critical translingual landscape in the elementary language arts classroom. *Language Arts*, 97(6), 384–390.

Zembylas, M. (2015). "Pedagogy of discomfort" and its ethical implications: The tensions of ethical violence in social justice education. *Ethics and Education*, 10(2), 163–174.

Zembylas, M., & Boler, M. (2002, August 12). On the spirit of patriotism: Challenges of a "pedagogy of discomfort." *Teachers College Record*. https://www.tcrecord.org/Content.asp?ContentId=11007

Index

Bold type indicates contributors to this volume.

ABC books photography project, 25
Abolitionist teaching (Love), 1
Absolutely True Diary of a Part-Time Indian, The (Alexie), 125
Adequate yearly progress (AYP), 9
Adichie, Chimamanda, 109
Adolescent and youth learners
  context and teacher positionalities, 54–55, 75–77, 97, 123–124
  The Corn Husk Doll (Schiller) based on CSSJP, 75–93
  disciplinary literacy practices, 53–73
  elevating youth critical consciousness in classrooms, 97, 107–119, 164–165
  Reading and Teaching Adolescent Literature course, 123–140
  Sachi (student expert) and, 75, 78, 85, 88–90, 93, 164
  and the Youth Equity Agent (YEA) Project, 97, 107–117
African American Language (AAL) pedagogy, 1–2, 6, 36, 58, 69–70
African American learners. *See* Black, Indigenous, and other people of color (BIPOC) learners
Ahmed, Riz, 132
Albro, J. J., 22
Alexie, S., 125
Alim, H. S., 5, 19, 21, 33–36, 39, 43–45, 47, 53, 57–59, 64, 70, 71, 95, 98, 107, 113, 126–128, 130, 141–143, 145, 147, 157, 162–164
Alina (Muslim student), 14, 39–49, 162–163
  described, 33, 46–47
  elementary school literacy vignettes, 39–46
  in the Names, Dreams, and Journeys project, 33–36, 39–49

All-American Boys (Reynolds & Kiely), 125
Allington, R., 35
Amanti, Cathy, 3, 4, 8, 88, 89, 92–93
Anchor charts, 20–21, 27, 30–31, 102
Antiracist Black language pedagogy (Baker-Bell), 1
Arabic Quilt, The (Khalil), 30
Arapostathis, M., 156
Arce-Boardman, A., 37, 145
Archaeology of Self technique (Sealey-Ruiz), 160–161
Ariely, D., 153
Arizpe, E., 35
Ascenzi-Moreno, L., 34
Assessment
  commercial reading programs and, 49
  Common Core State Standards (CCSS), 8, 9–10, 53, 78–79, 89–90, 151
  Race to the Top initiative, 8, 9–10
  reconceptualizing standards and, 151–154, 163–164
  White middle-class cultural norms in, 35, 36–37, 39, 45–49, 90, 151, 153
Asset-based pedagogies, 3–7
  collaborative curriculum excavation, 128–139, 160–161
  The Corn Husk Doll (Schiller) lesson, 75–93
  disciplinary literacies and, 53–73, 162–163
  funds of knowledge in, 3–4, 8, 78, 88–90, 92–93, 98–100
  linguistic and cultural resources in resisting deficit approaches, 10, 33–36, 39–49, 162–163
  for minoritized vs. White students, 11
  political right and, 11–12, 151–152, 166

About the Editors and Contributors

Dr. Susan V. Bennett is an associate professor in Literacy Studies at the College of Education at the University of South Florida–St. Petersburg and is on the board of the National Association of Multicultural Education. Her research and teaching focuses on multicultural children's literature, culturally sustaining pedagogy, teacher education, and community literacy, including individuals who are incarcerated.

Dr. Susan Chambers Cantrell is a professor of Literacy in the Department of Curriculum and Instruction at the University of Kentucky, where she teaches courses in literacy education. Her research is focused on teachers' professional learning, self-efficacy development, and instructional effectiveness, particularly toward creating more equitable classrooms. She is coeditor of *A Framework for Culturally Responsive Practices: Implementing the Culturally Responsive Instruction Observation Protocol (CRIOP) in K–8 Classrooms* (2021) with Rebecca Powell.

Dr. Kathleen M. Cowin's research focuses on the development of effective relational comentoring practices and the creation of comentoring circles among educational leadership students. Her current comentorship research is focused on culturally sustaining, socially just pedagogy enhanced by collaborative conversations between preservice teachers and aspiring school leaders. She served as a teacher and elementary and middle school principal for over 25 years and also completed her Superintendent Certification. Kathleen is the past chair for the American Educational Research Association Mentorship and Mentoring Practices Special Interest Group, and in 2020 she was selected as a member of the Washington State University President's Teaching Academy.

Heather Dunham is a doctoral candidate at The University of Texas at Austin in the Department of Curriculum and Instruction. She teaches courses on reading assessment, development, and instructional methods and supervises preservice teachers in the field. Her research interests include literacy teacher preparation, preservice teachers' communities of practice, and culturally sustaining approaches to literacy and language instruction.

Dr. AnnMarie Alberton Gunn is an associate professor at the University of South Florida in the area of Literacy Studies. She holds expertise in teacher education, multicultural education, and multicultural children's literature.

Dr. Steven M. Hart is professor of literacy in the Department of Literacy, Early, Bilingual, and Special Education and coordinator of the minor in urban civic education at California State University–Fresno, where he teaches courses in literacy education and service-learning pedagogy. His research is focused on investigating how critical literacy and service-learning can converge to frame culturally and linguistically sustaining literacy education for diverse student populations.

Dr. Aimee Hendrix-Soto is an assistant professor of literacy and learning at Texas Woman's University in Denton, Texas, where she teaches undergraduate and graduate courses on literacy and education. Her research focuses on adolescent literacy and preservice teacher preparation with a special focus on critical literacies and critical literacy instruction.

Dr. Erica Holyoke is an assistant professor of elementary and special education in the Education Department at Keene State College where she teaches courses in inclusive practices, literacy, and social studies education. Her research explores critical literacies, classroom communities, teacher and children's agency, and teaching practices that create more just and loving learning communities in elementary and preservice teacher education.

Dr. Britnie Delinger Kane is an assistant professor of literacy education at The Citadel's Zucker Family School of Education. Broadly, her research interests focus on teachers' professional learning about discipline-specific, conceptually rich, and equitable pedagogies. Recent publications have appeared in *Teachers College Record*, the *Journal of Teacher Education*, the *American Educational Research Journal,* and the *Journal of the Learning Sciences*.

Dr. Althier M. Lazar is professor of education at Saint Joseph's University in Philadelphia. Her research focuses on preparing teachers to nurture the literacies and languages of culturally diverse students. Her books include: *Schools of Promise for Multilingual Students: Transforming Literacies, Learning, and Lives* (2018) with coeditor Patricia Ruggino Schmidt; *Rethinking 21st-Century Diversity in K–12 Education: Promises, Perils, and Provocations* (2018) with coeditor Suniti Sharma; and *Bridging Literacy and Equity: The Essential Guide to Social Equity Teaching* (2012) with coauthors Patricia Edwards and Gwendolyn McMillon.

Dr. Chrystine Cooper Mitchell is an associate professor of elementary education at York College of Pennsylvania, where she teaches courses in literacy education methodology coursework and children's and adolescent literature. Her research is focused on culturally sustaining teaching practices, meaningful technology integration practices, professional learning communities, and exploring preservice teachers' passion projects as a form of teacher inquiry.

Dr. Olivia Murphy is a postdoctoral research fellow at the University of Maryland, College Park. Her research centers around critical literacy and social justice literacy practices, and she is interested in both curricula and educators that instructionally center these practices. She also teaches adolescent literacy methods classes in an urban teaching fellowship program because her passion is being in and talking about classrooms.

Dr. Sarah N. Newcomer is an associate professor in the Department of Teaching and Learning at Washington State University Tri-Cities. She earned her BA in Spanish at Northern Arizona University and her EdM and PhD in curriculum and instruction at Arizona State University. Her research and teaching center on language and literacy education, especially for culturally and linguistically diverse students. In particular, she investigates culturally sustaining and socially just literacy instructional practices, the ways in which family–school–community partnerships support literacy development, and strategies and resources for fostering geo-literacy.

Dr. Alexandra Panos is a former middle grades teacher and an assistant professor of literacy studies and affiliate faculty in measurement and research at the University of South Florida, where she focuses her research and teaching on the critical, spatial, and environmental dimensions of literacy. She has published numerous articles on these issues in journals such as *Linguistics and Education, Journal of Adolescent and Adult Literacy, Literacy UKLA, International Studies in Sociology of Education,* and *International Journal of Qualitative Studies in Education.*

Kelli A. Rushek is a visiting assistant professor of English education at iami University in Oxford, OH. Her research examines antiracist and ulturally sustaining ELA teacher education at the intersection of early career teachers and critical praxis.

Dr. Rachelle S. Savitz is an assistant professor of Adolescent Literacy at Clemson University. She is the recipient of the Association of Literacy Educators and Researchers' Jerry Johns Promising Researcher Award and the Early Career Literacy Scholar Award from the American Reading Forum. Her research interests and publications include focus on inquiry-based learning, analysis and use of young adult literature, teacher self-efficacy, and culturally sustaining pedagogy. She has coauthored *Teaching Hope and Resilience for Students Experiencing Trauma: Creating Safe and Nurturing Classrooms for Learning* (2019) with Douglas Fisher and Nancy Frey and has published in *Teaching and Teacher Education, Literacy Research and Instruction,* and *Journal of Adolescent & Adult Literacy.*

Ethan Seylar is a preservice teacher completing his BA in secondary English education in the College of Education at the University of Iowa. Upon entering the teaching force, he intends to mesh theory and practice in his classroom by employing strategies of culturally sustaining literacy Pedagogy to engage and honor students from culturally nondominant backgrounds.

Dr. Jenifer Jasinski Schneider is a professor of literacy studies in the College of Education at the University of South Florida. Her research focuses on children's composing processes including print-based writing development and multimodal composition in digital and embodied spaces as well as arts-based approaches to literacy education in which aspects of process drama, children's literature, and digital tools support youth's symbolic development and meaning-making strategies.

Dr. Jennifer D. Turner is an associate professor in reading education in the Department of Teaching and Learning, Policy and Leadership at the University of Maryland. Her research agenda centers on critical arts-based and visual research methods, Black and Brown youths' freedom dreaming and futurisms, critical multimodal literacies, and culturally responsive pedagogies in elementary schools.

Dr. Doris Walker-Dalhouse is professor of literacy in the College of Education at Marquette University, Milwaukee, Wisconsin and Professor Emerita of

Literacy, Minnesota State University–Moorhead. Her research conducted with preservice teachers and in after-school and community reading programs focuses on sociocultural factors impacting the literacy development and instruction of struggling readers and teachers' attitudes and beliefs in instructing underserved and marginalized students across multiple forms of diversity.

Dr. Melissa Mosley Wetzel is a professor of language and literacy studies in the Department of Curriculum and Instruction at The University of Texas at Austin, where she teaches courses in elementary reading and literacy, coaching and mentoring, and literacy leadership. Her research focuses on how teachers and students together design literacy practices that are transformative using antiracist and critical literacy approaches.

Dr. Kelly K. Wissman is an associate professor in the Department of Literacy Teaching and Learning at the University at Albany, State University of New York, and the director of the Capital District Writing Project there. Across her scholarship and teaching, she considers how children's literature, writing, and the arts can facilitate the creation of more equitable and humanizing educational spaces for all students.